CONTENTS

52nd Edition

Marine Publishin

P.O. Box 68, Sault Ste. Ma

(734) 668-473

roger@knowyoursh

KnowYourShips.com

ISBN: 978-1-891849-14-5   © 2011 Marine Publishing Co. Inc.

2

Editor/Publisher: Roger LeLievre

Researchers: Matt Miner (saltwater list), Wade P. Streeter, John Vournakis and George Wharton

Crew: Kathryn O'Gould (advertising), Nancy Kuharevicz, Audrey LeLievre, Neil Schultheiss and William Soleau

Founder: Tom Manse (1915-1994)

Cover: Detroit mailboat J.W. Westcott II passes American Mariner. The world's only floating post office with its own ZIP code, the Westcott delivers more than 100,000 pieces of mail to Great Lakes sailors each season. (Roger LeLievre)
Page 1: Canadian Provider upbound in the St. Marys River. (Roger LeLievre)
This page: Herbert C. Jackson loads taconite pellets at Marquette. (Luke Archer)

Kaye E. Barker, shown in Detroit's Rouge River, was back at work in 2010. (Wade P. Streeter)

Fleets & Vessels

2010 definitely a better season on the lakes

Cargo tonnages in 2010 saw strong increases over the previous year. Ore and grain in particular were up, with demand for the latter fueled by poor harvests in Russia and elsewhere in Europe. According to the Lake Carriers' Association, U.S.-flagged vessels on the Great Lakes carried 88.7 million tons of cargo in 2010, an increase of 33.4 percent over 2009. The St. Lawrence Seaway also reported an increase, with 2010 posting a 15 percent increase in cargo volume compared to the previous year. With the economy improving, many vessels that had been laid up in 2009 sailed in 2010 (see Lay-up Log on Page 6 for those that didn't), including Interlake's steamer *Kaye E. Barker*.

Canadian fleets add tonnage, with more to come

A new vessel, *Canadian Mariner*, built by the Chengxi Shipyard Co. Ltd. in Jiangyin City, China, is expected to enter service in July. This will not be the last new vessel built in China for Great Lakes/Seaway service, with several new hulls, some in partnership with the Canadian Wheat Board, on order. Meanwhile, Algoma and Canada Steamship Lines brought new purchases from saltwater into Canadian registry in 2010, the former adding *Algoma Guardian*, *Algoma Discovery* and *Algoma Spirit*, and the latter registering *Oakglen*, *Richelieu* and *Saguenay*.

Continued on Page 6

Algoma Central acquires Upper Lakes Group vessels

As *"Know Your Ships"* went to press it was announced that Algoma Central Marine (fleet A-3) had purchased the assets of Upper Lakes Group's Seaway Marine Transport (U-12). Algoma has acquired the 11 vessels owned by Upper Lakes, full interest in four vessels owned jointly by Algoma and Upper Lakes, and Upper Lakes' interest in the new *Canadian Mariner*. No renames had been released by press time, but will be posted on our Web site, **knowyourships.com**, as they become available. Upper Lakes traces its corporate roots on the Great Lakes / St. Lawrence Seaway back more than 80 years.

5

More power to 'em

Over the past winter, the steamer *Michipicoten* was dieselized at Sarnia, while *Edwin H. Gott* received a new set of diesels at Bay Shipbuilding Co.

K&K sells tug/barge combos

K&K Integrated Logistics sold its two self-unloading barges, *James L. Kuber* and *Lewis J. Kuber,* to Grand River Navigation in February. The dedicated tugs *Victory* and *Olive L. Moore* were also part of the deal.

Beeghly rename to honor Oberstar

Interlake Steamship Co.'s *Charles M. Beeghly* will be renamed *Hon. James L. Oberstar* this season, after the former chairman of the U.S. House Transportation and Infrastructure Committee.

Canadian fleets scrap 3 vessels

Three more vessels that have been familiar sights on the Great Lakes and St. Lawrence Seaway have been towed to overseas scrappers. *Algoisle, Agawa Canyon* and *Canadian Prospector* all made final port at Aliaga, Turkey, in fall 2010. Another vessel, *Canadian Leader*, was sent to the shipbreakers at Port Colborne, Ont., last October. *Algosteel* entered long-term lay-up at Montreal in December 2010

Ships still on the sidelines

Although business conditions improved dramatically over an abysmal 2009, several U.S.-flagged vessels did not return to service in 2010, including *American Courage* (laid up at Sturgeon Bay, but expected to sail in 2011), *American Valor* and *American Fortitude* (both at Toledo), *American Victory* (at Superior), *Adam E. Cornelius* (Superior) and *Edward L. Ryerson* (Superior). On the Canadian side, *Algontario* (Toronto), *Algonorth* (Thunder Bay), *Petrolia Desgagnés* (Montreal), *Canadian Ranger* (Toronto) and *Canadian Miner* (Toronto) remained idle. The *Miner* and *Ranger*, along with *Sauniere* and *Halifax* (both at Montreal), are reported headed for the scrap heap. *John Sherwin*, its rebuild canceled in 2008 by the economy, is still laid up at DeTour, Mich.

***Edward L. Ryerson* at Superior, Wis., in 2010.**
(Chris Mazzella)

Agawa Canyon at speed in Lake Huron (above) and being dismantled at the breaker's yard in Turkey (below) with Algoma fleetmate Algoisle. (John Belliveau, Selim San)

Canadian Prospector heads for scrapping at Aliaga, Turkey, in October 2010, under tow of the tug Simoon. (Michel Saint-Dennis)

Oakglen was brought under the Canadian flag in 2010 and given a refit at the Novadock facility in Halifax. (Mac Mackay)

Canadian Leader tow nears the scrapyard at Port Colborne on Nov. 6, 2010. Built in 1967 as Feux-Follets, she was the last steam-powered vessel constructed on the Lakes. (Bill Bird)

Historic Schoonmaker name returns to Great Lakes

An historic name returns to the bow of a Great Lakes freighter this summer at Toledo, Ohio, where a ceremony July 1 will restore the name *Col. James M. Schoonmaker* to a vessel originally christened in 1911.

Doing the honors will be James M. Schoonmaker II, the son of the vessel's namesake, who will break a bottle of champagne over the lake boat's bow exactly 100 years to the day when his mother, Gretchen V. Schoonmaker, christened the vessel in 1911.

Built by the Great Lakes Engineering Works in Ecorse, Mich., the showpiece steamer was the largest in the world when it was launched for the Shenango Furnace Co. The *Schoonmaker*, which made its 1911 maiden voyage to load a record cargo of coal at the same dock where she sits today as a museum, sailed the lakes under that name until 1969, when it was renamed *Willis B. Boyer*. Retired from active service in 1980, she has served as an interpretive display at Toledo since 1987, a role that will expand this year when she assumes her position as the centerpiece attraction of a new, national Great Lakes maritime museum in Toledo.

"Our goal is to create the Smithsonian of Great Lakes history," said Paul C. LaMarre III, manager of maritime affairs for the Toledo Port Authority, of the $3 million project. Under the plan, the Great Lakes Historical Society Maritime Museum, currently located in Vermilion, Ohio, will move into an already existing, 12,278-square-foot shoreside facility, with the *Col. James M. Schoonmaker* eventually moving to a permanent berth adjacent to the museum building.

John Belliveau

Col. James M. Schoonmaker in the Soo Locks, circa 1965.
(Tom Manse Collection)

Michipicoten heads in for a load of taconite at Marquette. The former steamer was repowered in early 2011. *(Rod Burdick)*

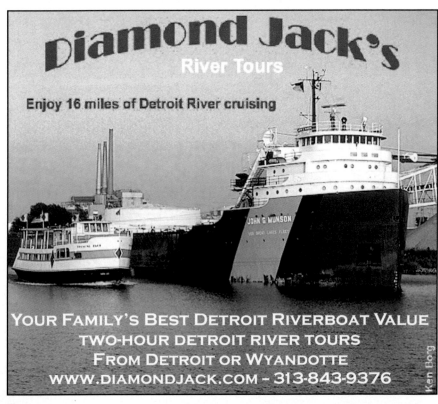

GREAT LAKES GLOSSARY

AAA CLASS – Vessel design popular on the Great Lakes in the early 1950s. *Arthur M. Anderson* is one example.

AFT – Toward the back, or stern, of a ship.

AHEAD – Forward.

AMIDSHIPS – The middle point of a vessel, referring to either length or width.

ARTICULATED TUG/BARGE (ATB) – Tug-barge combination. The two vessels are mechanically linked in one axis but with the tug free to move, or articulate, on another axis. *Jacklyn M/Integrity* is one example.

BACKHAUL – The practice of carrying a revenue-producing cargo (rather than ballast) on a return trip from hauling a primary cargo.

BARGE – Vessel with no engine, either pushed or pulled by a tug.

BEAM – The width of a vessel measured at the widest point.

BILGE – Lowest part of a hold or compartment, generally where the rounded side of a ship curves from the keel to the vertical sides.

BOW – Front of a vessel.

BOW THRUSTER – Propeller mounted transversely in a vessel's bow under the water line to assist in moving sideways. A stern thruster may also be installed.

BRIDGE – The platform above the main deck from which a ship is steered/navigated. Also: PILOTHOUSE or WHEELHOUSE.

BULKHEAD – Wall or partition that separates rooms, holds or tanks within a ship's hull.

BULWARK – The part of the ship that extends fore and aft above the main deck to form a rail.

DATUM – Level of water in a given area, determined by an average over time.

DEADWEIGHT TONNAGE – The actual carrying capacity of a vessel, equal to the difference between the light displacement tonnage and the heavy displacement tonnage, expressed in long tons (2,240 pounds or 1,016.1 kilograms).

DISPLACEMENT TONNAGE – The actual weight of the vessel and everything aboard her, measured in long tons. The displacement is equal to the weight of the water displaced by the vessel. Displacement tonnage may be qualified as light, indicating the weight of the vessel without cargo, fuel and stores, or heavy, indicating the weight of the vessel loaded with cargo, fuel and stores.

DRAFT – The depth of water a ship needs to float. Also, the distance from keel to water line.

FIT OUT – The process of preparing a vessel for service after a period of inactivity.

FIVE-YEAR INSPECTION – U.S. Coast Guard survey, conducted in a drydock every five years, of a vessel's hull, machinery and other equipment.

FLATBACK – Lakes slang for a non-self-unloader.

FOOTER – Lakes slang for 1,000-foot vessel.

FORECASTLE – (FOHK s'l) Area at the forward part of the ship and beneath the main cabins, often used for crew's quarters or storage.

FOREPEAK – The space below the forecastle.

FORWARD – Toward the front, or bow, of a ship.

FREEBOARD – The distance from the water line to the main deck.

GROSS TONNAGE – The internal space of a vessel, measured in units of 100 cubic feet (2.83 cubic meters) = a gross ton.

HATCH – An opening in the deck through which cargo is lowered or raised. A hatch is closed by securing a hatch cover over it.

HULL – The body of a ship, not including its superstructure, masts or machinery.

IMO # – Unique number issued by International Maritime Organization, or IMO, to each ship for identification purposes.

INTEGRATED TUG/BARGE (ITB) – Tug-barge combination in which the tug is rigidly mated to the barge. *Presque Isle* is one example.

IRON DECKHAND – Mechanical device that runs on rails on a vessel's main deck and is used to remove and replace hatch covers.

JONES ACT – A U.S. cabotage law that mandates that cargoes moved between American ports be carried by U.S.-flagged, U.S.-built and U.S.-crewed vessels.

KEEL – A ship's steel backbone. It runs along the lowest part of the hull.

LAID UP or **LAY-UP** – Out of service.

MARITIME CLASS – Style of lake vessel built during World War II as part of the nation's war effort. *Mississagi* is one example.

NET REGISTERED TONNAGE – The internal capacity of a vessel available for carrying cargo. It does not include the space occupied by boilers, engines, shaft alleys, chain lockers or officers' and crew's quarters. Net registered tonnage is usually referred to as registered tonnage or net tonnage and is used to calculate taxes, tolls and port charges.

RIVER CLASS SELF-UNLOADER – Group of vessels built in the 1970s to service smaller ports and negotiate narrow rivers such as Cleveland's Cuyahoga. *Manitowoc* is one example.

SELF-UNLOADER – Vessel able to discharge its own cargo using a system of conveyor belts and a movable boom.

STEM – The extreme forward end of the bow.

STEMWINDER – Vessel with all cabins aft (also sternwinder).

STERN – The back of the ship.

STRAIGHT-DECKER – A non-self-unloading vessel. *Edward L. Ryerson* is one example.

TACONITE – Processed, pelletized iron ore. Easy to load and unload, this is the primary type of ore shipped on the Great Lakes and St. Lawrence Seaway. Also known as pellets.

TRACTOR TUG – Highly maneuverable tug propelled by either a Z-drive or cycloidal system rather than the traditional screw propeller.

TURKEY TRAIL – Route from North Channel (above Manitoulin Island) into the St. Marys River, named for the many courses which zigzag through the area's islands, shoals and ports, much like the trail that wild turkeys might take.

vessel Index

Sea cadet training vessel Grayfox on the St. Marys River. (Roger LeLievre)

Vessel Name	Fleet #	Vessel Name	Fleet #	Vessel Name	Fleet #
Beluga Expectation	IB-1	Biscayne Bay	U-3	Brown, Prentiss	P-7
Beluga Faculty	IB-1	Black, Martha L.	C-3	Brutus I	T-9
Beluga Fairy	IB-1	Blacky	IN-1	Buckley	K-5
Beluga Family	IB-1	Block, Joseph L.	C-6	Buckthorn	U-3
Beluga Fanfare	IB-1	Blough, Roger	G-13	Buffalo	A-5
Beluga Fascination	IB-1	Blue Heron	U-9	Bunyan, Paul	U-2
Beluga Favourisation	IB-1	Blue Heron V	B-8	Burns Harbor	A-5
Beluga Federation	IB-1	Blue Quail	S-24	Busch, Edwin C.	B-18
Beluga Festival	IB-1	Bluebill	IN-1	Busch, Gregory J.	B-18
Beluga Fidelity	IB-1	Bluewing	IO-1	Busse, Fred A.	D-7
Beluga Fighter	IB-1	BMI-192	B-2	Buxton II	K-6
Beluga Flirtation	IB-1	BMI-FDD-1	B-2		
Beluga Formation	IB-1	BMT 3	B-18		
Beluga Fraternity	IB-1	Boatman No. 3	M-13		
Beluga Frequency	IB-1	Boatman No. 6	M-13	C.T.M.A. Vacancier	C-31
Beluga Fusion	IB-1	Boland, John J.	A-5	C.T.M.A. Voyageur	C-31
Beluga Legislation	IB-1	Bonnie B. III	M-13	Cabot {2}	IO-3
Beluga Recognition	IB-1	Boothe Sr., Ken	S-4	Cadillac	S-29
Beluga Resolution	IB-1	Bornholm	IH-7	California	G-14
Beluga Revolution	IB-1	Bowes, Bobby	D-3	Callaway, Cason J.	G-13
Bessie B	W-8	Boyd, David	G-19	Callie M.	M-9
Betsiamites	0-3	Bramble	P-8	Calliroe Patronicola	IO-4
Bide-A-Wee	S-13	Brant	IN-1	Callitsis, Athanasios G.	IC-2
BIG 503, BIG 543, BIG 546, BIG		Bras d'Or 400	M-30	Calumet	L-14
548, BIG 549, BIG 551	U-12	Breaker	N-5	Cameron O.	S-5
BIG 9708 B	U-12	Bright Laker	ID-2	Camille-Marcoux	S-12
BIG 9917 B	U-12	Bristol Bay	U-3	Canadian	M-15
Billmaier, D.L.	U-2	Bro Alma	IB-8	Canadian Argosy	M-15
Birchglen	C-2	Brochu	A-9	Canadian Empress	S-23

C

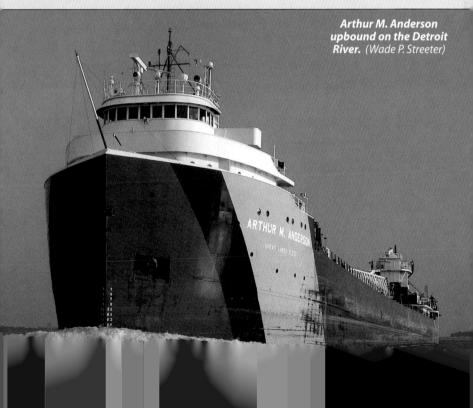

Arthur M. Anderson upbound on the Detroit River. *(Wade P. Streeter)*

BEFORE AND AFTER
Tug Pennsylvania assists CSL Tadoussac, sporting a new paint scheme, at Ironhead Shipyard in Toledo, Feb. 22, 2011. Inset shows her arriving at the shipyard on Dec. 20, 2010. (Paul C. LaMarre III)

Vessel Name	Fleet #	Vessel Name	Fleet #	Vessel Name	Fleet #
Diamond Belle	D-5	Drummond Islander II	M-1	Eider	IP-1
Diamond Jack	D-5	Drummond Islander III	E-1	Elikon	IH-4
Diamond Queen	D-5	Drummond Islander IV	E-1	Elizabeth	W-2
Diezeborg	IW-2	Duc d' Orleans II	D-10	Ellie	K-5
Dilly, William B.	M-15	Duga	0-3	Elliot, Benjamin	N-6
Dintelborg	IW-2	Duluth	G-11	Emerald Isle	B-7
Dobrush	IC-10	Durocher, Ray	D-12	Empire Sandy	N-3
Donald Bert	M-2	Dutch Runner	IG-2	Empire State	N-7
Donald C.	K-5			Empress of Canada	E-3
Donald Mac	G-10			Enchanter	IB-3
Dongeborg	IW-2	**E**		Endeavour	A-7
Donner, William H.	K-8			Energy 13502	H-8
Dool, Tim S.	A-3	Eagle	S-10	Energy 6506	H-8
Dora	IT-2	Eagle Service	H-8	English River	L-1
Dorothy Ann	I-5	Ecosse	N-1	Enterprise 2000	0-4
Dorsch	IC-9	Edelweiss II	M-26	Environaut	G-5
Dover	M-2	Edenborg	IW-2	Epinette II	E-6
Drake, Barney (The)	G-2	Edith J.	E-2	Erich	M-14
Drawsko	IP-5	Edna G.	L-3	Erie Explorer	0-5
Drechtborg	IW-2	Edson	S-1	Erie-West	M-13
Dredge Primrose	M-13	Edward H.	H-7	Escort	B-2
		Eemsborg	IW-2		

Vessel Name	Fleet #
Escorte	0-3
Eships Eagle	IE-2
Essayons	X-1
Evening Star	S-11
Everlast	M-12
Eyrarbakki	W-4

F

Vessel Name	Fleet #
Fairchem Colt	IF-1
Fairlane	IJ-2
Fairlift	IJ-2
Fairload	IJ-2
Falcon, G.W.	C-19
Federal Agno	IF-3
Federal Asahi {2}	IF-3
Federal Danube	II-2
Federal Elbe	II-2
Federal Ems	II-2
Federal Fuji	IV-1
Federal Hudson {3}	IF-3

Ice buildup on the American Integrity's mast. (Chris Mazzella)

Vessel Name	Fleet #
Federal Hunter {2}	IF-3
Federal Katsura	II-2
Federal Kivalina	IF-3
Federal Kumano	IF-3
Federal Kushiro	IF-3
Federal Leda	II-2
Federal Maas {2}	IF-3
Federal Mackinac	IF-3
Federal Manitou	IS-11
Federal Margaree	IF-3
Federal Matane	IS-11
Federal Mattawa	IR-4
Federal Miramichi	IS-11
Federal Nakagawa	IF-3
Federal Oshima	IF-3
Federal Patroller	II-2
Federal Pioneer	II-2
Federal Polaris	IV-1
Federal Power	II-2
Federal Progress	IF-3
Federal Rhine {2}	IF-3
Federal Rideau	IF-3
Federal Saguenay {2}	IF-3
Federal Sakura	II-2
Federal Schelde {3}	IF-3
Federal Seto	IF-3
Federal Shimanto	IF-10
Federal St. Laurent {3}	IF-3
Federal Venture	IF-3
Federal Welland	IF-3
Federal Weser	II-2
Federal Yoshino	IF-10
Federal Yukon	IF-3
Felicity	S-8
Felix-Antoine-Savard	S-12
Fen	IL-5
Finex	IF-8
Fivelborg	IW-2
Fjord Saguenay	R-2
Flevoborg	IW-2
Flinders, Capt. Matthew	M-10
Flinter Arctic	IF-6
Flinterduin	IF-6
Flintereems	IF-6
Flinterland	IF-6
Flintermaas	IF-6
Flintermar	IF-6
Flinterrebecca	IF-6
Flinterspirit	IF-6
Flinterstream	IF-6
Florence M.	M-13
Florida	G-14
Fodas Pescadores	IS-5
Ford, E.M.	P-13
Ford, J.B.	L-2
Forest City	W-6
Fox, Terry	C-3
Foxy Lady II	F-3
Frederick, Owen M.	U-2
Freedom Service	H-8
Friends Good Will	M-19

Vessel Name	Fleet #
Friendship	P-9
Frisian Spring	IB-6
Frontenac	C-2
Frontenac Howe Islander	M-27
Frontenac II	M-27
Ft. Dearborn	C-11
Futura	IN-3

G

Vessel Name	Fleet #
G.L.B. No. 2	P-13
Gadwall	IP-1
Garganey	IP-1
Gaynor, William C.	M-1
General	D-12
General Brock III	T-2
General Chemical No. 37	M-13
Georgian Queen	A-10
Gillen III, Edward E.	E-2
Giovanni DP	ID-1
Glen	IL-5
Glenada	T-3
Glenora	M-27
Global Carrier	II-3
Glory	IC-4
Goodtime I	L-4
Goodtime III	G-7
Gorthon, Alida	IT-5
Gorthon, Ingrid	IT-5
Gott, Edwin H.	G-13
Graham, H.E.	0-3
Graham, Sandy	B-6
Grand Baie	E-6
Grand Fleuve	C-28
Grand Island	P-4
Grand Portal	P-4
Grande Caribe	IB-4
Grande Mariner	IB-4
Grasse River	S-25
Grant, R.F.	0-3
Grayfox	U-8
Grayling	G-18
Great Blue Heron	B-8
Great Lakes	C-12
Great Lakes Trader	V-1
Green, Magdalena	IH-8
Green, Marinus	IH-8
Green, Marissa	IH-8
Green, Marlene	IH-8
Greenstone	B-2
Greenstone II	U-7
Greenwing	IO-1
Greta V	M-15
Gretchen B.	L-15
Griffon	C-3
Grue-des-Iles	S-12
Gull Isle	C-3

H

Vessel Name	Fleet #
Haida	H-5

21

Vessel Name	Fleet #	Vessel Name	Fleet #	Vessel Name	Fleet #
Hal Patriot	II-2	Holden, John	M-15	Inland Seas	I-3
Hal Pendant	II-2	Holiday	S-13, T-14	Innisfree	C-11
Hal Pride	II-2	Hollyhock	U-3	Innovation	L-2
Halifax	C-2	Hornell VC, David	T-9	Integrity	L-2
Hamilton Energy	U-12	Houghton	K-2	Intrepid III	N-1
Hamilton Harbour Queen	H-2	Howe Islander	C-27	Inviken	IV-1
Hammond Bay	L-12, U-2	Hulin	IC-6	Invincible	L-14
Handy Andy	M-15	Huron	A-11, P-8	Iowa	G-14
Hanlan II, Ned	C-16	Huron Belle	L-7	Irma	IP-5
Hannah 5101	X-1	Huron Explorer	G-12	Iroquois	M-24
Hannah, Daryl C.	C-1	Huron Explorer I	0-5	Irvin, William A.	D-11
Hannah, James A.	X-1	Huron Lady	M-5	Iryda	IP-5
Hannah, Mary E.	C-1	Huron Lady II	B-9	Isa	IP-5
Hannah, Mary Page	S-5	Huron Maid	L-7	Isadora	IP-5
Hannah, Peggy D.	C-1	Husky	P-11	Island Belle 1	K-7
Hannah, Susan W.	P-7			Island Clipper	V-7
Happy Ranger	IB-3			Island Duchess	U-1
Happy Rover	IB-3	**I**		Island Express	A-11
Harbor Seagull	M-25			Island Heritage	T-2
Harbour Clear	IC-8	I.V. No. 8	D-9	Island Princess	A-8
Harbour Cloud	IC-8	I.V. No. 9	D-9	Island Queen	M-3
Harbour Star	M-33	I.V. No. 10	D-9	Island Queen III	K-7
Harvey	U-2	I.V. No. 11	D-9	Island Queen V	T-13
Harvey, Ann	C-3	I.V. No. 13	D-9	Island Sauvage	M-15
Havasu II	N-5	I.V. No. 14	D-9	Island Skipper	IS-7
Hayden, Fischer	G-11	Ian Mac	M-2	Island Star	K-7
Heloise	IP-1	Ida M.	R-3	Island Wanderer	U-1
Henning	R-6	Ida M. II	R-3	Islander	B-3, M-23, R-5
Henry, Alexander	M-8	Idaho	G-14	Islay	X-1
Hiawatha	S-13	Iglehart, J.A.W.	I-2	Isle Rouge	C-3
Highlander Sea	A-2	Illinois	G-14	Isle Royale Queen III	P-12
Hoey, Carolyn	G-1	Indian Maiden	B-6	Isle Royale Queen IV	I-8
Hoey, Patricia	G-1	Indiana	G-14	Isolda	IP-5
Hogan, Joseph J.	J-1	Indiana Harbor	A-5		
		Inglis, William	C-16		

Algocanada in the Welland Canal.
(John C. Knecht)

Vessel Name	Fleet #	Vessel Name	Fleet #	Vessel Name	Fleet #

J

Jackman, Capt. Henry	A-3
Jackson, Herbert C.	I-5
Jackson, W.G.	G-9
Jacquelyn Nicole	S-5
Jacques-Cartier	C-29
Jamie L.	M-15
Jana	II-1
Jane Ann IV	T-1
Jarret M	M-13
Jean-Raymond	M-13
Jeanette M.	D-1
Jerry G.	O-3
Jet Express	P-14
Jet Express II	P-14
Jet Express III	P-14
Jet Express IV	P-14
Jette Theresa	IH-6
Jiimaan	M-27
Jill Marie	C-4
Jimmy L.	S-5
Jo Spirit	IJ-1
Joe Van	D-12
John Francis	G-6
John Henry	K-6
Johnson, Martin E.	P-13
Joliet	S-29
Jolliet, Louis	C-28
Joncaire, Daniel	N-5
Jos-Deschenes	S-12
Josee H.	O-3
Joseph-Savard	S-12
Jubilee Queen	J-4
Judge McCombs	H-3
Juleen I	C-26
Julia	II-1
Julie Dee	K-6
Juliet Alicia	K-3
Julietta	II-1
Jumbo Spirit	IJ-2
Jumbo Vision	IJ-2

K

Kaho	G-18
Kajama	G-17
Kamenitza	IN-2
Kaministiqua	L-13
Kane, M.R.	T-6
Kansas	G-14
Kasteelborg	IW-2
Katanni	I-4
Kathryn Spirit	M-13
Kathy Lynn	R-6
Katja	II-1
Katmai Bay	U-3
KCL Barracuda	IT-4
Keenosay	O-5
Keewanis	T-3
Keewatin	P-3

Keizersborg	IW-2
Kelso	C-3
Kendzora, Wally	F-4
Kenosha	U-2
Kent Sunrise	IK-1
Kenteau	G-2
Kentucky	G-14
Keweenaw Star	K-4
Kim R.D.	O-3
Kiyi	G-18
Knutsen, Ellen	IK-2
Knutsen, Hilda	IK-2
Knutsen, Pascale	IK-2
Knutsen, Sidsel	IK-2
Knutsen, Synnove	IK-2
Knutsen, Torill	IK-2
Knutsen, Turid	IK-2
Kobasic, Erika	B-2
Kom	IN-2
Koningsborg	IW-2
Kraynev, Khudozhnik	IF-2
Krios	IS-2
Krista S	C-1
Kristen D	P-5
Kristin J.	E-2
Kristina Theresa	IB-2
Kroonborg	IW-2
Krystal	B-2
Kuber, James L.	L-14
Kuber, Lewis J.	L-14
Kurt Paul	IB-7
Kwintebank	IP-6

L

La Croche	O-3
La Prairie	O-3
Lac Como	M-15
Lac Manitoba	N-1
Lac St-Francois	O-3
Lac Vancouver	M-15
Lady Kate	P-10
Lady Kim I	C-26
Laguna D	ID-1
Lake Char	M-18
Lake Explorer II	U-5
Lake Express	L-5
Lake Guardian	U-5
Lambert Spirit	M-13
Lapointe, Ernest	M-30
Lara	II-1
Larsen, Henry	C-3
LaSalle	S-29
Last Chance	C-18
Latitude Amsterdam	L-10
Laud, Sam	A-5
Laurentian	G-12
Lauzier, Louis M.	C-3
LCU 1680	N-4
Le Draveur	C-29
Le Phil D.	O-3

M

Leandra	II-1
Lee, Nancy A.	L-12
Lehmann, Edgar	IL-2
Lehmann, Hans	IL-2
Leitch, Gordon C.	U-12
Leitch, John D.	U-12
Leona B.	M-22
Le Voyageur	S-13
Liamare	IL-3
Lime Island	V-5
Limnos	C-3
Linda Jean	N-7
Linnea	W-5
Linnhurst	F-1
Little Rock	B-14
Loireborg	IW-2
Lomer-Gouin	S-12
Louie S.	R-4
Louisiana	G-14
LS Christine	IL-1
LS Jacoba	IL-1
LST-393	U-16
LT-5	H-1
Lucia	P-1
Lucien-L.	S-12
Ludington	C-15
Luebbert	II-1
Luedtke, Alan K.	L-15
Luedtke, Chris E.	L-15
Luedtke, Erich R.	L-15
Luedtke, Karl E.	L-15
Luedtke, Kurt R.	L-15

Macassa Bay	W-7
Maccoa	IN-1
MacKay, Tony	M-13
Mackenzie, William Lyon	T-7
Mackinac Express	A-11
Mackinac Islander	A-11
Mackinaw (WLBB-30)	U-3
Mackinaw (WAGB-83)	I-1
Mackinaw City	M-1
Madeline	M-3
Mado-Ray	O-3
Maemi	IC-8
Maid of the Mist IV	M-4
Maid of the Mist V	M-4
Maid of the Mist VI	M-4
Maid of the Mist VII	M-4
Maine	G-14
Maineborg	IW-2
Maisonneuve	M-28
Makeevka	IC-10
Malden	P-13
Malyovitza	IN-2
Manas	IC-6
Manatra	U-8
Mandarin	IO-1
Manistee	L-14

Vessel Name	Fleet #
Manitou	M-5, T-12
Manitou Isle	M-6
Manitowoc	K-8, L-14, U-2
Maple City	T-9
Maple Grove	0-1
Mapleglen	C-2
Margot	N-6
MarineLink Expolorer	U-12
Mariner 1	T-4
Mariposa Belle	M-10
Maritime Trader	V-8
Markborg	IW-2
Market, Wm.	M-23
Marlyn	S-11
Marneborg	IW-2
Marquette	C-11
Marquette II	S-29
Martin, Rt. Hon. Paul J.	C-2
Mary Ellen I	L-9
Marysville	G-1
Massachusetts	G-14
Mather, William G.	M-32
Matt Allen	K-6
Maumee	L-14
Maxima	II-1
McAllister 132	A-1
McAsphalt 401	M-12
McBride, Sam	C-16
McCarthy Jr., Walter J.	A-5
McCauley	U-2
McCleary's Spirit	K-1
McKee Sons	L-14
McKeil, Evans	M-13
McKeil, Jarret	M-13
McLane	G-16
McLeod, Norman	M-12
McQueen, F.R.	M-15
MCT Alioth	IM-4
MCT Almak	IM-4
MCT Altair	IM-4
MCT Arcturus	IM-4
Medemborg	IW-2
Menasha	M-16
Menier Consol	T-6
Merweborg	IW-2
Mesabi Miner	I-5
Meteor	S-20
Metis	E-10
Metsaborg	IW-2
Michigan	C-12
Michiganborg	IW-2
Michipicoten	L-13
Middle Channel	C-7
Miedwie	IP-5
Mighty Jake	G-6
Mighty Jessie	G-6
Mighty Jimmy	G-6
Mighty John III	G-6
Miles, Paddy	H-10
Milwaukee	G-14

Vessel Name	Fleet #
Milwaukee Clipper	S-21
Miners Castle	P-4
Minnesota	G-14
Miro D.	ID-1
Miseford	T-3
Mishe Mokwa	M-6
Misner, H.H.	F-5
Miss Buffalo II	B-16
Miss Edna	K-6
Miss Kim Simpson	T-10
Miss Laura	M-9
Miss Midland	M-21
Miss Munising	M-29
Miss Superior	P-4
Mississagi	L-13
Mississippi	G-14
Missouri	G-14
Missouriborg	IW-2
Mister Joe	M-15
Mobile Bay	U-3
Moby Dick	G-6
Mohawk	M-1
Molly M. 1	M-13
Montana	G-14
Montrealais	U-12
Moor	IL-5
Moore, Olive L.	L-14
Moore, William J.	K-1
Morgan	K-5
Morraborg	IW-2
Morro Bay	U-3
Mottler	IN-1
Mrs. C.	C-26
Mulberry, Marida	IM-1
Munson, John G.	G-13
Munteborg	IW-2
Musky II	G-18

N

Vessel Name	Fleet #
Namaycush	0-5
Nancy Anne	D-12
Nanny	IC-9
Nassauborg	IW-2
Nathan S	C-1
Nautica Queen	N-2
Navcomar No. 1	0-3
Neah Bay	U-3
Nebraska	G-14
Neebish Islander II	E-1
Neeskay	U-10
Nels J.	H-7
Neptune III	D-3
New Beginnings	T-10
New Jersey	G-14
New York	G-14
Newberry, Jerry	M-15
Niagara	E-8
Niagara Prince	IB-4
Niagara Queen II	0-6

Vessel Name	Fleet #
Niagara Spirit	M-13
Nichevo II	M-3
Nickelena	B-2
Nicolet	U-2
Niki S	C-1
Nina	II-1
Nipigon Osprey	0-5
No. 55	M-1
No. 56	M-1
Noble, Robert	W-4
Nogat	IP-5
Nokomis	S-13
Nordic Copenhagen	IN-6
Nordic Stockholm	IN-6
Nordik Express	G-20
Norgoma	S-28
Norisle	F-6
Norris, James	U-12
North Carolina	G-14
North Channel	C-7
North Dakota	G-14
North Fighter	IE-1
North Star	C-8
Northern Spirit I	M-10
Northwestern	G-15
Noyes, Hack	W-10

O

Vessel Name	Fleet #
Oakglen	C-2
Oatka	B-12
Oberstar, Hon. James L	I-5
Obsession III	C-30
Ocean Bertrand Jeansonne	0-3
Ocean Bravo	0-3
Ocean Charlie	0-3
Ocean Delta	0-3
Ocean Echo II	0-3
Ocean Express	0-3
Ocean Foxtrot	0-3
Ocean Georgie Bain	0-3
Ocean Golf	0-3
Ocean Henry Bain	0-3
Ocean Hercule	0-3
Ocean Intrepide	0-3
Ocean Jupiter	0-3
Ocean K. Rusby	0-3
Ocean Lima	0-3
Ocean Raymond Lemay	0-3
Ocean Serge Geois	0-3
Ocean Yvan Desgagnés	0-3
Oceanex Avalon	IO-3
Oceanex Sanderling	IO-3
Odra	IP-5
Ohio	G-14
Ojibway	L-13, M-1
Okapi	IF-5
Oklahoma	G-14
Old Mission	K-5
Olympic Melody	IO-4
Olympic Mentor	IO-4

Maritime Trader departing Duluth for Lake Superior. (Sam Lapinski)

CSL Assiniboine in the St. Marys River, summer 2010. *(Roger LeLievre)*

Lee A. Tregurtha anchored off Marquette. *(Lee Rowe)*

Vessel Name	Fleet #	Vessel Name	Fleet #	Vessel Name	Fleet #
Olympic Merit	IO-4	PML 357	P-13	Rochelle Kaye	R-6
Olympic Miracle	IO-4	PML 2501	P-13	Rocket	P-13
Omni-Atlas	O-3	PML 9000	P-13	Roman, Stephen B.	E-10
Omni-Richelieu	O-3	PML Alton	P-13	Rosaire	D-9
Onego Ponza	IR-2	PML Ironmaster	P-13	Rosalee D.	T-3
Onego Sementina	IM-3	PML Tucci	P-13	Rosemary	M-10
Ongiara	C-16	PML Tucker	P-13	Roxane D	O-3
Ontamich	B-10	Pochard	IH-2	Royal Pescadores	IS-5
Ontario Explorer	O-5	Point Valour	T-3	Ruddy	IN-1
Oriental Kerria	IS-4	Point Viking	C-25	Ryerson, Edward L.	C-6
Oriental Protea	IS-4	Polaris	I-7		
Oriole	M-10	Polydefkis	IA-4		
Orla	IP-5	Pomorze Zachodnie	IP-5	**S**	
Orsula	IA-5	Port City Princess	P-6		
Osborne, F.M.	O-7	Port Méchins	D-9	S/VM 86	M-13
OSC Vlistdiep	IH-3	Prairieland	G-6	Sabina	IE-4
Oshawa	M-15	Presque Isle	G-13	Sabrina	II-1
Ostrander, G.L.	L-2	Pride of Michigan	U-8	Sacre Bleu	S-8
Ottawa	A-11	Princess Wenonah	B-3	Saginaw	L-13
Ouilmette	W-5	Provmar Terminal	U-12	Saguenay	C-2
Outer Island	E-5	Provmar Terminal II	U-12	Sakarya	IC-6
OXL Lotus	IT-1	Puffin	IH-2	Salarium	C-2
		Purcell, Robert W.	A-7	Salvage Monarch	H-6
		Purves, John	D-8	Salvor	M-13
P		Purvis, W.I. Scott	P-13	Sandpiper	H-4
		Purvis, W.J. Isaac	P-13	Sandra Mary	M-15
Pacific Huron	IF-9	Purvis, W.J. Ivan	P-13	Santiago	IB-7
Palabora	IH-2	Put-In-Bay	M-23	Sarah B.	G-11
Palau	IH-2	Pyrgos	IF-5	Sauniere	A-3
Palembang	IH-2			Schlaeger, Victor L.	C-10
Palmerton	IH-2	**Q-R**		Schoening, Hermann	II-1
Pan Voyager	IS-10			Schoonmaker, Col. James M.	M-31
Panagia	IH-2	Qamutik	T-11	Schwartz, H.J	U-2
Panam Atlantico	IC-8	Quebecois	U-12	SCL Bern	IE-4
Pangani	IH-2	Quinte Loyalist	M-27	SE Verdant	IB-1
Papoose III	K-7	Racine	U-2	SE Verdigris	IB-1
Pathfinder	I-5	Radisson	S-12, S-29	SE Viridian	IB-1
Pathfinder	T-5	Radisson, Pierre	C-3	Sea Bear	S-3
Pearkes, George R.	C-3	Radium Yellowknife	B-13	Sea Chief	B-2
Pearl Mist	IP-2	Ramira	IA-2	Sea Eagle II	S-27
Pelee Islander	M-27	Randolph, Curtis	D-4	Sea Force	IP-4
Peninsula	G-10	Ranger III	U-7	Sea Fox II	T-2
Pennsylvania	G-14	Rapide Blanc	O-3	Sea Prince II	R-3
Penobscot Bay	U-3	Rebecca	II-1	Sea Service	H-8
Pere Marquette 41	P-2	Rebecca Lynn	A-7	Seahound	N-1
Perelik	IN-2	Red Witch	L-8	Seajon Enterprise	S-4
Performance	S-25	Redhead	IP-1	Segwun	M-34
Perrin, J.V.	O-3	Rega	IP-5	Selvick, Bonnie G.	C-1
Persenk	IN-2	Reiss	X-1	Selvick, Carla Anne	S-5
Pete, C. West	B-1	Reliance	P-13	Selvick, John M.	C-1
Petite Forte	S-27	Rennie, Thomas	C-16	Selvick, Kimberly	C-1
Pictured Rocks	P-4	Resko	IP-5	Selvick, Sharon M.	S-5
Pierson, Robert S.	L-13	Rest, William	T-9	Selvick, Steven	C-1
Pilica	IP-5	Rhode Island	G-14	Selvick, William C.	S-5
Pineglen	C-2	Richelieu	C-2	Seneca	IA-3
Pioneer	IC-12	Richter, Arni J.	W-4	Serena	II-1
Pioneer Princess	T-8	Ridgway, Benjamin	H-10	Service Boat No. 1	O-3
Pioneer Queen	T-8	Risley, Samuel	C-3	Service Boat No. 4	O-3
Pioneerland	G-6	Robert John	G-10	Seymour, Wilf	M-13
Pitts Carillon	G-2	Robert W.	T-3	Shamrock	J-3
Pitts No. 3	G-2	Robin Lynn	S-7	Shannon	G-1
Playfair	T-5	Robinson Bay	S-25	Sheila Kaye	M-7

Gordon C. Leitch at Port Weller Drydock on Oct. 2, 2010. (Matt Miner)

The information in this book, current as of March 1, 2011, was obtained from the U.S. Coast Guard, Lake Carriers' Association, Lloyd's Register of Shipping, Transport Canada, the U.S. Army Corps of Engineers, St. Lawrence Seaway Authority, Shipfax, Tugfax, The Tugboat Enthusiasts Society of the Americas, vessel owners/operators, BoatNerd.com and publications of the Toronto Marine Historical Society and the Marine Historical Society of Detroit.

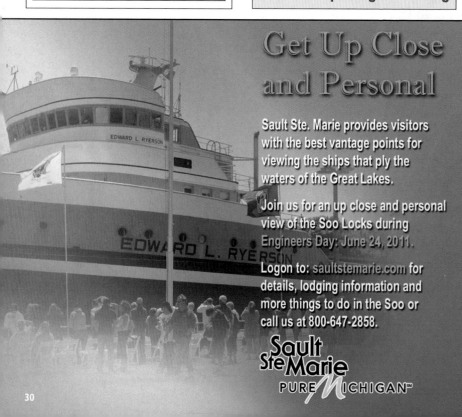

Fleet Listings

Canadian Transfer at Toledo's Cargill Dock.
(Paul C. LaMarre III)

GREAT LAKES / SEAWAY FLEETS

Listed after each vessel in order are: Type of Vessel, Year Built, Type of Engine, Maximum Cargo Capacity (at midsummer draft in long tons) or Gross Tonnage*, Overall Length, Breadth and Depth (from the top of the keel to the top of the upper deck beam) or Draft*. Only vessels over 30 feet long are included. The figures given are as accurate as possible and are given for informational purposes only. Vessels and owners are listed alphabetically as per American Bureau of Shipping and Lloyd's Register of Shipping format. Builder yard and location, as well as other pertinent information, are listed for major vessels; former names of vessels and years of operation under the former names appear in parentheses. A number in brackets following a vessel's name indicates how many vessels, including the one listed, have carried that name. Web addresses can change without notice.

KEY TO TYPE OF VESSEL

2B ....Brigantine	DS ....Spud Barge	PB .... Pilot Boat
2S ....2-Masted Schooner	DV ....Drilling Vessel	PF ....Passenger Ferry
3S ....3-Masted Schooner	DW .... Scow	PK ....Package Freighter
4S ....4-Masted Schooner	ES ....Excursion Ship	RR ....Roll On/Roll Off
AC ....Auto Carrier	EV ....Environmental Response	RT ....Refueling Tanker
AT ....Articulated Tug	FB ....Fireboat	RV ....Research Vessel
ATB ....Articulated Tug/Barge	FD ....Floating Dry Dock	SB ....Supply Boat
BC ....Bulk Carrier	FT ....Fishing Tug	SC .... Sand Carrier
BK ....Bulk Carrier/Tanker	GC ....General Cargo	SR .... Search and Rescue
BT ....Buoy Tender	GL ....Gate Lifter	SU ....Self-Unloader
CA ....Catamaran	GU .... Grain Self-Unloader	SV ....Survey Vessel
CC .... Cement Carrier	HL ....Heavy Lift Vessel	TB ....Tugboat
CF ....Car Ferry	IB ....Ice Breaker	TF ....Train Ferry
CO ....Container Vessel	IT ....Integrated Tug	TK ....Tanker
CS ....Crane Ship	ITB ....Integrated Tug/Barge	TW ....Towboat
DB ....Deck Barge	MB ....Mailboat	TT ....Tractor Tugboat
DH ....Hopper Barge	MU ....Museum Vessel	TV ....Training Vessel
DR ....Dredge	PA ....Passenger Vessel	

KEY TO PROPULSION

B ....Barge	R ....Steam – Triple Exp. Compound Engine
D ....Diesel	S ....Steam – Skinner "Uniflow" Engine
DE ....Diesel Electric	T ....Steam – Turbine Engine
Q ....Steam – Quad Exp. Compound Engine	W ....Sailing Vessel (Wind)

Fleet Name Vessel Name	IMO #	Vessel Type	Year Built	Engine Type	Cargo Cap. or Gross*	Overall Length	Breadth	Depth
A-1 **A. B. M. MARINE, THUNDER BAY, ON**								
McAllister 132		DB	1954	B	7,000	343'00"	63'00"	19'00"
Built: Burrard Dry Dock, N. Vancouver, BC (Powell No. 1 '54-'61, Alberni Carrier '61-'77, Genmar 132 '77-'79)								
W. N. Twolan	5384360	TB	1962	D	299*	106'00"	29'05"	15'00"
Built: George T. Davie & Sons, Lauzon, QC								
A-2 **ACHESON VENTURES LLC, PORT HURON, MI** (achesonventures.com)								
Highlander Sea		ES/2S	1927	W/D	140*	154'00"	25'06"	14'00"
Built: A.D. Story Shipyard, Essex, MA (Pilot '27-'76, Star Pilot '76-'98, Caledonia '98-'98)								
A-3 **ALGOMA CENTRAL CORP., ST. CATHARINES, ON** (www.algonet.com)								
Algobay	7711725	SU	1978	D	36,668	740'00"	77'11"	49'03"
Built: Collingwood Shipyards, Collingwood, ON; rebuilt with a new forebody at Chengxi Shipyard Co. Ltd.,								
Jiangyin City, China, in '09 (Algobay '78-'94, Atlantic Trader '94-'97)								
Algocape {2}	6703214	BC	1967	D	29,544	729'09"	75'00"	39'08"
Built: Davie Shipbuilding Co., Lauzon, QC (Richelieu {3} '67-'94)								
Algolake	7423093	SU	1977	D	32,807	730'00"	75'00"	46'06"
Built: Collingwood Shipyards, Collingwood, ON								
Algoma Discovery	8505848	BC	1987	D	34,380	729'00"	75'09"	48'05"
Built: 3 Maj Brodogradiliste d.d., Rijeka, Croatia (Malinska '87-'97, Daviken '97-'08)								
Algoma Guardian	8505850	BC	1987	D	34,380	729'00"	75'09"	48'05"
Built: 3 Maj Brodogradiliste d.d., Rijeka, Croatia (Omisalj '87-'97, Goviken '97-'08)								
Algoma Spirit	8504882	BC	1986	D	34,380	729'00"	75'09"	48'05"
Built: 3 Maj Brodogradiliste d.d., Rijeka, Croatia (Petka '86-'00, Sandviken '00-'08)								

Fleet Name / Vessel Name	IMO #	Vessel Type	Year Built	Engine Type	Cargo Cap. or Gross*	Overall Length	Breadth	Depth
Algomarine	6816607	SU	1968	D	26,755	730' 00"	75' 00"	39' 08"

Built: Davie Shipbuilding Co., Lauzon, QC; converted to a self-unloader by Port Weller Dry Docks, St. Catharines, ON, in '89 (Lake Manitoba '68-'87)

Algonorth	7028104	BC	1971	D	28,750	729' 10"	75' 02"	42' 11"

Built: Upper Clyde Shipbuilders, Govan, Scotland; laid up at Thunder Bay, ON, since Jan. 1, 2009 (Temple Bar '71-'76, Lake Nipigon '76-'84, Laketon {2} '84-'86, Lake Nipigon '86-'87)

Algontario	5301980	BC	1960	D	29,100	730' 00"	75' 09"	40' 02"

Built: Schlieker-Werft, Hamburg, West Germany; rebuilt and lengthened with new forebody at Davie Shipyard, Lauzon, QC, in '77; entered long-term lay-up at Toronto, ON, on July 4, 2009.
([Fore Section] Cartiercliffe Hall '76-'88, Winnipeg {2} '88-'94 [Stern Section] Ruhr Ore '60-'76)

Algorail {2}	6805531	SU	1968	D	23,810	640' 05"	72' 00"	40' 00"

Built: Collingwood Shipyards, Collingwood, ON

Algosoo {2}	7343619	SU	1974	D	30,284	730' 00"	75' 00"	44' 06"

Built: Collingwood Shipyards, Collingwood, ON; last Great Lakes vessel built with cabins at the bow

Algosteel {2}	6613299	SU	1966	D	26,949	730' 00"	75' 00"	39' 08"

Built: Davie Shipbuilding Co., Lauzon, QC; converted to a self-unloader by Port Weller Dry Docks, St. Catharines, ON, in '89; entered long-term lay-up at Montreal, QC, on Dec. 27, 2010 (A. S. Glossbrenner '66-'87, Algogulf {1} '87-'90)

Algoway {2}	7221251	SU	1972	D	23,812	646' 06"	72' 00"	40' 00"

Built: Collingwood Shipyards, Collingwood, ON

Algowood	7910216	SU	1981	D	32,253	740' 00"	75' 11"	46' 06"

Built: Collingwood Shipyards, Collingwood, ON; lengthened 10' in '00 at Port Weller Dry Docks, St. Catharines, ON

Capt. Henry Jackman	8006323	SU	1981	D	30,590	730' 00"	75' 11"	42' 00"

Built: Collingwood Shipyards, Collingwood, ON; converted to a self-unloader by Port Weller Dry Docks, St. Catharines, ON, in '96 (Lake Wabush '81-'87)

John B. Aird	8002432	SU	1983	D	31,000	730' 00"	75' 10"	46' 06"

Built: Collingwood Shipyards, Collingwood, ON

Peter R. Cresswell	8016641	SU	1982	D	30,590	730' 00"	75' 11"	42' 00"

Built: Collingwood Shipyards, Collingwood, ON; converted to a self-unloader by Port Weller Dry Docks, St. Catharines, ON, in '98 (Algowest '82-'01)

Sauniere	7028489	SU	1970	D	23,430	642' 10"	74' 10"	42' 00"

Built: Lithgows Ltd., East Yard, Glasgow, Scotland; lengthened 122' by Swan Hunter Ship Repairers, North Shields, UK, in '75; converted to a self-unloader by Herb Fraser & Associates, Port Colborne, ON, in '76; entered long-term lay-up at Montreal, QC, March 1, 2009 (Bulknes '70-'70, Brooknes '70-'76, Algosea {1} '76-'82)

Tim S. Dool	6800919	BC	1967	D	31,054	730' 00"	77' 11"	39' 08"

Built: Saint John Shipbuilding & Drydock Co., Saint John, NB; widened by 3' at Port Weller Dry Docks, St. Catharines, ON, in '96 (Senneville '67-'94, Algoville '94-'08)

▶ *New construction: Algoma Central Corp. has five "Equinox" class vessels on order from Chengxi Shipyard Co. Ltd., Jiangyin City, China, the first of which is expected to enter service in 2013.*

▶ *New acquisitions: At press time, Algoma Central Corp. was in the process of purchasing the 11 vessels operated by Upper Lakes Group's Seaway Marine Transport division (fleet U-12).*

ALGOMA TANKERS LTD., ST. CATHARINES, ON – DIVISION OF ALGOMA CENTRAL CORP.

Algocanada	9378591	TK	2008	D	11,453	426' 01"	65' 00"	32' 08"

Built: Eregli Shipyard, Zonguldak, Turkey

Algoeast	7526924	TK	1977	D	10,350	431' 05"	65' 07"	35' 05"

Built: Mitsubishi Heavy Industries Ltd., Shimonoseki, Japan; converted from single to double hull by Port Weller Dry Docks, St. Catharines, ON, in '00 (Texaco Brave {2} '77-'86, Le Brave '86-'97, Imperial St. Lawrence {2} '97-'97)

Algoma Dartmouth	9327516	RT	2007	D	3,512	296' 11"	47' 11"	24' 11"

Built: Turkter Shipyard, Tuzla, Turkey; vessel is engaged in bunkering operations at Halifax, NS| (Clipper Bardolino '07 - '08, Samistal Due '08 - '09)

Algonova {2}	9378589	TK	2008	D	11,453	426' 01"	65' 00"	32' 08"

Built: Eregli Shipyard, Zonguldak, Turkey (Eregli 04 '07-'08)

Algosar {2}	7634288	TK	1978	D	12,000	434' 06"	65' 00"	29' 04"

Built: Levingston Shipbuilding Co., Orange, TX (Gemini '78-'05)

Algoscotia	9273222	TK	2004	D	19,160	488' 03"	78' 00"	42' 00"

Built: Jiangnan Shipyard (Group) Co. Ltd., Shangahi, China

Algosea {2}	9127198	TK	1998	D	17,258	472' 07"	75' 04"	40'08"

Built: Alabama Shipyard Inc., Mobile, AL (Aggersborg '98-'05)

A-4   AMERICAN MARINE CONSTRUCTORS INC., BENTON HARBOR, MI (americanmarineconstructors.com)

AMC 100		DB	1977	B	1,361*	200' 00"	54' 00"	14'00"
AMC 200		DB	1977	B	1,361*	200' 00"	54' 00"	14'00"
AMC 300		DB	1977	B	1,047*	180' 00"	54' 00"	12'00"
Alice E		TB	1944	D	146*	86' 00"	25' 00"	9' 08"

Built: George Lawley & Son Corp., Neponset, MA

Fleet Name / Vessel Name	IMO #	Vessel Type	Year Built	Engine Type	Cargo Cap. or Gross*	Overall Length	Breadth	Depth
Defiance		TW	1966	D	39*	48' 00"	18' 00"	6' 03"
Wisconsin		CS	1965	B	309*	103' 00"	50' 00"	14' 00"

A-5   AMERICAN STEAMSHIP CO., WILLIAMSVILLE, NY (americansteamship.com)

Fleet Name / Vessel Name	IMO #	Vessel Type	Year Built	Engine Type	Cargo Cap. or Gross*	Overall Length	Breadth	Depth
Adam E. Cornelius {4}	7326245	SU	1973	D	29,200	680' 00"	78' 00"	42' 00"
Built: American Shipbuilding Co., Toledo, OH (Roger M. Kyes '73-'89)								
American Century	7923196	SU	1981	D	80,900	1,000' 00"	105' 00"	56' 00"
Built: Bay Shipbuilding Co., Sturgeon Bay, WI (Columbia Star '81-'06)								
American Courage	7634226	SU	1979	D	24,300	636' 00"	68' 00"	40' 00"
Built: Bay Shipbuilding Co., Sturgeon Bay, WI (Fred R. White Jr. '79-'06)								
American Fortitude	5105843	T	1953		23,400	690' 00"	70' 00"	37' 00"
Built: American Shipbuilding Co., Lorain, OH; converted to a self-unloader by Bay Shipbuilding, Sturgeon Bay, WI, in '81; entered long-term-layup Nov. 11, 2008 at Toledo, OH (Ernest T. Weir {2} '53-'78, Courtney Burton '78-'06)								
American Integrity	7514696	SU	1978	D	80,900	1,000' 00"	105' 00"	56' 00"
Built: Bay Shipbuilding Co., Sturgeon Bay, WI (Lewis Wilson Foy '78-'91, Oglebay Norton '91-'06)								
American Mariner	7812567	SU	1980	D	37,300	730' 00"	78' 00"	42' 00"
Built: Bay Shipbuilding Co., Sturgeon Bay, WI (Laid down as Chicago {3})								
American Republic	7914236	SU	1981	D	25,600	634' 10"	68' 00"	39' 07"
Built: Bay Shipbuilding Co., Sturgeon Bay, WI								
American Spirit	7423392	SU	1978	D	62,400	1,004' 00"	105' 00"	50' 00"
Built: American Shipbuilding Co., Lorain, OH (George A. Stinson '78-'04)								
American Valor	5024738	SU	1953	T	26,200	767' 00"	70' 00"	36' 00"
Built: American Shipbuilding Co., Lorain, OH; lengthened 120' by Fraser Shipyard, Superior, WI, in '74, converted to a self-unloader in '82; entered long-term-layup Nov. 13, 2008 at Toledo, OH (Armco '53-'06)								
American Victory	5234395	SU	1942	T	26,700	730' 00"	75' 00"	39' 03"
Built: Bethlehem Shipbuilding and Drydock Co., Sparrows Point, MD; converted from saltwater tanker to a Great Lakes bulk carrier by Maryland Shipbuilding in '61; converted to a self-unloader by Bay Shipbuilding Co., Sturgeon Bay, WI, in '82; entered long-term-layup Nov. 12, 2008 at Superior, WI								
(Laid down as Marquette. USS Neshanic [AO-71] '42-'47, Gulfoil '47-'61, Pioneer Challenger '61-'62, Middletown '62-'06)								
Buffalo {3}	7620653	SU	1978	D	24,300	634' 10"	68' 00"	40' 00"
Built: Bay Shipbuilding Co., Sturgeon Bay, WI								
Burns Harbor {2}	7514713	SU	1980	D	80,900	1,000' 00"	105' 00"	56' 00"
Built: Bay Shipbuilding Co., Sturgeon Bay, WI								
H. Lee White {2}	7366362	SU	1974	D	35,400	704' 00"	78' 00"	45' 00"
Built: Bay Shipbuilding Co., Sturgeon Bay, WI								
Indiana Harbor	7514701	SU	1979	D	80,900	1,000' 00"	105' 00"	56' 00"
Built: Bay Shipbuilding Co., Sturgeon Bay, WI								
John J. Boland {4}	7318901	SU	1973	D	34,000	680' 00"	78' 00"	45' 00"
Built: Bay Shipbuilding Co., Sturgeon Bay, WI (Charles E. Wilson '73-'00)								
Sam Laud	7390210	SU	1975	D	24,300	634' 10"	68' 00"	40' 00"
Built: Bay Shipbuilding Co., Sturgeon Bay, WI								
St. Clair {3}	7403990	SU	1976	D	44,800	770' 00"	92' 00"	52' 00"
Built: Bay Shipbuilding Co., Sturgeon Bay, WI								
Walter J. McCarthy Jr.	7514684	SU	1977	D	80,500	1,000' 00"	105' 00"	56' 00"
Built: Bay Shipbuilding Co., Sturgeon Bay, WI (Belle River '77-'90)								

A-6   AMHERSTBURG FERRY CO. INC, AMHERSTBURG, ON

Fleet Name / Vessel Name	IMO #	Vessel Type	Year Built	Engine Type	Cargo Cap. or Gross*	Overall Length	Breadth	Depth
The Columbia V		PA/CF	1946	D	46*	65' 00"	28' 10"	8' 06"
Built: Champion Auto Ferries, Algonac, MI (Crystal O, St. Clair Flats)								
The Ste. Claire V		PA/CF	1997	D	82*	86' 06"	32' 00"	6' 00"
Built: Les Ateliers Maurice Bourbonnais Ltée, Gatineau, QC (Courtney O., M. Bourbonnais)								

A-7   ANDRIE INC., MUSKEGON, MI (andrie.com)

Fleet Name / Vessel Name	IMO #	Vessel Type	Year Built	Engine Type	Cargo Cap. or Gross*	Overall Length	Breadth	Depth
A-390		TK	1982	B	2,346*	310' 00"	60' 00"	17' 00"
Built: St. Louis Shipbuilding & Steel Co., St. Louis, MO (Canonie 40 '82-'92)								
A-397		TK	1962	B	2,928*	270' 00"	60' 01"	22' 05"
Built: Dravo Corp., Pittsburgh, PA (Auntie Mame '62-'91, Iron Mike '91-'93)								
A-410		TK	1955	B	3,793*	335' 00"	54' 00"	17' 00"
Built: Ingalls Shipbuilding Corp., Birmingham, AL (Methane '55-'63, B-6400 '63-'71, Kelly '71-'86, Canonie 50 '86-'93)								
Barbara Andrie	5097187	TB	1940	D	298*	122' 00"	29' 07"	16' 00"
Built: Pennsylvania Shipyards Inc., Beaumont, TX (Edmond J. Moran '40-'76)								
Endeavour		TK	2009	B	7,232*	360' 00"	60' 00"	24' 00"
Built: Jeffboat LLC, Jeffersonville, IN								
Karen Andrie {2}	6520454	TB	1965	D	516*	120' 00"	31' 06"	16' 00"
Built: Gulfport Shipbuilding, Port Arthur, TX (Sarah Hays '65-'93)								

American Spirit leaves Duluth, seen from the Aerial Lift Bridge. (Mike Sipper)

Fleet Name Vessel Name	IMO #	Vessel Type	Year Built	Engine Type	Cargo Cap. or Gross*	Overall Length	Breadth	Depth
Rebecca Lynn	6511374	TB	1964	D	433*	112' 07"	31' 06"	16' 00"
Built: Gulfport Shipbuilding, Port Arthur, TX (Kathrine Clewis '64-'96)								
Robert W. Purcell		TB	1943	D	29*	45' 02"	12' 10"	7' 08"
Built: Sturgeon Bay Shipbuilding, Sturgeon Bay, WI								
Ronald J. Dahlke		TB	1903	D	58*	63' 04"	17' 06"	9' 00"
Built: Johnston Bros., Ferrysburg, MI (Bonita '03-'14, Chicago Harbor No. 4 '14-'60, Eddie B. '60-'69, Seneca Queen '69-'70, Ludington '70-'96, Seneca Queen '96-'04)								

A-8 APOSTLE ISLANDS CRUISE SERVICE, BAYFIELD, WI *(apostleisland.com)*

Island Princess {2}		ES	1973	D	63*	65' 07"	20' 05"	7' 03"
Built: Defoe Shipbuilding Co., Bay City, MI								

A-9 ARCELORMITTAL MINES CANADA, PORT CARTIER, QC *(www.arcelormittal.com/minescanada)*

Brochu	7305899	TT	1973	D	390*	98' 11"	36' 00"	12' 04"
Built: Star Shipyards Ltd., New Westminster, BC								
Vachon	7305904	TT	1973	D	390*	98' 11"	36' 00"	12' 04"
Built: Star Shipyards Ltd., New Westminster, BC								

A-10 ARGEE BOAT CRUISES LTD., PENETANGUISHENE, ON *(georgianbaycruises.com)*

Georgian Queen		ES	1918	D	249*	119' 00"	36' 00"	16' 06"
Built: Port Arthur Shipbuilding, Port Arthur, ON (Victoria '18-'18, Murray Stewart '18-'48, David Richard '48-'79)								

A-11 ARNOLD TRANSIT CO., MACKINAC ISLAND, MI *(arnoldline.com)*

Algomah		PF/PK	1961	D	81*	93' 00"	29' 08"	5' 02"
Built: Paasch Marine Services Inc., Erie, PA								
Beaver		CF	1952	D	84*	64' 09"	30' 02"	6' 05"
Built: Lock City Machine/Marine, Sault Ste. Marie, MI								
Chippewa {6}		PF/PK	1962	D	81*	93' 00"	29' 08"	5' 02"
Built: Paasch Marine Services Inc., Erie, PA								
Corsair		CF	1955	D	98*	94' 06"	33' 01"	8' 01"
Built: Blount Marine Corp., Warren, RI								
Huron {5}		PF/PK	1955	D	99*	91' 06"	25' 00"	7' 00"
Built: Paasch Marine Services Inc., Erie, PA								
Island Express		PF/CA	1988	D	90*	82' 07"	28' 06"	8' 04"
Built: Gladding-Hearn Shipbuilding, Somerset, MA								
Mackinac Express		PF/CA	1987	D	90*	82' 07"	28' 04"	8' 04"
Built: Gladding-Hearn Shipbuilding, Somerset, MA								

Saguenay inbound to load grain at Toledo. *(Jim Hoffman)*

	Fleet Name Vessel Name	IMO #	Vessel Type	Year Built	Engine Type	Cargo Cap. or Gross*	Overall Length	Breadth	Depth
	Mackinac Islander		CF	1947	D	99*	84' 00"	30' 00"	8' 02"
	Built: Sturgeon Bay Shipbuilding, Sturgeon Bay, WI (Drummond Islander '47-'02)								
	Ottawa {2}		PF/PK	1959	D	81*	93' 00"	29' 08"	5' 02"
	Built: Paasch Marine Services Inc., Erie, PA								
	Straits Express		PF/CA	1995	D	99*	101' 00"	28' 08"	10' 00"
	Built: Marinette Marine Corp., Marinette, WI								
	Straits of Mackinac II		PF/PK	1969	D	89*	89' 11"	27' 00"	8' 08"
	Built: Blount Marine Corp., Warren, RI								
A-12	**ASHLAND BAYFIELD CRUISE LINE INC., WASHBURN, WI**								
	Ashland Bayfield Express		PA	1995	D	13*	49' 00"	18' 05"	5' 00"
	Built: Bellecraft Industries, Naples, FL (Sea Venture II)								
A-13	**ASI GROUP LTD., ST. CATHARINES, ON** *(asi-group.com)*								
	ASI Clipper		SV	1939	D	64*	70' 00"	23' 00"	6' 06"
	Built: Port Colborne Iron Works, Port Colborne, ON (Stanley Clipper '39-'94, Nadro Clipper '94-'08)								
B-1	**B & L TUG SERVICE, THESSALON, ON**								
	C. West Pete		TB	1958	D	29*	65' 00"	17' 05"	6' 00"
	Built: Erieau Shipbuilding & Drydock Co. Ltd., Erieau, ON								
B-2	**BASIC MARINE INC., ESCANABA, MI** *(basicmarine.com)*								
	BMI-192		DB	2009	B	1219*	220' 02"	55' 00"	12' 00"
	Built: Basic Marine Inc., Escanaba, MI								
	BMI-FDD-1		FD	1981		301*	160' 02"	65' 00"	8 08"
	Danicia	8991774	TB	1943	DE	240*	110' 02"	26' 04"	14' 08"
	Built: Ira S. Bushy and Sons Inc., Brooklyn, NY; inactive at Escanaba, MI *(USCGC Chinook [WYT / WYTM-96] '44-'86, Tracie B '86-'98)*								
	Erika Kobasic		TB	1939	DE	226*	110' 00"	25' 01"	14' 03"
	Built: Gulfport Shipbuilding, Port Arthur, TX (USCGC Arundel [WYT / WYTM-90] '39-'84, Karen Andrie {1} '84-'90)								
	Escort		TB	1969	D	26*	50' 00"	14' 00"	6' 03"
	Built: Jakobson Shipyard, Oyster Bay, NY								
	Greenstone		TK	1977	B	114*	81' 00"	24' 00"	7' 09"
	Krystal		TB	1954	D	23*	45' 02"	12' 08"	6' 00"
	Built: Roamer Boat Co., Holland, MI (ST-2168 '54-'62, Thunder Bay '62-'02)								
	Nickelena		TB	1973	D	240*	109' 00"	30' 07"	15' 08"
	Built: Marinette Marine Corp., Marinette, WI (USS Chetek [YTB-827] '73-'96, Chetek '96-'00, Koziol '00-'08)								

Tanker Esta Desgagnés, the former Emerald Star. (Paul Beesley)

Fleet Name / Vessel Name	IMO #	Vessel Type	Year Built	Engine Type	Cargo Cap. or Gross*	Overall Length	Breadth	Depth
Sea Chief	8991633	TB	1952	D	196*	107' 00"	26' 06"	15' 00"

Built: Avondale Marine Ways Inc., Westwego, LA; inactive at Escanaba, MI
(U. S. Army LT-1944 '52-'62, USCOE Washington '62-'00)

B-3 BAY CITY BOAT LINES LLC, BAY CITY, MI *(baycityboatlines.com)*

Islander {1}		ES	1946	D	39*	53' 04"	19' 09"	5' 04"

Built: Knudsen Brothers Shipbuilding Co., Superior, WI

Princess Wenonah		ES	1954	D	96*	64' 09"	31' 00"	7' 03"

Built: Sturgeon Bay Shipbuilding Co., Sturgeon Bay, WI (William M. Miller '54-'98)

B-4 BAY SHIPBUILDING CO., STURGEON BAY, WI *(bayshipbuildingcompany.com)*

Bayship		TB	1943	D	19*	45' 00"	12' 04"	5' 03"

Built: Sturgeon Bay Shipbuilding Co., Sturgeon Bay, WI (Sturshipco)

B-5 BAYSAIL, BAY CITY, MI *(baysailbaycity.org)*

Appledore IV		2S/ES	1989	W/D	48*	85' 00"	18' 08"	8' 08"

Built: Treworgy Yachts, Palm Coast, FL

Appledore V		2S/ES	1992	W/D	34*	65' 00"	14' 00"	8' 06"

Built: Treworgy Yachts, Palm Coast, FL (Westwind, Appledore)

B-6 BEAUSOLEIL FIRST NATION TRANSPORTATION, CHRISTIAN ISLAND, ON *(chimnissing.ca)*

Indian Maiden		PA/CF	1987	D	91.5*	73' 06"	23' 00"	8' 00"

Built: Duratug Shipyard & Fabricating Ltd., Port Dover, ON

Sandy Graham		PA/CF	1957	D	212*	125' 07"	39' 09"	8' 00"

Built: Barbour Boat Works Inc., New Bern, NC

B-7 BEAVER ISLAND BOAT CO., CHARLEVOIX, MI *(bibco.com)*

Beaver Islander		PF/CF	1963	D	95*	96' 03"	27' 02"	8' 03"

Built: Sturgeon Bay Shipbuilding, Sturgeon Bay, WI

Emerald Isle {2}		PF/CF	1997	D	95*	130' 00"	38' 00"	12' 00"

Built: Washburn & Doughty Associates Inc., East Boothbay, ME

B-8 BLUE HERON CO., TOBERMORY, ON *(blueheronco.com)*

Blue Heron V		ES	1983	D	24*	54' 06"	17' 05"	7' 02"

Built: Kanter Yacht Corp., St. Thomas, ON

Great Blue Heron		ES	1994	D	112*	79' 00"	22' 00"	6' 05"

Built: Hike Metal Products, Wheatley, ON

B-9 BLUEWATER EXCURSIONS INC., FORT GRATIOT, MI *(huronlady.com)*

Huron Lady II		ES	1993	D	82*	65' 00"	19' 00"	10' 00"

Built: Navigator Boat Works (Lady Lumina '93-'99)

B-10 BLUE WATER FERRY CO., SOMBRA, ON *(bluewaterferry.com)*

Daldean		CF	1951	D	145*	75' 00"	35' 00"	7' 00"

Built: Erieau Shipbuilding & Drydock Co. Ltd., Erieau, ON

Ontamich		CF	1939	D	55*	65' 00"	28' 10"	8' 06"

Built: Champion Auto Ferries, Harsens Island, MI (Harsens Island '39-'73)

B-11 BRIGANTINE INC., KINGSTON, ON *(brigantine.ca)*

St. Lawrence II		TV	1954	W/D	34*	72' 00"	15' 00"	8' 06"

Built: Kingston Shipyards, Kingston, ON

B-12 BRUCE VON RIEDEL, CORNUCOPIA, WI

Oatka		TB	1935	D	8*	40' 00"	10' 00"	3' 01"

B-13 BUCHANAN FOREST PRODUCTS LTD., THUNDER BAY, ON

Radium Yellowknife	5288956	TB	1948	D	235*	120' 00"	28' 00"	6' 00"

Built: Yarrow's Ltd., Esquimalt, BC

B-14 BUFFALO AND ERIE COUNTY NAVAL & MILITARY PARK, BUFFALO, NY *(buffalonavalpark.org)*

Croaker		MU	1944	D	1,526*	311' 07"	27' 02"	33' 09"

Former U. S. Navy "Gato" class submarine IXSS-246; open to the public at Buffalo, NY

Little Rock		MU	1945	T	10,670*	610' 01"	66' 04"	25' 00"

Former U. S. Navy "Cleveland / Little Rock" class guided missile cruiser; open to the public at Buffalo, NY

The Sullivans		MU	1943	T	2,500*	376' 06"	39' 08"	22' 08"

Former U. S. Navy "Fletcher" class destroyer; open to the public at Buffalo, NY (Launched as USS Putnam)

B-15 BUFFALO DEPARTMENT OF PUBLIC WORKS, BUFFALO, NY

Edward M. Cotter		FB	1900	D	208*	118' 00"	24' 00"	11' 06"

Built: Crescent Shipbuilding, Elizabeth, NJ (W. S. Grattan 1900-'53, Firefighter '53-'54)

Fleet Name Vessel Name	IMO #	Vessel Type	Year Built	Engine Type	Cargo Cap. or Gross*	Overall Length	Breadth	Depth

B-16 BUFFALO HARBOR CRUISES, BUFFALO, NY (buffaloharborcruises.com)

Miss Buffalo II		ES	1972	D	88*	81' 09"	24' 00"	6' 00"

B-17 BUFFALO SAILING ADVENTURES INC., AMHERST, NY (spiritofbuffalo.com)

Spirit of Buffalo		2S/ES	1992	D/W	34*	73' 00"	15' 06"	7' 02"

Built: Rover Marine Lines Inc., Norfolk, VA (Jolly Rover)

B-18 BUSCH MARINE INC., CARROLLTON, MI (buschmarine.com)

BMT 3		DB	1965	B	280*	120' 01"	36' 01"	7' 06"

Built: Hillman Barge & Construction Co., Brownsville, PA (BC 12 '65 - '09)

Edwin C. Busch		TB	1935	D	18*	42' 06"	11' 11"	5' 00"

Built: Manitowoc Shipbuilding Co., Manitowoc, WI (Paul L. Luedtke '35-'02, Joanne '02-'09)

Gregory J. Busch	5156725	TB	1919	D	299*	151' 00"	27' 06"	14' 07"

Built: Whitney Bros. Co., Superior, WI (Humaconna '19-'77)

STC 2004		TK	1963	B	1,230*	250' 00"	50' 00"	12' 00"

Built: St. Louis Shipbuilding & Steel Co., St. Louis, MO

C-1 CALUMET RIVER FLEETING INC., CHICAGO, IL (g-lakes.com)

Bonnie G. Selvick		TB	1981	D	45*	57' 08"	17' 00"	6' 01"

(Captain Robbie '81-'90, Philip M. Pearse '90-'97, Chris Ann '97-'09)

Daryl C. Hannah {2}		TW	1956	D	268*	102' 00"	28' 00"	8' 00"

Built: Calumet Shipyard & Drydock Co., Chicago, IL (Cindy Jo '56-'66, Katherine L. '66-'93)

John M. Selvick	8993370	TB	1898	D	256*	118' 00"	24' 03"	16' 00"

Built: Chicago Shipbuilding Co., Chicago, IL (Illinois {1} 1898-'41, John Roen III '41-'74)

Kimberly Selvick		TW	1975	D	93*	57' 07"	28' 00"	10' 00"

Built: Grafton Boat Co., Grafton, IL (Scout '75-'02)

Krista S		TB	1954	D	93*	67' 09"	20' 01"	7' 07"

Built: Pascagoula, MS (Sea Wolf '54-'01, Jimmy Wray '01-'08)

Mary E. Hannah		TB	1945	D	612*	149' 00"	33' 00"	16' 00"

Built: Marietta Manufacturing, Marietta, GA (U. S. Army LT-821 '45-'47, Brooklyn '47-'66, Lee Reuben '66-'75)

Nathan S		TB	1951	D	144*	84' 01"	23' 06"	9'06"

Built: Ira S. Bushey & Sons Inc., Brooklyn, NY (Huntington '51-'05, Spartacus '05-'06, Huntington '06-'08)

Niki S		TW	1971	D	39*	42' 00"	18' 00"	6' 00"

Built: Scully Bros. Boat Builders, Morgan City, LA (Miss Josie '71-'79, Matador VI '79-'08)

Peggy D. Hannah		TB	1920	D	145*	108' 00"	25' 06"	14' 00"

Built: Whitney Bros. Co., Superior, WI (William A. Whitney '20-'92)

Steven Selvick		TB	1954	D	120*	82' 00"	23' 06"	9' 09"

Built: Defoe Shipbuilding Co., Bay City, MI (John A. McGuire '54-'87, William Hoey {1} '87-'94, Margaret Ann '94-'08)

Zuccolo		TB	1954	D	76*	66' 00"	19' 00"	9' 00"

(Sanita '54-'77, Soo Chief '77-'81, Susan M. Selvick '81-'96, Nathan S. '96-'02, John M. Perry '02-'08)

C-2 CANADA STEAMSHIP LINES INC., MONTREAL, QC (csl.ca)
(VESSELS MANAGED BY V.SHIPS CANADA INC., MONTREAL, QC)

Atlantic Erie	8016639	SU	1985	D	37,411	736' 07"	75' 10"	50' 00"

Built: Collingwood Shipyards, Collingwood, ON (Hon. Paul Martin '85-'88)

Atlantic Huron {2}	8025680	SU	1984	D	34,860	736' 07"	77' 11"	46' 04"

Built: Collingwood Shipyards, Collingwood, ON; converted to a self-unloader in '89 and widened 3' in '03 at Port Weller Dry Docks, St. Catharines, ON (Prairie Harvest '84-'89, Atlantic Huron {2} '89-'94, Melvin H. Baker II {2} '94-'97)

Atlantic Superior	7927805	SU	1982	D	36,219	730' 00"	75' 10"	50' 00"

Built: Collingwood Shipyards, Collingwood, ON (Atlantic Superior '82-'97, M. H. Baker III '97-'03)

Birchglen {2}	8119273	BC	1983	D	33,824	730' 01"	75' 09"	48' 00"

Built: Govan Shipyards, Glasgow, Scotland
(Canada Marquis '83-'91, Federal Richelieu '91-'91, Federal MacKenzie '91-'01, MacKenzie '01-'02)

Cedarglen {2}	5103974	BC	1959	D	29,518	730' 00"	75' 09"	40' 04"

Built: Schlieker-Werft, Hamburg, West Germany; rebuilt, lengthened with a new forebody at Davie Shipbuilding Co., Lauzon, QC, in '77 ([Stern Section] Ems Ore '59-'76, [Fore Section] Montcliffe Hall '76-'88, Cartierdoc '88-'02)

CSL Assiniboine	7413218	SU	1977	D	36,768	739' 10"	78' 00"	48' 05"

Built: Davie Shipbuilding Co., Lauzon, QC; rebuilt with a new forebody at Port Weller Dry Docks, St. Catharines, ON, in '05 (Jean Parisien '77-'05)

CSL Laurentien	7423108	SU	1977	D	37,795	739' 10"	78' 00"	48' 05"

Built: Collingwood Shipyards, Collingwood, ON; rebuilt with new forebody in '01 at Port Weller Dry Docks, St. Catharines, ON (Stern section: Louis R. Desmarais '77-'01)

CSL Niagara	7128423	SU	1972	D	37,694	739' 10"	78' 00"	48' 05"

Built: Collingwood Shipyards, Collingwood, ON; rebuilt with a new forebody in '99 at Port Weller Dry Docks, St. Catharines, ON (Stern section: J. W. McGiffin '72-'99)

Cement carrier *Stephen B. Roman* in the Welland Canal. *(Paul Beesley)*

Fleet Name Vessel Name	IMO #	Vessel Type	Year Built	Engine Type	Cargo Cap. or Gross*	Overall Length	Breadth	Depth
CSL Tadoussac	6918716	SU	1969	D	30,051	730'00"	77'11"	41'11"

Built: Collingwood Shipyards, Collingwood, ON; rebuilt with new midbody, widened 3' at Port Weller Dry Docks, St. Catharines, ON, in '01 (Tadoussac {2} '69-'01)

Frontenac {5}	6804848	SU	1968	D	26,822	729'07"	75'00"	39'08"

Built: Davie Shipbuilding Co., Lauzon, QC; converted to a self-unloader by Collingwood Shipyards, Collingwood, ON, in '73

Halifax	5120075	SU	1963	T	29,283	730'02"	75'00"	45'02"

Built: Davie Shipbuilding Co., Lauzon, QC; converted to a self-unloader, deepened 6' at Port Arthur Shipbuilding, Thunder Bay, ON, in '80; entered long-term lay-up at Montreal, QC, Dec. 28, 2008 (Frankcliffe Hall {2} '63-'88)

Mapleglen {3}	7910163	BC	1981	D	35,067	729'11"	75'10"	47'01"

Built: Cockerill Yards N.V., Hoboken, Belgium (Federal Maas {1} '81-'95, Lake Michigan '95-'09)

Oakglen {3}	7901148	BC	1980	D	35,067	729'11"	75'10"	47'01"

Built: Boelwerf Vlaanderen Shipbuilding N.V., Temse, Belgium (Federal Danube '80-'95, Lake Ontario '95-'09)

Pineglen {2}	8409331	BC	1985	D	33,197	736'07"	75'11"	42'00"

Built: Collingwood Shipyards, Collingwood, ON (Paterson '85-'02)

Richelieu {3}	7901150	BC	1980	D	35,067	729'11"	75'10"	47'01"

Built: Boelwerf Vlaanderen Shipbuilding N.V., Temse, Belgium (Federal Ottawa '80-'95, Lake Erie '95-'09)

Rt. Hon. Paul J. Martin	7324405	SU	1973	D	37,694	739'07"	77'11"	48'04"

Built: Collingwood Shipyards, Collingwood, ON; rebuilt with a new forebody in '00 at Port Weller Dry Docks, St. Catharines, ON (Stern section: H. M. Griffith '73-'00)

Saguenay {4}	7910175	BC	1981	D	35,067	729'11"	75'10"	47'01"

Built: Boelwerf Vlaanderen Shipbuilding N.V., Temse, Belgium (Federal Thames '81-'95, Lake Superior '95-'09)

Salarium	7902233	SU	1980	D	35,123	730'00"	75'11"	46'06"

Built: Collingwood Shipyards, Collingwood, ON (Nanticoke '80-'09)

Spruceglen {2}	8119261	BC	1983	D	33,824	730'01"	75'09"	48'00"

Built: Govan Shipyards, Glasgow, Scotland
  (Selkirk Settler '83-'91, Federal St. Louis '91-'91, Federal Fraser {2} '91-2001, Fraser '01-'02)

C-3   CANADIAN COAST GUARD (FISHERIES AND OCEANS CANADA), OTTAWA, ON

(www.ccg-gcc.gc.ca) **CENTRAL AND ARCTIC REGION, SARNIA, ON**

Vessel Name	IMO #	Vessel Type	Year Built	Engine Type	Cargo Cap. or Gross*	Overall Length	Breadth	Depth
Cape Chaillon		SR	2004	D	34*	47'09"	14'00"	4'05"
Cape Commodore		SR	2004	D	34*	47'09"	14'00"	4'05"
Cape Discovery		SR	2004	D	34*	47'09"	14'00"	4'05"
Cape Dundas		SR	2004	D	39*	47'09"	14'00"	4'05"
Cape Hearne		SR	2004	D	34*	47'09"	14'00"	4'05"
Cape Hurd		SR	1982	D	55*	70'10"	18'00"	8'09"
(CG 126 '82-'85)								
Cape Lambton		SR	2000	D	34*	47'09"	14'00"	4'05"
Cape Mercy		SR	2000	D	34*	47'09"	14'00"	4'05"
Cape Providence		SR	2004	D	34*	47'09"	14'00"	4'05"
Cape Storm		SR	1999	D	34*	47'09"	14'00"	4'05"
Caribou Isle		BT	1985	D	92*	75'06"	19'08"	7'04"

Built: Breton Industrial & Marine Ltd., Port Hawkesbury, NS

Cove Isle		BT	1980	D	80*	65'07"	19'08"	7'04"

Built: Canadian Dredge & Dock Co. Ltd., Kingston, ON

Griffon	7022887	IB	1970	D	2,212*	234'00"	49'00"	21'06"

Built: Davie Shipbuilding Co., Lauzon, QC

Gull Isle		BT	1980	D	80*	65'07"	19'08"	7'04"

Built: Canadian Dredge & Dock Co. Ltd., Kingston, ON

Isle Rouge		SR	1980	D	58*	70'08"	18'00"	5'02"
Kelso		RV	2009	D	63*	57'07"	17'01"	4'09"
Limnos	6804903	RV	1968	D	489*	147'00"	32'00"	12'00"

Built: Port Weller Dry Docks, St. Catharines, ON

Samuel Risley	8322442	IB	1985	D	1,988*	228'09"	47'01"	21'09"

Built: Vito Steel Boat & Barge Construction Ltd., Delta, BC

Thunder Cape		SR	2000	D	34*	47'09"	14'00"	4'05"

LAURENTIAN REGION, QUÉBEC, QC (Vessels over 100' only have been listed)

Amundsen	7510846	IB	1978	D	5,910*	295'09"	63'09"	31'04"

Built: Burrard Dry Dock Co., North Vancouver, BC (Sir John Franklin '78-'03)

Des Groseilliers	8006385	IB	1983	D	5,910*	322'07"	64'00"	35'06"

Built: Port Weller Dry Docks, St. Catharines, ON

F. C. G. Smith	8322686	SV	1985	D	439*	114'02"	45'11"	11'02"

Built: Georgetown Shipyard, Georgetown, PEI

Martha L. Black	8320432	IB	1986	D	3,818*	272'04"	53'02"	25'02"

Built: Versatile Pacific Shipyards, Victoria, BC

Stewart J. Cort *discharging taconite at Burns Harbor, Ind.,*
using its one-of-a-kind unloading system. (Mike Sipper)

Side view of the Cort's unloader, which retracts into the deckhouse when not in use. (Mike Sipper)

Pierre Radisson	7510834	IB	1978	D	5,910*	322' 00"	62' 10"	35' 06"
Built: Burrard Dry Dock Co., North Vancouver, BC								
Tracy	6725432	BT	1968	D	837*	181' 01"	38' 00"	16' 00"
Built: Port Weller Dry Docks, St. Catharines, ON								

NEWFOUNDLAND REGION, QUÉBEC, QC (Only vessels over 100' have been listed)

Ann Harvey	8320468	IB	1987	D	3,853*	272' 03	53' 01"	20' 04"
Built: Halifax Dartmouth Industries Ltd., Halifax, NS								
George R. Pearkes	8320444	IB	1986	D	3,809*	272' 04"	53' 02"	25' 02"
Built: Versatile Pacific Shipyards, Victoria, BC								
Henry Larsen	8409329	IB	1987	D	6,166*	327' 04"	64' 00"	23' 06"
Built: Versatile Pacific Shipyards, Victoria, BC								
Louis M. Lauzier	7635995	SR	1976	D	346*	100' 02	26' 09"	11' 02"
Louis S. St-Laurent	6705937	IB	1969	D	11,345*	393' 04"	80' 00"	32' 01"
Built: Canadian Vickers, Montreal, QC								
Terry Fox	8127799	IB	1983	D	4,234*	288' 07"	58' 04"	27' 02"
Built: Burrard Yarrows Corporation, North Vancouver, BC								

C-4 CAUSLEY MARINE CONTRACTING LLC, BAY CITY, MI

Jill Marie		TB	1891	D	24*	60' 00"	12' 06"	6' 00"
Built: Cleveland Shipbuilding Co., Cleveland, OH (Cisco 1891-1952, Capama-S '52-'07)								

C-5 CEMBA MOTOR SHIPS LTD., PELEE ISLAND, ON

Cemba		TK	1960	D	17*	50' 00"	15' 06"	7' 06"
Built: Elmer Haikala, Wheatley, ON								

C-6 CENTRAL MARINE LOGISTICS INC., GRIFFITH, IN (centralmarinelogistics.com)

Edward L. Ryerson	5097606	BC	1960	T	27,500	730' 00"	75' 00"	39' 00"
Built: Manitowoc Shipbuilding Co., Manitowoc, WI; in lay-up, Superior, WI, most of 2009 and all of 2010 season								
Joseph L. Block	7502320	SU	1976	D	37,200	728' 00"	78' 00"	45' 00"
Built: Bay Shipbuilding Co., Sturgeon Bay, WI								
Wilfred Sykes	5389554	SU	1949	T	21,500	678' 00"	70' 00"	37' 00"
Built: American Shipbuilding Co., Lorain, OH; converted to a self-unloader by Fraser Shipyards, Superior, WI, in '75								

C-7 CHAMPION MARINE INC., ALGONAC, MI

Champion		CF	1941	D	69*	65' 00"	25' 09"	5' 08"
Built: Arthur R. Champion, Algonac, MI								

Maumee inbound ...

Fleet Name / Vessel Name	IMO #	Vessel Type	Year Built	Engine Type	Cargo Cap. or Gross*	Overall Length	Breadth	Depth
Middle Channel		CF	1997	D	81*	79' 00"	30' 00"	6' 05"
Built: T.D. Vinette Co., Escanaba, MI								
North Channel		CF	1967	D	67*	75' 00"	30' 04"	6' 01"
Built: Blount Marine Corp., Warren, RI								
South Channel		CF	1973	D	94*	79' 00"	30' 03"	6' 01"
Built: Blount Marine Corp., Warren, RI								

C-8 CHARITY ISLAND TRANSPORT INC., AU GRES, MI *(charityisland.net)*

North Star		PA	1949	D	14*	50' 05"	14' 06"	3' 06"
Shirley Ann		PA	2007	D	11*	45' 00"	14' 00"	3' 05"

C-9 CHARLEVOIX COUNTY TRANSPORTATION AUTHORITY, CHARLEVOIX, MI

Charlevoix {1}		CF	1926	D	43*	47' 00"	30' 00"	3' 08"

C-10 CHICAGO FIRE DEPARTMENT, CHICAGO, IL *(chicagofireboat.com)*

Victor L. Schlaeger		FB	1949	D	350*	92' 06"	24' 00"	11' 00"
New Construction		FB	2011	D				
Built: Hike Metal Products Ltd., Wheatley, ON								

C-11 CHICAGO FROM THE LAKE INC., CHICAGO, IL *(chicagoline.com)*

Ft. Dearborn		ES	1985	D	72*	64' 10"	22' 00"	7' 03"
Built: Blount Marine Corp., Warren, RI								
Innisfree		ES	1980	D	35*	61' 09"	15' 06"	5' 07"
Built: Blount Marine Corp., Warren, RI (Lady Fenwick)								
Marquette {6}		ES	1957	D	39*	50' 07"	15' 00"	5' 05"
Built: Burger Boat Co., Manitowoc, WI (Caloosa, Harbor Escort)								

C-12 CHIGAGO MARINE ASSET MANAGEMENT, CHICAGO, IL *(chicago-marine.com)*

Great Lakes {2}		TK	1982	B	5,024*	414' 00"	60' 00"	30' 00"
Built: Bay Shipbuilding Co., Sturgeon Bay, WI (Amoco Great Lakes '82-'85)								
Michigan {10}	8121795	AT	1982	D	293*	107' 08"	34' 00"	16' 00"
Built: Bay Shipbuilding Co., Sturgeon Bay, WI (Amoco Michigan '82-'85)								
[ATB Michigan / Great Lakes {2} OA dimensions together]						454' 00"	60' 00"	30' 00"

C-13 CHICAGO WATER PUMPING STATION, CHICAGO, IL

James J. Versluis		TB	1957	D	126*	83' 00"	22' 00"	11' 02"
Built: Sturgeon Bay Shipbuilding Co., Sturgeon Bay, WI								

... and outbound at Cleveland, Dec. 17, 2010. (Rex Cassidy)

	Fleet Name Vessel Name	IMO #	Vessel Type	Year Built	Engine Type	Cargo Cap. or Gross*	Overall Length	Breadth	Depth
C-14	**CHIEF SHINGWAUK MARINE LTD., SAULT STE. MARIE, ON**								
	Chief Shingwauk		ES	1965	D	109*	70' 00"	24' 00"	4' 06"
	Built: Hike Metal Products Ltd., Wheatley, ON; company is closed and vessel laid up at Sault Ste. Marie, ON								
C-15	**CITY OF KEWAUNEE, KEWAUNEE, WI** *(cityofkewaunee.org)*								
	Ludington		MU	1943	D	249*	115' 00"	26' 00"	13' 08"
	Built: Jakobson Shipyard, Oyster Bay, NY; former U.S. Army Corps of Engineers tug is open to the public as a marine museum at Kewaunee, WI (Major Wilbur F. Browder [LT-4] '43-'47)								
C-16	**CITY OF TORONTO, TORONTO, ON** *(toronto.ca/parks)*								
	Ned Hanlan II		TB	1966	D	22*	41' 06"	14' 01"	5' 05"
	Built: Erieau Shipbuilding & Drydock Co. Ltd., Erieau, ON								
	Ongiara	6410374	PA/CF	1963	D	180*	78' 00"	12' 04"	9' 09"
	Built: Russel Brothers Ltd., Owen Sound, ON								
	Sam McBride		PF	1939	D	387*	129' 00"	34' 11"	6' 00"
	Built: Toronto Dry Dock Co. Ltd., Toronto, ON								
	Thomas Rennie		PF	1951	D	387*	129' 00"	32' 11"	6' 00"
	Built: Toronto Dry Dock Co. Ltd., Toronto, ON								
	Trillium		PF	1910	R	564*	150' 00"	30' 00"	8' 04"
	Built: Poulson Iron Works, Toronto, ON; last sidewheel-propelled vessel on the Great Lakes was 100 years old in 2010								
	William Inglis		PF	1935	D	238*	99' 00"	24' 10"	6' 00"
	Built: John Inglis Co. Ltd., Toronto, ON (Shamrock {2} '35-'37)								
C-17	**CJC CRUISES INC., GRAND LEDGE, MI** *(detroitprincess.com)*								
	Detroit Princess		PA	1993	D	1,430*	222' 00"	62' 00"	11' 01"
	Built: Leevac Shipyards Inc., Jennings, LA (Players Riverboat Casino II '93-'04)								
C-18	**CLAYTON FIRE DEPARTMENT, CLAYTON, NY**								
	Last Chance		FB	2003	D		36' 00"	13' 00"	2' 04"
C-19	**CLEARWATER MARINE LLC, HOLLAND, MI** *(clearwatermarinellc.com)*								
	G.W. Falcon		TB	1936	D	22*	49' 07"	13' 08"	6' 02"
	(J.W. Walsh, Anna Marie)								
C-20	**CLEVELAND FIRE DEPARTMENT, CLEVELAND, OH**								
	Anthony J. Celebrezze		FB	1961	D	42*	66' 00"	17' 00"	5' 00"
	Built: Paasch Marine Services Inc., Erie, PA								
C-21	**CLINTON RIVER CRUISE CO., MOUNT CLEMENS, MI** *(clintonrivercruisecompany.com)*								
	Captain Paul II		PA	1960	D	14*	44' 07"	11' 00"	4' 00"
	Clinton		PA	1949	D	10*	63' 07"	15' 03"	4' 08"
	Clinton Friendship		PA	1984	D	43*	64' 08"	22' 00"	4' 05"
C-22	**CLUB CANAMAC CRUISES, TORONTO, ON** *(canamac.com)*								
	Aurora Borealis		ES	1983	D	277*	101' 00"	24' 00"	6' 00"
	Built: Ralph Hurley, Port Burwell, ON								
	Stella Borealis		ES	1989	D	356*	118 '00"	26' 00"	7' 00"
	Built: Duratug Shipyard & Fabricating Ltd., Port Dover, ON								
C-23	**COBBY MARINE (1985) INC., KINGSVILLE, ON**								
	Vida C.		TB	1960	D	17*	46' 03"	15' 05"	3' 02"
C-24	**COLUMBIA YACHT CLUB, CHICAGO, IL** *(columbiayachtclub.com)*								
	Abegweit		CF	1947	D	6,694*	372' 06"	61' 00"	24' 09"
	Built: Marine Industries Ltd., Sorel, QC; former CN Marine Inc. vessel last operated in 1981; in use as a private, floating clubhouse in Chicago, IL (Abegweit '47- 81, Abby '81-'97)								
C-25	**CONSTRUCTION POLARIS INC., L'ANCIENNE-LORETTE, QC** *(constructionpolaris.com)*								
	Point Viking	5118840	TB	1962	D	207*	98' 05"	27' 10"	13' 05"
	Built: Davie Shipbuilding Co., Lauzon, QC (Foundation Viking '62-'75)								
C-26	**COOPER MARINE LTD., SELKIRK, ON**								
	J.W. Cooper		PB	1984	D	25*	48' 00"	14' 07"	5' 00"
	Juleen I		PB	1972	D	23*	46' 00"	14' 01"	4' 05"
	Lady Kim I		PB	1974	D	20*	44' 00"	13' 00"	4' 00"
	Mrs. C.		PB	2006	D	26*	50' 00"	14' 05"	4' 05"
	Stacey Dawn		TB	1993	D	14*	35' 09"	17' 04"	3' 05"
	Wilson T. Cooper		DB	2009	D	58*	56' 08"	23' 06"	5' 08"
	Built: Cooper Marine Ltd., Selkirk, ON								

Fleet Name Vessel Name	IMO #	Vessel Type	Year Built	Engine Type	Cargo Cap. or Gross*	Overall Length	Breadth	Depth
C-27 CORPORATION OF THE TOWNSHIP OF FRONTENAC ISLANDS, WOLFE ISLAND, ON								
Howe Islander		CF	1946	D	13*	53' 00"	12' 00"	3' 00"
Built: Canadian Dredge & Dock Co. Ltd., Kingston, ON								
Simcoe Islander		PF	1964	D	24*	47' 09"	18' 00"	3' 06"
Built: Canadian Dredge & Dock Co. Ltd., Kingston, ON								
C-28 CROISIÈRES AML INC., QUÉBEC, QC (croisieresaml.com)								
Cavalier des Mers	7431430	ES	1974	D	161*	91' 08"	21' 03"	8' 05"
Built: Camcraft Inc., Crown Point, LA (Marine Sprinter '74-'84)								
Cavalier Maxim	5265904	ES	1962	D	752*	191' 02"	42' 00"	11' 07"
Built: John I. Thornycroft & Co., Wollston, Southampton, England (Osborne Castle '62-'78, Le Gobelet D' Argent '78-'88, Gobelet D' Argent '88-'89, Le Maxim '89-'93)								
Cavalier Royal		ES	1971	D	283*	125' 00"	24' 00"	5' 00"
Built: Beaux's Bay Craft, Loreauville, LA (Bob Cat)								
Grand Fleuve		ES	1987	D	499*	145' 00"	30' 00"	5' 06"
Built: Kanter Yacht Co., St. Thomas, ON								
Louis Jolliet	5212749	ES	1938	R	2,436*	170' 01"	70' 00"	17' 00"
Built: Davie Shipbuilding Co., Lauzon, QC								
Transit		ES	1992	D	102*	66' 00"	22' 00"	2' 08"
Built: Chantier AML Inc., Ile-Aux-Coudres, QC								
C-29 CROISIÈRES M/S JACQUES-CARTIER, TROIS-RIVIERES, QC (croisieres.qc.ca)								
Jacques-Cartier		ES	1924	D	457*	135' 00"	35' 00"	10' 00"
Built: Davie Shipbuilding Co., Lauzon, QC								
Le Draveur		ES	1992	D	79*	58' 07"	22' 00"	5' 24"
Built: Chantier Naval Matane Inc., Matane, QC								
C-30 CRUISE TORONTO INC., TORONTO ON (cruisetoronto.com)								
Obsession III		ES	1967	D	160*	66' 00"	25' 00"	6' 01"
Built: Halter Marine Services, New Orleans, LA (Mystique)								
C-31 CTMA GROUP, CAP-AUX-MEULES, QC (ctma.ca)								
C.T.M.A. Vacancier	7310260	PA/RR	1973	D	11,481*	388' 04"	70' 02"	43' 06"
Built: J.J. Sietas KG Schiffswerft, Hamburg, Germany (Aurella '80-'82, Saint Patrick II '82-'98, Egnatia II '98-'00, Ville de Sete '00-'01, City of Cork '01-'02)								
C.T.M.A. Voyageur	7222229	PA/RR	1972	D	4,526*	327' 09"	52' 06"	31' 07"
Built: Trosvik Versted A/S, Brevik, Norway (Anderida)								
D-1 DAN MINOR & SONS INC., PORT COLBORNE, ON								
Andrea Marie I		TB	1963	D	87*	75' 02"	24' 07"	7' 03"
Built: Dan Minor & Sons Inc., Port Colborne, ON								
Jeanette M.		TB	1981	D	31*	62' 09"	20 01"	4' 05"
Built: Hike Metal Products, Wheatley, ON								
Susan Michelle		TB	1995	D	89*	79' 10"	20' 11"	6' 02"
Built: Vic Powell Welding Ltd., Dunnville, ON								
Welland		TB	1954	D	94*	86' 00"	20' 00"	8' 00"
Built: Russel-Hipwell Engines, Owen Sound, ON								
D-2 DANN MARINE TOWING, CHESAPEAKE CITY, MD (dannmarinetowing.com)								
Zeus	9506071	TB	1964	D	98*	104' 02"	29' 03"	13' 05"
Built: Houma Shipbuilding Co., Houma, LA (Usually paired with barge Robert F. Deegan)								
D-3 DEAN CONSTRUCTION CO. LTD., BELLE RIVER, ON (deanconstructioncompany.com)								
Americo Dean		TB		D	15*	45' 00"	15' 00"	5' 00"
Annie M. Dean		TB	1981	D	58*	50' 00"	19' 00"	5' 00"
Built: Dean Construction Co. Ltd., Tecumseh, ON								
Bobby Bowes		TB	1944	D	11*	37' 04"	10' 02"	3' 06"
Built: Russel Brothers Ltd., Owen Sound, ON (La Praxis)								
Canadian Jubilee		DR	1978	B	896*	149' 09"	56' 01"	11' 01"
Built: Omnimar Inc., Sorel, QC								
Neptune III		TB	1939	D	23*	53' 10"	15' 06"	5' 00"
Built: Harold Cromwell, London, ON								
D-4 DETROIT CITY FIRE DEPARTMENT, DETROIT, MI								
Curtis Randolph		FB	1979	D	85*	77' 10"	21' 06"	9' 03"
Built: Peterson Builders Inc., Sturgeon Bay, WI								

J.W. Shelley in the St. Marys River, 2010.
(Roger LeLievre)

Vessel Spotlight

If there were a category for the most unexpected reprieve from the scrappers, it surely must belong to the *J.W. Shelley*.

When the former Algoma Central bulk carrier *Algocen* was sold to an Eastern U.S. company in 2005 for use as a spoils barge, it was assumed that when that service ended, the 1968-built motorship would be cut up. However in a surprise move, the vessel was bought, refurbished and brought back to the Lakes for further trading under the banner of Vanguard Shipping (Great Lakes) in 2008. As *J.W. Shelley*, named in honor of John Shelley Sr., for many years a principal of Sarnia's Shelley Machine and Marine, the vessel has been busy in the grain trade ever since.

Algocen in 1971.

Launched on June 18, 1968 for the Algoma Central Corp., Sault Ste. Marie, Ont., the 730-foot-long bulker proved to be the last traditional-styled (fore/aft cabin design) bulk carrier built at Collingwood Shipyards.

Algocen entered service on Sept. 20, 1968. She set a barley record at Superior, Wis., on May 6, 1970, carrying 1,061,300 bushels, followed by a Great Lakes corn record, loading 1,014,000 bushels at Milwaukee, Wis., on Nov. 5, 1971. In fact, she was the first vessel to load in excess of one million bushels of this product. On July 3, 1974, *Algocen* set a Great Lakes soybean record, loading 946,000 bushels of soybeans at Superior bound for Quebec City.

The 2004 navigation season appeared to be *Algocen*'s last, clearing Duluth with her final load on Dec. 18, bound for Port Cartier, Que. By January 2005, her new owner was Recycling Technologies, Inc. In 2008, her service as a spoils barge at an end, the vessel was re-registered Canadian under the new name *J.W. Shelley*.

After being towed from New Jersey to a Brooklyn, N.Y., shipyard for repairs, *Shelley* left on Aug. 30, 2008, under her own power bound for Montreal and the Great Lakes. It is believed that this voyage from New York to the Great Lakes was a first for any classic laker. – **George Wharton**

Fleet Name / Vessel Name	IMO #	Vessel Type	Year Built	Engine Type	Cargo Cap. or Gross*	Overall Length	Breadth	Depth

D-5 DIAMOND JACK'S RIVER TOURS, DETROIT, MI (diamondjack.com)

Diamond Belle		ES	1958	D	93*	93'06"	25'00"	7'00"
Built: Hans Hansen Welding Co., Toledo, OH (Mackinac Islander {2} '58–'90, Sir Richard '90–'91)								
Diamond Jack		ES	1955	D	82*	72'00"	25'00"	7'03"
Built: Christy Corp., Sturgeon Bay, WI (Emerald Isle {1} '55–'91)								
Diamond Queen		ES	1956	D	94*	92'00"	25'00"	7'02"
Built: Marinette Marine Corp., Marinette, WI (Mohawk '56–'96)								

D-6 DISCOVERY WORLD AT PIER WISCONSIN, MILWAUKEE, WI (voyage.pierwisconsin.org)

Denis Sullivan		TV/ES	2000	W/D	99*	138'00"	22'08"	10'06"
Built: Wisconsin Lake Schooner, Milwaukee, WI								

D-7 DOOR COUNTY CRUISES LLC, STURGEON BAY, WI (doorcountyfireboatcruises.com)

Fred A. Busse		ES	1937	D	99*	92'00"	22'04"	9'06"
Built: Defoe Boat & Motor Works, Bay City, MI; former Chicago fireboat offers cruises at Sturgeon Bay, WI								

D-8 DOOR COUNTY MARITIME MUSEUM & LIGHTHOUSE PRESERVATION SOCIETY INC., STURGEON BAY, WI (dcmm.org)

John Purves		TB/MU	1919	D	436*	150'00"	27'06"	16'08"
Built: Bethlehem Steel Co., Elizabeth, NJ; former Roen/Andrie Inc. tug has been refurbished as a museum display at Sturgeon Bay, WI (Butterfield '19–'42, LT-145 '42–'57)								

D-9 DRAGAGE VERREAULT INC., LES MÉCHINS, QC (dragageverreault.com)

I.V. No. 8		DR	1967	B	348*	96'03"	36'00"	8'05"
Built: Verreault Navigation Inc., Les Méchins, QC								
I.V. No. 9		GC	1936	D	148*	106'08"	23'10"	8'05"
Built: Geo. T. Davie & Sons, Lauzon, QC (A.C.D. '36–'69)								
I.V. No. 10		GC	1936	D	320*	110'00"	23'10"	8'05"
Built: Geo. T. Davie & Sons, Lauzon, QC (G.T.D. '36–'69)								
I.V. No. 11		GC	1935	D	144*	106'08"	24'00"	8'00"
Built: Geo. T. Davie & Sons, Lauzon, QC (Donpaco '35–'72)								
I.V. No. 13		GC	1936	D	148*	106'08"	24'00"	8'00"
Built: Geo. T. Davie & Sons, Lauzon, QC (Newscarrier '36–'72)								
I.V. No. 14		GC	1937	D	229*	113'00"	22'05"	8'06"
Built: Geo. T. Davie & Sons, Lauzon, QC (Kermic '37–'74)								
Port Méchins		DR	1949	R	1,321*	200'00"	40'02"	18'00"
Built: Lobnitz & Co., Renfrew, Scotland (Haffar '49–'88, Lockeport '88–'92)								
Rosaire		DR	1952	B	714*	137'07"	44'06"	9'01"
Built: Saint John Drydock Co., Saint John, NB								

D-10 DUC D' ORLEANS CRUISE BOAT, CORUNNA, ON (ducdorleans.com)

Duc d' Orleans II		ES	1987	D	120*	71'03	23'02"	7'07"
Built: Blount Marine Corp., Warren, RI (Spirit of Newport '87–'06)								

D-11 DULUTH ENTERTAINMENT CONVENTION CENTER, DULUTH, MN (decc.org/omnimax-irvin)

William A. Irvin		MU	1938	T	14,050	610'09"	60'00"	32'06"
Built: American Shipbuilding Co., Lorain, OH; former United States Steel Corp. bulk carrier last operated Dec. 16, 1978; open to the public at Duluth, MN								

D-12 DUROCHER MARINE, DIV. OF KOKOSING CONSTRUCTION CO., CHEBOYGAN, MI (kokosing.biz)

Champion {3}		TB	1974	D	125*	75'00"	23'05"	9'05"
Built: Service Machine & Shipbuilding Co., Amelia, LA								
General {2}		TB	1954	D	119*	71'00"	19'06"	10'00"
Built: Missouri Valley Bridge & Iron Works, Leavenworth, KS (U. S. Army ST-1999 '54–'61, USCOE Au Sable '61–'84, Challenger {3} '84–'87)								
Joe Van		TB	1955	D	32*	57'09"	15'00"	7'00"
Built: W.J. Hingston, Buffalo, NY								
Nancy Anne		TB	1969	D	73*	60'00"	20'00"	8'00"
Built: Houma Shipbuilding Co., Houma, LA								
Ray Durocher		TB	1943	D	20*	45'06"	12'05"	7'06"
Valerie B.		TB	1981	D	101*	65'00"	25'06"	10'00"
Built: Rayco Shipbuilders & Repairers, Bourg, LA (Mr. Joshua, Michael Van)								

E-1 EASTERN UPPER PENINSULA TRANSPORTATION AUTHORITY, SAULT STE. MARIE, MI (www.eupta.net)

Drummond Islander III		CF	1989	D	96*	108'00"	37'00"	7'02"
Built: Moss Point Marine Inc., Escatawpa, MS								

Fleet Name Vessel Name	IMO #	Vessel Type	Year Built	Engine Type	Cargo Cap. or Gross*	Overall Length	Breadth	Depth
Drummond Islander IV		CF	2000	D	97*	148' 00"	40' 00"	12' 00"
Built: Basic Marine Inc., Escanaba, MI								
Neebish Islander II		CF	1946	D	90*	89' 00"	25' 09"	5' 08"
Built: Lock City Machine/Marine, Sault Ste. Marie, MI (Sugar Islander '46-'95)								
Sugar Islander II		CF	1995	D	90*	114' 00"	40' 00"	10' 00"
Built: Basic Marine Inc., Escanaba, MI								

E-2 EDWARD E. GILLEN CO., MILWAUKEE, WI (gillenco.com)

Andrew J.		TB	1950	D	25*	47' 00"	15' 07"	8' 00"
Edith J.		TB	1962	D	18*	45' 03"	13' 00"	8' 00"
Edward E. Gillen III		TB	1988	D	97*	75' 00"	26' 00"	9' 06"
Built: Terrebonne Shipbuilders Inc., Houma, LA								
Kristin J.		TB	1963	D	60*	52' 06"	19' 01"	7' 04"
Built: St. Charles Steel Works, Thibodaux, LA (Jason A. Kadinger '63-'06)								

E-3 EMPRESS OF CANADA ENTERPRISES LTD., TORONTO, ON (empressofcanada.com)

Empress of Canada		ES	1980	D	399*	116' 00"	28' 00"	6' 06"
Built: Hike Metal Products, Wheatley, ON (Island Queen V {2} '80-'89)								

E-4 ENTREPRISE MARISSA INC., QUEBEC, QC

Cape Crow		TB	1951	D	14*	37' 08"	10' 05"	5' 00"
Cap Brulé		TB		D	12*	39' 09"	10' 00"	2' 00"
Soulanges		TB	1905	D	72*	77' 00"	17' 00"	8' 00"
Built: Cie Pontbriand Ltee., Sorel, QC (Dandy '05-'39)								

E-5 ERICSON MARINE FREIGHT INC., BAYFIELD, WI

Outer Island		PK	1942	D	173*	112' 00"	32' 00"	8' 06"
(LCT 203 '42-'46, Pluswood '46-'53)								

E-6 EQUIPMENTS VERREAULT INC., LES MÉCHINS, QC

Epinette II		TB	1965	D	75*	61' 03"	20' 01"	8' 05"
Built: Russel Brothers Ltd., Owen Sound, ON								
Grande Baie		TT	1972	D	194*	86' 06"	30' 00"	12' 00"
Built: Prince Edward Island Lending Authority, Charlottetown, PEI								

E-7 ERIE ISLANDS PETROLEUM INC., PUT-IN-BAY, OH

Cantankerus		TK	1955	D	43*	56' 00"	14' 00"	6' 06"
Built: Marinette Marine Corp., Marinette, WI								

Saginaw at sunset. (Rod Burdick)

Fleet Name Vessel Name	IMO #	Vessel Type	Year Built	Engine Type	Cargo Cap. or Gross*	Overall Length	Breadth	Depth
E-8	**ERIE MARITIME MUSEUM, ERIE, PA** *(flagshipniagara.org)*							
Niagara		MU/2B	1988	W	295*	198' 00"	32' 00"	10' 06"
Reconstruction of Oliver Hazard Perry's U. S. Navy brigantine from the War of 1812								
E-9	**ERIE SAND AND GRAVEL CO., ERIE, PA** *(eriesandandgravel.com)*							
J. S. St. John	5202524	SC	1945	D	415*	174' 00"	31' 09"	15' 00"
Built: Smith Shipyards & Engineering Corp., Pensacola, FL (USS YO-178 '45-'51, Lake Edward '51-'67)								
E-10	**ESSROC CANADA INC., MISSISSAUGA, ON** *(essroc.com)*							
	VESSELS MANAGED BY SEAWAY MARINE TRANSPORT							
Metis	5233585	CC	1956	B	5,800	331' 00"	43' 09"	26' 00"
Built: Davie Shipbuilding Co., Lauzon, QC; lengthened 72', deepened 3'06" in '59 and converted to a self-unloading cement barge in '91 by Kingston Shipbuilding & Dry Dock Co., Kingston, ON								
Stephen B. Roman	6514900	CC	1965	D	7,600	488' 09"	56' 00"	35' 06"
Built: Davie Shipbuilding Co., Lauzon, QC; converted to a self-unloading cement carrier by Collingwood Shipyards, Collingwood, ON, in '83 (Fort William '65-'83)								
E-11	**EVERETTE J. GAYTON, OAK PARK, MI**							
Titan		TB	1940	D	31*	56' 03"	15' 08"	7' 00"
F-1	**FAUST CORP., ST. CLAIR SHORES, MI**							
Linnhurst		TB	1930	D	11*	37' 05"	10' 05"	4' 08"
Built: Great Lakes Engineering Works, Ecorse, MI (G.L.E. WKS, Toledoan, Grosse Ile)								
F-2	**FEDNAV LTD., MONTREAL, QC** *(fednav.com)*							
	CANARCTIC SHIPPING CO. LTD. – DIVISION OF FEDNAV LTD. SEE ALSO SALTWATER FLEET IF-3							
Arctic	7517507	GC	1978	D	26,440	692' 04"	75' 05"	49' 05"
Built: Port Weller Dry Docks, Port Weller, ON								
Umiak I	9334715	BC	2006	D	31,992	619' 04"	87' 02"	51' 50"
Built: Universal Shipbuilding Corp., Kawasaki, Japan								
F-3	**FOXY LADY CRUISES, GREEN BAY, WI** *(foxyladycruises.com)*							
Foxy Lady II		ES	2003	D	61*	73' 05"	20' 00"	5' 05"
(Marco Island Princess)								
F-4	**FRASER SHIPYARDS INC., SUPERIOR, WI** *(frasershipyards.com)*							
Maxine Thompson		TB	1959	D	30*	47' 04"	13' 00"	6' 06"
(Susan A. Fraser '59-'78)								
Wally Kendzora		TB	1956	D	24*	43' 00"	12' 00"	5' 06"

	Fleet Name Vessel Name	IMO #	Vessel Type	Year Built	Engine Type	Cargo Cap. or Gross*	Overall Length	Breadth	Depth

F-5 FRED SMITH, PORT DOVER, ON

	H. H. Misner		TB	1946	D	28*	66' 09"	16' 04"	4' 05"

Built: George Gamble, Port Dover, ON

F-6 FRIENDS OF THE NORISLE, MANITOWANING, ON *(norisle.com)*

	Norisle		MU	1946	R	1,668*	215' 09"	36' 03"	16' 00"

Built: Collingwood Shipyards, Collingwood, ON; former Ontario Northland Transportation Commission passenger vessel last operated in 1974; open to the public at Manitowaning, Manitoulin Island, ON

G-1 GAELIC TUGBOAT CO., DETROIT, MI *(gaelictugboat.com)*

	Carolyn Hoey	5029946	TB	1951	D	149*	88' 06"	25' 06"	11' 00"
	Marysville		TK	1973	B	1,136*	200' 00"	50' 00"	12' 06"
	Patricia Hoey {2}		TB	1949	D	146*	88' 06"	25' 06"	11' 00"
	Shannon	8971669	TB	1944	D	145*	101' 00"	25' 08"	13' 00"

Built: Alexander Shipyard Inc., New Orleans, LA (Atlas '51-'84, Susan Hoey {1} '84-'85, Atlas '85-'87)
(N.M.S. No. 102 '73-'81)
Built: Alexander Shipyard Inc., New Orleans, LA (Propeller '49-'82, Bantry Bay '82-'91)
Built: Consolidated Shipbuilding Corp., Morris Heights, NY (USS Connewango [YT / YTB / YTM-388] '44-'77)

G-2 GALCON MARINE LTD., TORONTO, ON *(galconmarine.com)*

	Barney Drake (The)		TB	1954	D	10*	31' 02"	9 05"	3' 04"
	Batchawana		TB	1912	D	40*	49' 00"	13' 00"	7' 08"
	Kenteau		TB	1937	D	15*	54' 07"	16' 04"	4' 02"
	Pitts Carillon		DB	1959	B	260*	91' 08"	39' 00"	8' 01"
	Pitts No. 3		DB	1961	B	107*	78' 02"	32' 00"	5' 05"

Built: Toronto Dry Dock Co Ltd., Toronto ON (T.T.&S. No. 9)
Built: Polson Iron Works Ltd., Toronto, ON
Built: George Gamble, Port Dover, ON
Built: Walter Young Machinery & Equipment Ltd., Waubaushine, ON (Omar D.S. 34 '59 - '80)
Built: Thomas Storey Engineers Ltd., Stockport, England

G-3 GALLAGHER MARINE CONSTRUCTION CO. INC., ESCANABA, MI

	Bee Jay		TB	1939	D	19*	45' 00"	13' 00"	7' 00"

G-4 GANANOQUE BOAT LINE LTD., GANANOQUE, ON *(ganboatline.com)*

	Thousand Islander	7227346	ES	1972	D	200*	96' 11"	22' 01"	5' 05"
	Thousand Islander II	7329936	ES	1973	D	200*	99' 00"	22' 01"	5' 00"
	Thousand Islander III		ES	1975	D	376*	118' 00"	28' 00"	6' 00"
	Thousand Islander IV	7947984	ES	1976	D	347*	110' 09"	28' 04"	10' 08"
	Thousand Islander V		ES	1979	D	246*	88' 00"	24' 00"	5' 00"

Built: Marlin Yachts Co., Gananoque, ON
Built: Gananoque Boat Line Ltd., Gananoque, ON
Built: Gananoque Boat Line Ltd., Gananoque, ON
Built: Gananoque Boat Line Ltd., Gananoque, ON
Built: Algan Shipyards Ltd., Gananoque, ON (Concordia '79-'97)

G-5 GANNON UNIVERSITY, ERIE, PA *(www.gannon.edu)*

	Environaut		RV	1950	D	13*	36' 05"	12' 00"	5' 00"

Built: Paasch Marine Services Inc., Erie, PA (Little Toot)

G-6 GEO. GRADEL CO., TOLEDO, OH *(geogradelco.com)*

	Crow		DB	1955	B	416*	110' 00"	42' 00"	9' 06"
	John Francis		TB	1965	D	99*	75' 00"	22' 00"	9' 00"
	Mighty Jake		TB	1969	D	15*	36' 00"	12' 03"	7' 03"
	Mighty Jessie		TB	1954	D	57*	61' 02"	18' 00"	7' 03"
	Mighty Jimmy		TB	1945	D	34*	56' 00"	15' 10"	6' 05"
	Mighty John III		TB	1962	D	24*	45' 00"	15' 00"	5' 10"
	Moby Dick		DB	1952	B	835	121' 00"	33' 02"	10' 06"
	Pioneerland		TB	1943	D	53*	58' 00"	16' 08"	8' 00"
	Prairieland		TB	1955	D	35*	49' 02"	15' 02"	6' 00"
	Timberland		TB	1946	D	20*	41' 03"	13' 01"	7' 00"

Built: Bollinger Shipbuilding Inc., Lockport, LA (Dad '65-'98, Creole Eagle '98-'03)
(Niagara Queen '62-'99)

G-7 GOODTIME CRUISE LINE INC., CLEVELAND, OH *(goodtimeiii.com)*

	Goodtime III		ES	1990	D	95*	161' 00"	40' 00"	11' 00"

Bulit: Leevac Shipyards Inc., Jennings, LA

Fleet Name Vessel Name	IMO #	Vessel Type	Year Built	Engine Type	Cargo Cap. or Gross*	Overall Length	Breadth	Depth
G-8	**GRAND PORTAGE / ISLE ROYALE TRANSPORTATION LINE, SUPERIOR, WI** *(isleroyaleboats.com)*							
Voyageur II		ES	1970	D	40*	63' 00"	18' 00"	5' 00"
Wenonah		ES	1960	D	91*	70' 07"	19' 04"	9' 07"

Built: Dubuque Boat & Boiler Works, Dubuque, IA (Jamaica '60-'64)

GRAND RIVER NAVIGATION CO. – SEE LOWER LAKES TRANSPORTATION CO. L-13

G-9	**GRAND VALLEY STATE UNIVERSITY, ANNIS WATER RESOURCES, MUSKEGON, MI** *(gvsu.edu/wri)*							
D. J. Angus		RV	1986	D	16*	45' 00"	14' 00"	4' 00"
W. G. Jackson		RV	1996	D	80*	64' 10"	20' 00"	5' 00"

G-10	**GRAVEL AND LAKE SERVICES LTD., THUNDER BAY, ON**							
Donald Mac		TB	1914	D	69*	71' 00"	17' 00"	10' 00"

Built: Thor Iron Works Ltd., Toronto, ON

| George N. Carleton | | TB | 1943 | D | 97* | 82' 00" | 21' 00" | 11' 00" |

Built: Russel Brothers, Owen Sound, ON (HMCS Glenlea [W-25] '43-'45, Bansaga '45-'64)

| Peninsula | | TB | 1944 | D | 261* | 111' 00" | 27' 00" | 13' 00" |

Built: Montreal Drydock Ltd., Montreal, QC (HMCS Norton [W-31] '44-'45, W.A.C. 1 '45-'46)

| Robert John | | TB | 1945 | D | 98* | 82' 00" | 20' 01" | 11' 00" |

Built: Canadian Dredge & Dock Co., Kingston, ON (HMCS Gleneagle [W-40] '45-'46, Bansturdy '46-'65)

| Wolf River | | BC | 1956 | D | 5,880 | 349' 02" | 43' 07" | 25' 04" |

Built: Port Weller Dry Docks, Port Weller, ON; last operated in 1998; laid up at Thunder Bay, ON
(Tecumseh {2} '56-'67, New York News {3} '67-'86, Stella Desgagnés '86-'93, Beam Beginner '93-'95)

G-11	**GREAT LAKES DOCK & MATERIALS LLC, MUSKEGON, MI** *(greatlakesdock.com)*							
Duluth		TB	1954	D	87*	70' 01"	19' 05"	9' 08"

Built: Missouri Valley Bridge & Iron Works, Leavenworth, KS (U. S. Army ST-2015 '54-'62)

| Fischer Hayden | | TB | 1967 | D | 64* | 54' 00" | 22' 01" | 7' 01" |

Built: Main Iron Works Inc., Houma, LA (Gloria G. Cheramie, Joyce P. Crosby)

| Sarah B. | | TB | 1953 | D | 23* | 45' 00" | 13' 00" | 7' 00" |

Built: Nashville Bridge Co., Nashville, TN (ST-2161 '53-'63, Tawas Bay '63-'03)

G-12	**GREAT LAKES ENVIRONMENTAL RESEARCH LABORATORY, MUSKEGON, MI** *(www.glerl.noaa.gov)*							
Huron Explorer		RV	1979	D	15*	41' 00"	14' 08"	4' 08"
Laurentian		RV	1974	D	129*	80' 00"	21' 06"	11' 00"
Shenehon		SV	1953	D	90*	65' 00"	17' 00"	6' 00"

G-13	**GREAT LAKES FLEET INC. / KEY LAKES INC., DULUTH, MN (MANAGER)** *(www.keyship.com)*							
Arthur M. Anderson	5025691	SU	1952	T	25,300	767' 00"	70' 00"	36' 00"

Built: American Shipbuilding Co., Lorain, OH; lengthened 120' in '75 and converted to a self-unloader in '82 at Fraser Shipyards, Superior, WI

| Cason J. Callaway | 5065392 | SU | 1952 | T | 25,300 | 767' 00" | 70' 00" | 36' 00" |

Built: Great Lakes Engineering Works, River Rouge, MI; lengthened 120' in '74 and converted to a self-unloader in '82 at Fraser Shipyards, Superior, WI

| Edgar B. Speer | 7625952 | SU | 1980 | D | 73,700 | 1,004' 00" | 105' 00" | 56' 00" |

Built: American Shipbuilding Co., Lorain, OH

| Edwin H. Gott | 7606061 | SU | 1979 | D | 74,100 | 1,004' 00" | 105' 00" | 56' 00" |

Built: Bay Shipbuilding Co., Sturgeon Bay, WI; converted from shuttle self-unloader to deck-mounted self-unloader at Bay Shipbuilding, Sturgeon Bay, WI, in '96

| John G. Munson {2} | 5173670 | SU | 1952 | T | 25,550 | 768' 03" | 72' 00" | 36' 00" |

Built: Manitowoc Shipbuilding Co., Manitowoc, WI; lengthened 102' at Fraser Shipyards, Superior, WI, in '76

| Philip R. Clarke | 5277062 | SU | 1952 | T | 25,300 | 767' 00" | 70' 00" | 36' 00" |

Built: American Shipbuilding Co., Lorain, OH; lengthened 120' in '74 and converted to a self-unloader in '82 at Fraser Shipyards, Superior, WI

| Presque Isle {2} | 7303877 | IT | 1973 | D | 1,578* | 153' 03" | 54' 00" | 31' 03" |

Built: Halter Marine Services, New Orleans, LA

| Presque Isle {2} | | SU | 1973 | B | 57,500 | 974' 06" | 104' 07" | 46' 06" |

Built: Erie Marine Inc., Erie, PA

| **[ITB Presque Isle OA dimensions together]** | | | | | | 1,000' 00" | 104' 07" | 46' 06" |
| Roger Blough | 7222138 | SU | 1972 | D | 43,900 | 858' 00" | 105' 00" | 41' 06" |

Built: American Shipbuilding Co., Lorain, OH

G-14	**THE GREAT LAKES GROUP, CLEVELAND, OH** *(thegreatlakesgroup.com)*							
	THE GREAT LAKES TOWING CO., CLEVELAND, OH – DIVISION OF THE GREAT LAKES GROUP							
Arizona		TB	1931	D	98*	84' 04"	20' 00"	12' 06"
Arkansas {2}		TB	1909	D	98*	81' 00"	21' 03"	12' 05"
(Yale '09-'48)								

Tugs

Patricia Hoey on the Detroit River. (Wade P. Streeter)

Wendy Anne departs Charlevoix, Mich. (Roger LeLievre)

Kurt R. Luedtke. (Jim Hoffman)

Tug Missouri assists Cedarglen through brash ice in the Rock Cut, December 2010. (Roger LeLievre)

Fleet Name Vessel Name	IMO #	Vessel Type	Year Built	Engine Type	Cargo Cap. or Gross*	Overall Length	Breadth	Depth
California		TB	1926	DE	98*	81' 00"	20' 00"	12' 06"
Colorado		TB	1928	D	98*	84' 04"	20' 00"	12' 06"
Delaware {4}		TB	1924	DE	98*	81' 00"	20' 00"	12' 06"
Florida		TB	1926	D	99*	81' 00"	20' 00"	12' 06"
(Florida '26-'83, Pinellas '83-'84)								
Idaho		TB	1931	DE	98*	84' 00"	20' 00"	12' 06"
Illinois {2}		TB	1914	D	99*	81' 00"	20' 00"	12' 06"
Indiana		TB	1911	DE	97*	81' 00"	20' 00"	12' 06"
Iowa		TB	1915	D	98*	81' 00"	20' 00"	12' 06"
Kansas		TB	1927	D	98*	81' 00"	20' 00"	12' 06"
Kentucky {2}		TB	1929	D	98*	84' 04"	20' 00"	12' 06"
Louisiana		TB	1917	D	98*	81' 00"	20' 00"	12' 06"
Maine {1}		TB	1921	D	96*	81' 00"	20' 00"	12' 06"
(Maine {1} '21-'82, Saipan '82-'83, Hillsboro '83-'84)								
Massachusetts		TB	1928	D	98*	84' 04"	20' 00"	12' 06"
Milwaukee		DB	1924	B	1,095	172' 00"	40' 00"	11' 06"
Minnesota {1}		TB	1911	D	98*	81' 00"	20' 00"	12' 06"
Mississippi		TB	1916	DE	98*	81' 00"	20' 00"	12' 06"
Missouri {2}		TB	1927	D	149*	88' 04"	24' 06"	12' 03"
(Rogers City {1} '27-'56, Dolomite {1} '56-'81, Chippewa {7} '81-'90)								
Montana		TB	1929	DE	98*	84' 04"	20' 00"	12' 06"
Nebraska		TB	1929	D	98*	84' 04"	20' 00"	12' 06"
New Jersey		TB	1924	D	98*	81' 00"	20' 00"	12' 06"
(New Jersey '24-'52, Petco-21 '52-'53)								
New York		TB	1913	D	98*	81' 00"	20' 00"	12' 06"
North Carolina {2}		TB	1952	DE	145*	87' 09"	24' 01"	10' 07"
(Limestone '52-'83, Wicklow '83-'90)								
North Dakota		TB	1910	D	97*	81' 00"	20' 00"	12' 06"
(John M. Truby '10-'38)								
Ohio {3}	6507440	TB	1903	D	194*	101' 02"	26' 00"	13' 07"
Built: Great Lakes Towing Co., Chicago, IL (M.F.D. No. 15 '03-'52, Laurence C. Turner '52-'73)								
Oklahoma		TB	1913	DE	97*	81' 00"	20' 00"	12' 06"
(T. C. Lutz {2} '13-'34)								
Pennsylvania {3}		TB	1911	D	98*	81' 00"	20' 00"	12' 06"
Rhode Island		TB	1930	D	98*	84' 04"	20' 00"	12' 06"
South Carolina		TB	1925	D	102*	86' 00"	21' 00"	11' 00"
(Welcome {2} '25-'53, Joseph H. Callan '53-'72, South Carolina '72-'82, Tulagi '82-'83)								
Superior {3}		TB	1912	D	147*	97' 00"	22' 00"	12' 00"
(Richard Fitzgerald '12-'46)								
Tennessee		TB	1917	D	98*	81' 00"	20' 00"	12' 06"
Texas		TB	1916	DE	97*	81' 00"	20' 00"	12' 06"
Vermont		TB	1914	D	98*	81' 00"	20' 00"	12' 06"
Virginia {2}		TB	1914	DE	97*	81' 00"	20' 00"	12' 06"
Washington {1}		TB	1925	DE	97*	81' 00"	20' 00"	12' 06"
Wisconsin {4}		TB	1897	D	105*	90' 03"	21' 00"	12' 03"
(America {3}, Midway)								
Wyoming		TB	1929	D	104*	84' 04"	20' 00"	12' 06"

G-15 GREAT LAKES MARITIME ACADEMY – NORTHWESTERN MICHIGAN COLLEGE, TRAVERSE CITY, MI

(nmc.edu/maritime)

Anchor Bay		TV	1953	D	23*	45' 00"	13' 00"	7' 00"
Built: Roamer Boat Co., Holland, MI (ST-2158 '53-'62)								
Northwestern {2}		TV	1969	D	12*	55' 00"	15' 00"	6' 06"
Built: Paasch Marine Services Inc., Erie, PA (USCOE North Central '69-'98)								
State of Michigan		TV	1985	D	1,914*	224' 00"	43' 00"	20' 00"
Built: Tacoma Boatbuilding Co., Tacoma, WA (USNS Persistent '85-'98, USCG Persistent '98-'02)								

G-16 GREAT LAKES NAVAL MEMORIAL & MUSEUM, MUSKEGON, MI *(glnmm.org)*

McLane		MU	1927	D	289*	125' 00"	24' 00"	12' 06"
Built: American Brown Boveri Electric Co., Camden, NJ; former U.S. Coast Guard Buck & A Quarter class medium endurance cutter; on display at Muskegon, MI (USCGC McLane [WSC / WMEC-146] '27-'70, Manatra II '70-'93)								
Silversides		MU	1941	D/V	1,526*	311' 08"	27' 03"	33' 09"
Built: Mare Island Naval Yard, Vallejo, CA; former U.S. Navy Albacore (Gato) class submarine AGSS-236; open to the public at Muskegon, MI								

Fleet Name Vessel Name	IMO #	Vessel Type	Year Built	Engine Type	Cargo Cap. or Gross*	Overall Length	Breadth	Depth
G-17	**GREAT LAKES SCHOONER CO., TORONTO, ON** (greatlakesschooner.com)							
Challenge		ES	1980	W/D	76*	96' 00"	16' 06"	8' 00"
Built: Kanter Yachts Company, Port Stanley, ON								
Kajama		ES	1930	W/D	263*	128' 09"	22' 09"	11' 08"
Built: Nobis Krug, Rensburg, Germany								
G-18	**GREAT LAKES SCIENCE CENTER, ANN ARBOR, MI** (www.glsc.usgs.gov)							
Grayling		RV	1977	D	198*	75' 00"	22' 00"	9' 10"
Kaho		RV	1961	D	83*	64' 10"	17' 10"	9' 00"
Kiyi		RV	1999	D	290*	107' 00"	27' 00"	12' 02"
Musky II		RV	1960	D	25*	45' 00"	14' 04"	5' 00"
Sturgeon		RV	1977	D	325*	100' 00"	25' 05"	10' 00"
New construction - 2 vessels		RV	2011	D				
Built: Great Lakes Shipyard, Cleveland, OH								
G-19	**GREAT LAKES SHIPWRECK HISTORICAL SOCIETY, SAULT STE. MARIE, MI** (shipwreckmuseum.com)							
David Boyd		RV	1982	D	26*	47' 00"	17' 00"	3' 00"*
G-20	**GROUPE DESGAGNÉS INC., QUÉBEC CITY, QC** (groupedesgagnes.com)							
	ALL VESSELS OPERATED BY SUBSIDIARY TRANSPORT DESGAGNÉS							
Amelia Desgagnés	7411167	GC	1976	D	7,349	355' 00"	49' 00"	30' 06"
Built: Collingwood Shipyards, Collingwood, ON (Soodoc {2} '76-'90)								
Anna Desgagnés	8600507	RR	1986	D	17,850	569' 03"	75' 07"	44' 11"
Built: Kvaerner Warnow Werft GmbH, Rostock, Germany; re-registered in the Bahamas in 2006								
(Truskavets '86-'96, Anna Desgagnés '96-'98, PCC Panama '98-'99)								
Camilla Desgagnés	8100595	GC	1982	D	6,889	436' 04"	67' 07"	46' 03"
Built: Kroeger Werft GmbH & Co. KG, Rendsburg, Germany (Camilla 1 '82-'04)								
Catherine Desgagnés	5133979	GC	1962	D	8,394	410' 03"	55' 06"	31' 00"
Built: Hall, Russel and Co., Aberdeen, Scotland (Gosforth '62-'72, Thorold {4} '72-'85)								
Melissa Desgagnés	7356501	GC	1975	D	7,500	355' 00"	49' 00"	30' 06"
Built: Collingwood Shipyards, Collingwood, ON (Ontadoc {2} '75-'90)								
Rosaire A. Desgagnés	9363534	GC	2007	D	12,575	453' 00"	68' 11"	36' 01"
Built: Quingshan/Jiangdong/Jiangzhou Shipyards, Jiangzhou, China (Beluga Fortification '07-'07)								
Sedna Desgagnés	9402093	GC	2009	D	12,413	456' 00"	68' 11"	36' 01"
Built: Quingshan/Jiangdong/Jiangzhou Shipyards, Jiangzhou, China (Beluga Festivity '09-'09)								
Zelada Desgagnés	9402081	GC	2008	D	12,413	453' 00"	68' 11"	36' 01"
Built: Quingshan/Jiangdong/Jiangzhou Shipyards, Jiangzhou, China (Beluga Freedom '09-'09)								
	THE FOLLOWING VESSELS CHARTERED TO PETRO-NAV INC., MONTREAL, QC,							
	A SUBSIDIARY OF GROUPE DESGAGNÉS INC.							
Dara Desgagnés	9040089	TK	1992	D	10,511	405' 10"	58' 01"	34' 09"
Built: MTW Shipyard, Wismar, Germany (Elbestern '92-'93, Diamond Star, '93-'10)								

Ojibway in Soo Harbor. (Terry LeLievre)

Fleet Name / Vessel Name	IMO #	Vessel Type	Year Built	Engine Type	Cargo Cap. or Gross*	Overall Length	Breadth	Depth
Esta Desgagnés	9040077	TK	1992	D	10,511	405' 10"	58' 01"	34' 09"
Built: MTW Shipyard, Wismar, Germany (Emsstern '92-'92, Emerald Star '92-'10)								
Jana Desgagnés	9046564	TK	1993	D	10,511	405' 10"	58' 01"	34' 09"
Built: MTW Shipyard, Wismar, Germany (Jadestern '93-'94, Jade Star '94-'10)								
Maria Desgagnés	9163752	TK	1999	D	13,199	393' 08"	68' 11"	40' 05"
Built: Qiuxin Shipyard, Shanghai, China (Kilchem Asia '99-'99)								
Petrolia Desgagnés	7382976	TK	1975	D	9,712	441' 05"	56' 05"	32' 10"
Built: Ankerlokken Verft Glommen, Fredrikstad, Norway (Jorvan '75-'79, Lido '79-'84, Ek-Sky '84-'98)								
Sarah Desgagnés	9352171	TK	2007	D	18,000	483'11"	73' 06"	41' 04"
Built: Gisan Shipyard, Tuzla, Turkey (Besiktas Greenland '07 - '08)								
Thalassa Desgagnés	7382988	TK	1976	D	9,748	441' 05"	56' 05"	32' 10"
Built: Ankerlokken Verft Glommen, Fredrikstad, Norway (Joasla '76-'79, Orinoco '79-'82, Rio Orinoco '82-'93)								
Véga Desgagnés	7927960	TK	1982	D	11,548	461'11"	69' 07"	35' 01"
Built: Kvaerner Masa-Yards, Helsinki, Finland (Shelltrans '82-'94, Acila '94-'99, Bacalan '99-'01)								

THE FOLLOWING VESSEL CHARTERED TO RELAIS NORDIC INC., RIMOUSKI, QC A SUBSIDIARY OF GROUPE DESGAGNÉS INC.

Fleet Name / Vessel Name	IMO #	Vessel Type	Year Built	Engine Type	Cargo Cap. or Gross*	Overall Length	Breadth	Depth
Bella Desgagnés	9511519	GC/PA	2011	D	6,500	312'00"	63' 06"	22' 08"
Built: Shipyard Kraljevica, Croatia								
Nordik Express	7391290	GC/CF	1974	D	1,697	219'11"	44' 00"	16' 01"
Built: Todd Pacific Shipyards Corp., Seattle, WA (Theriot Offshore IV '74-'77, Scotoil 4 '77-'79, Tartan Sea '79-'87)								

H-1 H. LEE WHITE MARINE MUSEUM, OSWEGO, NY (hleewhitemarinemuseum.com)

LT-5		MU	1943	D	305*	115'00"	28' 00"	14' 00"
Built: Jakobson Shipyard, Oyster Bay, NY; former U.S. Army Corps of Engineers tug last operated in 1989; open to the public at Oswego, NY (Major Elisha K. Henson '43-'47, U.S. Army LT-5 '47-'47, Nash '47-'95)								

H-2 HAMILTON HARBOUR QUEEN CRUISES, HAMILTON, ON (hamiltonwaterfront.com)

Hamilton Harbour Queen		ES	1956	D	252*	100'00"	22' 00"	4' 05"
Built: Russel-Hipwell Engines, Owen Sound, ON (Johnny B. '56-'89, Garden City '89-'00, Harbour Princess '00-'05)								

H-3 HAMILTON PORT AUTHORITY, HAMILTON, ON (hamiltonport.ca)

Judge McCombs		TB	1948	D	10*	33'01"	10' 03"	4' 00"
Built: Northern Shipbuilding & Repair Co. Ltd., Bronte, ON (Bronte Sue '48-'50)								

H-4 HARBOR LIGHT CRUISE LINES INC., TOLEDO, OH (sandpiperboat.com)

Sandpiper		ES	1984	D	21*	65'00"	16' 00"	3' 00"

H-5 HMCS HAIDA NATIONAL HISTORICAL SITE, HAMILTON, ON (hmcshaida.ca)

Haida		MU	1943	T	2,744*	377'00"	37' 06"	15' 02"
Former Royal Canadian Navy Tribal class destroyer G-63 / DDE-215; open to the public at Hamilton, ON								

H-6 HERITAGE HARBOUR MARINE LTD., LONDON, ON

Salvage Monarch	5308275	TB	1959	D	219*	97'09"	29' 00"	13' 06"
Built: P.K. Harris Ltd., Appledore, England								

H-7 HERITAGE MARINE, TWO HARBORS, MN

Edward H.		TB	1944	D	142*	86'00"	23' 00"	10' 03"
Built: Equitable Equipment Co., Madisonville, LA (ST-707 '44-'60, Forney '60-'07)								
Nels J.		TB	1958	D	194*	103'00"	26 06"	12' 00"
Built: Gulfport Shipbuilding Co., Port Arthur, TX (Gatco Alabama, Ares)								

H-8 HORNBECK OFFSHORE SERVICES, COVINGTON, LA (hornbeckoffshore.com)

Bayridge Service	8101654	TB	1981	D	194*	100'00"	30' 00"	14' 05"
Built: Bollinger Shipyard Inc., Lockport, LA								
Eagle Service	9117260	TB	1996	D	195*	124'08"	37' 00"	18' 00"
Built: Bollinger Shipyard Inc., Lockport, LA								
Energy 13502	9328871	TK	2005	D	9,878*	445'00"	78' 00"	37' 05"
Energy 6506		TK	2007	B	5,778*	362'00"	60' 00"	23' 07"
Freedom Service	8207599	TB	1983	B	169*	126'00"	37' 00"	16' 04"
Built: McDermott Shipyards, Morgan City, LA								
Sea Service	7643708	TB	1975	D	173*	109'00"	31' 00"	16' 05"
Built: Halter Marine, New Orleans, LA								
Tradewind Service	7612307	TB	1975	D	183*	104'07"	30' 00"	12' 08"
Built: Bollinger Shipyard Inc., Lockport, LA								

H-9 HORNE TRANSPORTATION LTD., WOLFE ISLAND, ON (wolfeisland.com/ferry.php)

William Darrell		CF	1952	D	66*	66'00"	28' 00"	6' 00"
Built: Harry Gamble, Port Dover, ON								

H-10 HUFFMAN EQUIPMENT RENTAL INC., EASTLAKE, OH

Fleet Name / Vessel Name	IMO #	Vessel Type	Year Built	Engine Type	Cargo Cap. or Gross*	Overall Length	Breadth	Depth
Benjamin Ridgway		TW	1969	D	51*	53' 00"	18' 05"	7' 00"
Hamp Thomas		TB	1968	D	22*	43' 00"	13' 00"	4' 00"
Paddy Miles		TB	1934	D	16*	45' 04"	12' 04"	4' 07"

H-11 HYDRO-QUEBEC, MONTREAL, QC

R.O. Sweezy		TB	1991	D	29*	41' 09"	14' 00"	5' 07"

Built: Jean Fournier, Quebec City, QC (Citadelle I '91 - '92)

I-1 ICEBREAKER MACKINAW MARITIME MUSEUM INC., MACKINAW CITY, MI (themackinaw.org)

Mackinaw [WAGB-83]		MU	1944	D	5,252*	290' 00"	74' 00"	29' 00"

Built: Toledo Shipbuilding Co., Toledo, OH; former U.S. Coast Guard icebreaker was decommissioned in 2006; open to the public at Mackinaw City, MI (Launched as USCGC Manitowoc [WAG-83])

I-2 INLAND LAKES MANAGEMENT INC., ALPENA, MI

Alpena {2}	5206362	CC	1942	T	13,900	519' 06"	67' 00"	35' 00"

Built: Great Lakes Engineering Works, River Rouge, MI; shortened by 120' and converted to a self-unloading cement carrier at Fraser Shipyards, Superior, WI, in '91 (Leon Fraser '42-'91)

J. A. W. Iglehart	5139179	CC	1936	T	12,500	501' 06"	68' 03"	37' 00"

Built: Sun Shipbuilding and Drydock Co., Chester, PA; converted from a saltwater tanker to a self-unloading cement carrier at American Shipbuilding Co., South Chicago, IL , in '65; last operated Oct. 29, 2006; in use as a cement storage/transfer vessel at Superior, WI (Pan Amoco '36-'55, Amoco '55-'60, H. R. Schemm '60-'65)

Paul H. Townsend	5272050	CC	1945	D	7,850	447' 00"	50' 00"	29' 00"

Built: Consolidated Steel Corp., Wilmington, DE; converted from a saltwater cargo vessel to a self-unloading cement carrier at Bethlehem Steel Co., Shipbuilding Div., Hoboken, NJ, & Calumet Shipyard, Chicago, IL, in '52 / '53; lengthened at Great Lakes Engineering Works, Ashtabula, OH, in '58; last operated Dec. 5, 2005; in use as a cement storage/transfer vessel at Muskegon, MI (USNS Hickory Coll '45-'46, USNS Coastal Delegate '46-'52)

S. T. Crapo	5304011	CC	1927	B	8,900	402' 06"	60' 03"	29' 00"

Built: Great Lakes Engineering Works, River Rouge, MI; last operated Sept. 4, 1996; in use as a cement storage and transfer vessel at Green Bay, WI

I-3 INLAND SEAS EDUCATION ASSOCIATION, SUTTONS BAY, MI (schoolship.org)

Inland Seas		RV	1994	W	41*	61' 06"	17' 00"	7' 00"

Built: Treworgy Yachts, Palm Coast, FL

I-4 INLAND TUG & BARGE LTD., BROCKVILLE, ON

Katanni		TB	1991	D	19*	34' 08"	14' 05"	5' 05"

I-5 INTERLAKE STEAMSHIP CO., RICHFIELD, OH (interlakesteamship.com)

Dorothy Ann	8955732	AT/TT	1999	D	1,090*	124' 03"	44' 00"	24' 00"

Built: Bay Shipbuilding Co., Sturgeon Bay, WI

Herbert C. Jackson	5148417	SU	1959	T	24,800	690' 00"	75' 00"	37' 06"

Built: Great Lakes Engineering Works, River Rouge, MI; converted to a self-unloader at Defoe Shipbuilding Co., Bay City, MI, in '75

Hon. James L. Oberstar	5322518	SU	1959	D	31,000	806' 00"	75' 00"	37' 06"

Built: American Shipbuilding Co., Lorain, OH; lengthened 96' in '72; converted to a self-unloader in '81 at Fraser Shipyards, Superior, WI (Shenango II '59-'67, Charles M. Beeghly '67-'11)

James R. Barker	7390260	SU	1976	D	63,300	1,004' 00"	105' 00"	50' 00"

Built: American Shipbuilding Co., Lorain, OH

Mesabi Miner	7390272	SU	1977	D	63,300	1,004' 00"	105' 00"	50' 00"

Built: American Shipbuilding Co., Lorain, OH

Pathfinder {3}	5166768	SU	1953	B	26,700	606' 02"	70' 00"	36' 00"

Built: Great Lakes Engineering Works, River Rouge, MI; converted from a powered vessel to a self-unloading barge at Bay Shipbuilding Co., Sturgeon Bay, WI, in '98 (J. L. Mauthe '53-'98)

[ATB Dorothy Ann / Pathfinder {3} OA dimensions together]						700' 00"	70' 00"	36' 00"
Paul R. Tregurtha	7729057	SU	1981	D	68,000	1,013' 06"	105' 00"	56' 00"

Built: American Shipbuilding Co., Lorain, OH (William J. DeLancey '81-'90)

Stewart J. Cort	7105495	SU	1972	D	58,000	1,000' 00"	105' 00"	49' 00"

Built: Erie Marine Inc., Erie, PA; was the first 1,000-footer to enter Great Lakes service

LAKES SHIPPING CO. INC., RICHFIELD, OH – DIVISION OF INTERLAKE STEAMSHIP CO.

John Sherwin {2}	5174428	BC	1958	T	31,500	806' 00"	75' 00"	37' 06"

Built: American Steamship Co., Lorain, OH; lengthened 96' at Fraser Shipyards, Superior, WI, in '73; last operated Nov. 16, 1981; repowering and conversion to a self-unloader was begun at Bay Shipbuilding Co., Sturgeon Bay, WI, in 2008 but was cancelled pending an improvement in the economy; moved to DeTour, MI, Oct. 17, 2009 for continued lay-up.

Philip R. Clarke, from the Aerial Lift Bridge at Duluth. (Mike Sipper)

Fleet Name / Vessel Name	IMO #	Vessel Type	Year Built	Engine Type	Cargo Cap. or Gross*	Overall Length	Breadth	Depth
Kaye E. Barker	5097450	SU	1952	T	25,900	767' 00"	70' 00"	36' 00"

Built: American Shipbuilding Co., Toledo, OH; lengthened 120' at Fraser Shipyards, Superior, WI, in '76; converted to a self-unloader at American Shipbuilding Co., Toledo, OH, in '81 (Edward B. Greene '52-'85, Benson Ford {3} '85-'89)

Lee A. Tregurtha	5385625	SU	1942	D	29,360	826' 00"	75' 00"	39' 00"

Built: Bethlehem Shipbuilding and Drydock Co., Sparrows Point, MD; converted from a saltwater tanker to a Great Lakes bulk carrier in '61; lengthened 96' in '76 and converted to a self-unloader in '78, all at American Shipbuilding Co., Lorain, OH; repowered in '06 (laid down as Mobiloil; launched as Samoset). USS Chiwawa [AO-68] '42-'46, Chiwawa '46-'61, Walter A. Sterling '61-'85, William Clay Ford {2} '85-'89)

I-6 INTERNATIONAL MARINE SALVAGE INC., PORT COLBORNE, ON (rawmaterials.com)

Charlie E.		TB	1943	D	32*	63' 00"	16' 06"	7' 06"

Built: W.F. Kolbe & Co. Ltd., Port Dover, ON (Kolbe '43-'86, Lois T. '86-'02)

At scrap dock: Canadian Leader (bulk carrier), Windoc (barge), Techno St. Laurent (tug)

I-7 ISLAND FERRY SERVICES CORP., CHEBOYGAN, MI

Polaris		PF	1952	D	99*	60' 02"	36' 00"	8' 06"

Built: Weldship Corp., Bethlehem, PA

I-8 ISLE ROYALE LINE INC., COPPER HARBOR, MI (isleroyale.com)

Isle Royale Queen IV		PA/PK	1980	D	93*	98 09"	22' 01"	7' 00"

Built: Neuville Boat Works Inc., New Iberia, LA (American Freedom, John Jay, Shuttle V, Danielle G, Harbor Commuter V)

J-1 J. W. WESTCOTT CO., DETROIT, MI (jwwestcott.com)

J. W. Westcott II		MB	1949	D	14*	46' 01"	13' 03"	4' 05"

Built: Paasch Marine Service, Erie, PA; floating post office has its own U.S. ZIP code, 48222

Joseph J. Hogan		MB	1957	D	16*	40' 00"	12' 05"	5' 00"

Backup mailboat and water taxi for vessels docked at Great Lakes Steel / Zug Island (USCOE Ottawa '57-'95)

J-2 JEFF FOSTER, SUPERIOR, WI

Sundew		IB	1944	DE	1,025*	180' 00"	37' 05"	17' 04"

Built: Marine Ironworks and Shipbuilding Corp., Duluth, MN; former U.S. Coast Guard cutter WLB-404 was decommissioned in 2004 and turned into a marine museum. Vessel was returned to private ownership in 2009.

J-3 JOSEPH B. MARTIN, BEAVER ISLAND, MI

Shamrock		TB	1933	D	60*	64' 00"	18' 00"	7' 03"

Built: Pennsylvania Shipyard Inc., Beaumont, TX

Tanker II		TK	1964	B	60*	64' 00"	18' 00"	6' 00"

Built: Christy Corp, Sturgeon Bay, WI

J-4 JUBILEE QUEEN CRUISES, TORONTO, ON (jubileequeencruises.ca)

Jubilee Queen		ES	1986	D	269*	122' 00"	23' 09"	5' 05"

Built: Robin Lane Hanson, Oromocto, NB (Pioneer Princess III '86-'89)

J-5 JULIO CONTRACTING CO., HANCOCK, MI

Winnebago		TW	1945	D	14*	40' 00"	10' 02"	4' 06"

K-1 K-SEA CANADA CORP., HALIFAX, NS (k-sea.com)
VESSELS OPERATED BY McKEIL MARINE, CHARTERED TO PETRO-NAV INC., MONTREAL, QC

McCleary's Spirit	8967424	TK	1969	B	6,888*	379' 09"	63' 03"	33' 08"

Built: Boelwerf, Belgium (LeVent '69-'02)

William J. Moore	7030444	TB	1970	D	564*	135' 00"	34' 09"	19' 04"

Built: Adelaide Ship Construction Pty. Ltd., Port Adelaide, South Australia (Warrawee '70-'76, Seaspan Raider '76-'87, Raider '87-'87, Raider IV '87-'88, Alice A. '88-'02)

K-2 KEHOE MARINE CONSTRUCTION CO., LANSDOWNE, ON

Houghton		TB	1944	D	15*	45' 00"	13' 00"	6' 00"

K-3 KELLEYS ISLAND BOAT LINES, MARBLEHEAD, OH (kelleysislandferry.com)

Carlee Emily		PA/CF	1987	D	98*	101' 00"	34' 06"	10' 00"

Built: Blount Marine Corp., Warren, RI (Endeavor '87-'02)

Juliet Alicia		PA/CF	1969	D	95*	88' 03"	33' 00"	6' 08"

Built: Blount Marine Corp., Warren, RI (Kelley Islander)

Shirley Irene		PA/CF	1991	D	68*	160' 00"	46' 00"	9' 00"

Built: Ocean Group Shipyard, Bayou La Batre, AL

K-4 KEWEENAW EXCURSIONS INC., AHMEEK, MI (keweenawexcursions.com)

Keweenaw Star	631711	ES	1981	D	97*	110' 00"	23' 04"	6' 03"

Built: Camcraft Inc., Crown Point, LA (Atlantic Star, Privateer, De De Bruce)

Fleet Name Vessel Name	IMO #	Vessel Type	Year Built	Engine Type	Cargo Cap. or Gross*	Overall Length	Breadth	Depth
K-5	**KINDRA LAKE TOWING LP, CHICAGO, IL** (kindralake.com)							
Buckley		TW	1958	D	94*	95' 00"	26' 00"	11' 00"
Built: Parker Bros. Shipyard, Houston, TX (Linda Brooks '58-'67, Eddie B. {2} '67-'95)								
Donald C.	8841967	TB	1962	D	198*	91' 00"	29' 00"	11' 06"
Built: Main Iron Works Inc., Houma, LA (Donald C. Hannah '62-'09)								
Ellie		TB	1970	D	29*	39' 07"	16' 00"	4' 06"
Built: Big River Shipbuilding Inc., Vicksburg, MS (Miss Bissy '09)								
Morgan		TB	1974	D	134*	90' 00"	30' 00"	10' 06"
Built: Peterson Builders Inc., Sturgeon Bay, WI (Donald O'Toole '74-'86, Bonesey B. '86-'95)								
Old Mission		TB	1945	D	94*	85' 00"	23' 00"	10' 04"
Built: Sturgeon Bay Shipbuilding, Sturgeon Bay, WI (U. S. Army ST-880 '45-'47, USCOE Avondale '47-'64, Adrienne B. '64-'95)								
Tanner		TB	1976	D	62*	56' 06"	22' 00"	6' 06"
K-6	**KING CO. INC., HOLLAND, MI**							
Barry J		TB	1943	D	26*	46' 00"	13' 00"	7' 00"
Built: Sturgeon Bay Shipbuilding & Dry Dock Co., Sturgeon Bay, WI								
Buxton II		DR	1976	B	147*	130' 02"	28' 01"	7' 00"
Built: Barbour Boat Works Inc., Holland, MI								
Carol Ann		TB	1981	D	86*	61' 05"	24' 00"	8' 07"
Built: Rodriguez Boat Builders, Bayou La Batre, AL								
John Henry		TB	1954	D	66*	65' 04"	19' 04"	9' 06"
Built: Missouri Valley Steel, Leavenworth, KS (U. S. Army ST-2013 '54-'80)								
Julie Dee		TB	1937	D	64*	68' 08"	18' 01"	7' 06"
Built: Herbert Slade, Beaumont, TX (Dernier, Jerry O'Day, Cindy B)								
Matt Allen		TB	1961	D	146*	80' 04"	24' 00"	11' 03"
Built: Nolty Theriot Inc., Golden Meadow, LA (Gladys Bea '61-'73, American Viking '73-'83, Maribeth Andrie '83-'05)								
Miss Edna		TB	1935	D	13*	36' 08"	11' 02"	4' 08"
Built: Levingston Shipbuilding, Orange, TX								
K-7	**KINGSTON 1,000 ISLANDS CRUISES, KINGSTON, ON** (1000islandscruises.on.ca)							
Island Belle I		ES	1988	D	150*	65' 00"	22' 00"	8' 00"
Built: Kettle Creek Boat Works, Port Stanley, ON (Spirit of Brockville '88-'91)								

Great Lakes Science Center's research vessel Sturgeon. (Steve Hogler)

	Fleet Name Vessel Name	IMO #	Vessel Type	Year Built	Engine Type	Cargo Cap. or Gross*	Overall Length	Breadth	Depth
	Island Queen III		ES	1975	D	300*	96' 00"	26' 00"	11' 00"

Built: Marlin Yachts Co. (1974) Ltd., Summerstown, ON

| | Island Star | | ES | 1994 | D | 220* | 97' 00" | 30' 00" | 10' 00" |

Built: Bateau-Mouche Au Vieux Port Inc., Montreal, QC (Le Bateau Mouche II)

| | Papoose III | | ES | 1968 | D | 110* | 64' 08" | 23' 03" | 7' 03" |

Built: Hike Metal Products Ltd., Wheatley, ON (Peche Island II)

K-8 KK INTEGRATED LOGISTICS, MENOMINEE, MI (kkwarehousing.com/shipping.html)

| | William H. Donner | | CS | 1914 | B | 9,400 | 524' 00" | 54' 00" | 30' 00" |

Built: Great Lakes Engineering Works, Ashtabula, OH; last operated in 1969; in use as a cargo transfer vessel at Marinette, WI

VIKING I LLC, MENOMINEE, MI

| | Manitowoc | | DB | 1926 | B | 3,080* | 371' 03" | 67' 03" | 22' 06" |

Built: Manitowoc Shipbuilding Co., Manitowoc, WI; laid up at Marinette, WI

| | Snohomish | 8971384 | TB | 1943 | DE | 195* | 110' 00" | 26' 06" | 12' 06" |

Built: Ira S. Bushey & Sons Inc., Brooklyn, NY (WYTM-98 Snohomish, Dami Dew)

| | Viking I | 5018246 | CF | 1925 | D | 2,713* | 360' 00" | 56' 03" | 21' 06" |

Built: Manitowoc Shipbuilding Co., Manitowoc, WI; laid up at Marinette, WI (Ann Arbor No. 7 '25-'64, Viking {2} '64-'96)

L-1 LAFARGE CANADA INC., MONTREAL, QC
THE FOLLOWING VESSEL MANAGED BY CANADA STEAMSHIP LINES INC.

| | English River | 5104382 | CC | 1961 | D | 7,450 | 404' 03" | 60' 00" | 36' 06" |

Built: Canadian Shipbuilding and Engineering Ltd., Collingwood, ON; converted to a self-unloading cement carrier by Port Arthur Shipbuilding, Port Arthur (now Thunder Bay), ON, in '74

L-2 LAFARGE NORTH AMERICA INC., BINGHAM FARMS, MI (lafargenorthamerica.com)

| | J. B. Ford | | CC | 1904 | R | 8,000 | 440' 00" | 50' 00" | 28' 00" |

Built: American Ship Building Co., Lorain, OH; converted to a self-unloading cement carrier in '59; last operated Nov. 15, 1985; most recently used as a cement storage and transfer vessel at Superior, WI, and now laid up at that port (Edwin F. Holmes '04-'16, E. C. Collins '16-'59)

THE FOLLOWING VESSELS MANAGED BY ANDRIE INC., MUSKEGON, MI (andrie.com)

| | G. L. Ostrander | 7501106 | AT | 1976 | D | 198* | 140' 02" | 40' 01" | 22' 03" |

Built: Halter Marine, New Orleans, LA (Andrew Martin '76-'90, Robert L. Torres '90-'94, Jacklyn M '94-'04)

| | Integrity | 8637213 | CC | 1996 | B | 14,000 | 460' 00" | 70' 00" | 37' 00" |

Built: Bay Shipbuilding Co., Sturgeon Bay, WI

| | **[ATB G.L. Ostrander / Integrity OA dimensions together]** | | | | | | 543' 00" | 70' 00" | 37' 00" |
| | Innovation | 9082336 | CC | 2006 | B | 7,320* | 460' 00" | 70' 00" | 37' 00" |

Built: Bay Shipbuilding Co., Sturgeon Bay, WI

| | Samuel de Champlain | 7433709 | AT | 1975 | D | 299* | 140' 02" | 39' 02" | 20' 00" |

Built: Mangone Shipbuilding, Houston, TX (Musketeer Fury '75- '78, Tender Panther '78- '79, Margarita '79- '83, Vortice '83- '99, Norfolk '99-'06)

L-3 LAKE COUNTY HISTORICAL SOCIETY, TWO HARBORS, MN (lakecountyhistoricalsociety.org)

| | Edna G. | | MU | 1896 | R | 154* | 102' 00" | 23' 00" | 14' 06" |

Built: Cleveland Shipbuilding Co., Cleveland, OH; former Duluth, Missabe & Iron Range Railroad tug last operated in 1981; open to the public at Two Harbors, MN

L-4 LAKE ERIE ISLAND CRUISES LLC, SANDUSKY, OH (goodtimeboat.com)

| | Goodtime I | | ES | 1960 | D | 81* | 111' 00" | 29' 08" | 9' 05" |

Built: Blount Marine Corp., Warren, RI

L-5 LAKE EXPRESS LLC, MILWAUKEE, WI (lake-express.com)

| | Lake Express | 9329253 | PA/CF | 2004 | D | 96* | 179' 02" | 57' 07" | 16' 00" |

Built: Austal USA, Mobile, AL; high-speed ferry service from Milwaukee, WI, to Muskegon, MI; capacity is 250 passengers, 46 autos

L-6 LAKE MICHIGAN CARFERRY SERVICE INC., LUDINGTON, MI (ssbadger.com)

| | Badger | 5033583 | PA/CF | 1953 | S | 4,244* | 410' 06" | 59' 06" | 24' 00" |

Built: Christy Corp., Sturgeon Bay, WI; traditional ferry service from Ludington, MI, to Manitowoc, WI; capacity is 520 passengers, 180 autos; vessel is the last coal-fired steamship on the Great Lakes

| | Spartan | | PA/CF | 1952 | S | 4,244* | 410' 06" | 59' 06" | 24' 00" |

Built: Christy Corp., Sturgeon Bay, WI; last operated Jan. 20, 1979; in long-term lay-up at Ludington, MI

L-7 LAKES PILOTS ASSOCIATION, PORT HURON, MI (lakespilots.com)

| | Huron Belle | | PB | 1979 | D | 38* | 50' 00" | 15' 07" | 7' 09" |

Built: Gladding-Hearn Shipbuilding, Somerset, MA; vessel offers pilot service at Port Huron, MI

Fleet Name / Vessel Name	IMO #	Vessel Type	Year Built	Engine Type	Cargo Cap. or Gross*	Overall Length	Breadth	Depth
Huron Maid		PB	1977	D	26*	46' 00"	12' 05"	3' 05"

Built: Hans Hansen Welding Co., Toledo, OH; vessel offers pilot service at Detroit, MI

L-8   LAKESHORE SAIL CHARTERS LLC, CHICAGO, IL (redwitch.com)

Red Witch		ES/2S	1986	W	41*	77' 00"	17' 06"	6' 05"

Built: Nathaniel Zirlott, Bayou La Batre, AL

L-9   LAMBTON MARINE LTD., PORT LAMBTON, ON

Mary Ellen I		TB	2008	D	18*	41' 08"	14' 02"	7' 04"

L-10   LATITUDE 45° NORD INC. , SALABERR-DE-VALLEYFIELD, QC (www.latitude45n.com)

Latitude Amsterdam		PA	1996	D	170*	70' 05"	21' 08"	6' 03"

Built: Duratug Shipyard & Fabricating Ltd., Port Dover, ON (Georgian Clipper '96–'09)

L-11   LE SAULT DE SAINTE MARIE HISTORIC SITES INC., SAULT STE. MARIE, MI (saulthistoricsites.com)

Valley Camp {2}		MU	1917	R	12,000	550' 00"	58' 00"	31' 00"

Built: American Shipbuilding Co., Lorain, OH; former Hanna Mining Co./Wilson Marine Transit Co./Republic Steel Corp. bulk carrier last operated in 1966; open to the public at Sault Ste. Marie, MI (Louis W. Hill '17–'55)

L-12   LEE MARINE LTD., PORT LAMBTON, ON (hammondbaycruises.com)

Hammond Bay		ES	1992	D	31*	54' 00"	16' 00"	5' 00"
Nancy A. Lee		TB	1939	D	9*	40' 00"	12' 00"	3' 00"

Built: Donald Mummery, Port Dover, ON (Scrimp & Scrounge '92–'95) (Hammond Bay)

L-13   LOWER LAKES TOWING LTD., PORT DOVER, ON (randlogisticsinc.com)

Cuyahoga	5166392	SU	1943	D	15,675	620' 00"	60' 00"	35' 00"
Kaministiqua	8119285	BC	1983	D	34,500	730' 01"	75' 09"	48' 00"
Michipicoten {2}	5102865	SU	1952	D	22,300	698' 00"	70' 00"	37' 00"
Mississagi	5128467	SU	1943	D	15,800	620' 06"	60' 00"	35' 00"
Ojibway	5105831	BC	1952	D	20,668	642' 03"	67' 00"	35' 00"
Robert S. Pierson	7366403	SU	1974	D	19,650	630' 00"	68' 00"	36' 11"
Saginaw {3}	5173876	SU	1953	D	20,200	639' 03"	72' 00"	36' 00"

Cuyahoga — Built: American Shipbuilding Co., Lorain, OH; converted to a self-unloader by Manitowoc Shipbuilding Co., Manitowoc, WI, in '74; repowered in '01 (J. Burton Ayers '43–'95)

Kaministiqua — Built: Govan Shipyards, Glasgow, Scotland (Saskatchewan Pioneer '83–'95, Lady Hamilton '95–'06, Voyageur Pioneer '06–'08)

Michipicoten — Built: Bethlehem Shipbuilding & Drydock Co., Sparrows Point, MD; lengthened 72' by American Shipbuilding Co, S. Chicago, IL, in '57; converted to a self-unloader by American Shipbuilding Co., Toledo, OH, in '80; repowered in '11 (Elton Hoyt 2nd '52–'03)

Mississagi — Built: Great Lakes Engineering Works, River Rouge, MI; converted to a self-unloader by Fraser Shipyards, Superior, WI, in '67; repowered in '85 (Hill Annex '43–'43, George A. Sloan '43–'01)

Ojibway — Built: Defoe Shipbuilding Co., Bay City, MI; repowered in '05 (Charles L. Hutchinson {3} '52–'62, Ernest R. Breech '62–'88, Kinsman Independent '88–'05, Voyageur Independent '05–'08)

Robert S. Pierson — Built: American Shipbuilding Co., Lorain, OH (Wolverine {2} '74–'08)

Saginaw — Built: Manitowoc Shipbuilding Co., Manitowoc, WI, repowered in '08 (John J. Boland {3} '53–'99)

L-14   LOWER LAKES TRANSPORTATION CO., WILLIAMSVILLE, NY
A DIVISION OF LOWER LAKES TOWING LTD.

GRAND RIVER NAVIGATION CO., AVON LAKE, OH – OWNER – AN AFFILIATE OF LOWER LAKES TOWING LTD.

Calumet {3}	7329314	SU	1973	D	19,650	630' 00"	68' 00"	36' 11"
CTC No. 1		CC	1943	R	16,300	620' 06"	60' 00"	35' 00"
Invincible	7723819	ATB	1979	D	180*	100' 00"	35' 00"	22' 06"
James L. Kuber	5293341	SU	1953	B	25,500	703' 08"	70' 00"	36' 00"
Lewis J. Kuber	5336351	SU	1952	B	22,300	616' 10"	70' 00"	37' 00"

Calumet — Built: American Shipbuilding Co., Lorain, OH (William R. Roesch '73–'95, David Z. Norton {3} '95–'07, David Z. '07–'08)

CTC No. 1 — Built: Great Lakes Engineering Works, River Rouge, MI; last operated Nov. 12, 1981; former cement storage/transfer vessel is laid up at South Chicago, IL (Launched as McIntyre. Frank Purnell {1} '43–'64, Steelton {3} '64–'78, Hull No. 3 '78–'79, Pioneer {4} '79–'82)

Invincible — Built: Atlantic Marine Inc., Fort George Island, FL (R. W. Sesler '79–'91)

James L. Kuber — Built: Great Lakes Engineering Works, River Rouge, MI; lengthened 120' by Fraser Shipyards, Superior, WI, in '75; converted to a self-unloader by Bay Shipbuilding, Sturgeon Bay, WI, in '83; converted to a barge by the owners in '07 (Reserve '53–'08)

Lewis J. Kuber — Built: Bethlehem Steel Corp., Sparrows Point, MD; lengthened 72' by American Shipbuilding, South Chicago, IL, in '58; converted to a self-unloader by Fraser Shipyards, Superior, WI, in '80; converted to a barge by Erie Shipbuilding, Erie, PA, in '06; (Sparrows Point '52–'90, Buckeye {3} '90–'06)

Montrealais passing under a Welland Canal lift bridge. *(Roger LeLievre)*

Fleet Name / Vessel Name	IMO #	Vessel Type	Year Built	Engine Type	Cargo Cap. or Gross*	Overall Length	Breadth	Depth
Manistee	5294307	SU	1943	D	14,900	620' 06"	60' 03"	35' 00"

Built: Great Lakes Engineering Works, River Rouge, MI; converted to a self-unloader by Manitowoc Shipbuilding Co., Manitowoc, WI, in '64; repowered in '76 (Launched as Adirondack. Richard J. Reiss {2} '43-'86, Richard Reiss '86-'05

Manitowoc	7366398	SU	1973	D	19,650	630' 00"	68' 00"	36' 11"

Built: American Shipbuilding Co., Lorain, OH (Paul Thayer '73-'95, Earl W. Oglebay '95-'07, Earl W. '07-'08)

Maumee	5057709	SU	1929	D	12,650	604' 09"	60' 00"	32' 00"

Built: American Shipbuilding Co., Lorain, OH; converted to a self-unloader by Manitowoc Shipbuilding Co., Manitowoc, WI, in '61; repowered in '64; (William G. Clyde '29-'61, Calcite II '61-'01)

Olive L. Moore	8635227	AT	1928	D	524*	125' 00"	39' 02"	13' 09"

Built: Manitowoc Shipbuilding Co., Manitowoc, WI (John F. Cushing '28-'66, James E. Skelly '66-'66)

Victory	8003292	TB	1980	D	194*	140' 00"	43' 01"	18' 00"

Built: McDermott Shipyard Inc., Amelia, LA

LAKE SERVICE SHIPPING CO., GROSSE POINTE FARMS, MI – OWNER

McKee Sons	5216458	SU	1945	B	19,900	579' 02"	71' 06"	38' 06"

Built: Sun Shipbuilding and Drydock Co., Chester, PA; converted from saltwater vessel to a self-unloading Great Lakes bulk carrier by Maryland Drydock, Baltimore, MD, in '52; completed as a self-unloader by Manitowoc Shipbuilding Co., Manitowoc, WI, in '53; engine removed and converted to a self-unloading barge by Upper Lakes Towing, Escanaba, MI, in '91; (USNS Marine Angel '45-'52)

[ATB McKee Sons / Invincible OA dimensions together]						615' 00"	71' 06"	38' 06"

L-15 LUEDTKE ENGINEERING CO., FRANKFORT, MI *(luedtke-eng.com)*

Alan K. Luedtke		TB	1944	D	149*	86' 04"	23' 00"	10' 03"

Built: Allen Boat Co., Harvey, LA (U. S. Army ST-527 '44-'55, USCOE Two Rivers '55-'90)

Ann Marie		TB	1954	D	81*	71' 00"	19' 05"	9' 06"

Built: Smith Basin & Drydock, Pensacola, FL (ST-9684 '54- '80, Lewis Castle '80-'97, Apache '97-'01)

Chris E. Luedtke		TB	1936	D	18*	42' 05"	11' 09"	5' 00"
Erich R. Luedtke		TB	1939	D	18*	42' 05"	11' 09"	5' 00"
Gretchen B.		TB	1943	D	18*	41' 09"	12' 05"	6' 00"
Karl E. Luedtke		TB	1928	D	32*	55' 02"	14' 09"	6' 00"

Buit: Leathem D. Smith Dock Co., Sturgeon Bay, WI

Kurt R. Luedtke		TB	1956	D	95*	72' 00"	22' 06"	7' 06"

Built: Lockport Shipyard, Lockport, LA (Jere C. '56-'90)

M-1 MCM MARINE INC., SAULT STE. MARIE, MI *(mcmmarine.com)*

Beaver State		TB	1935	D	18*	43' 07"	12' 00"	5' 02"
Drummond Islander II		TB	1961	D	97*	65' 00"	36' 00"	9' 00"

Built: Marinette Marine Corp., Marinette, WI

Mackinaw City		TB	1943	D	23*	38' 00"	11' 05"	4' 07"
Mohawk		TB	1945	D	46*	65' 00"	19' 00"	10' 06"

Built: Robert Jacob Inc., City Island, NY

No. 55		DR	1927	DE	721*	165' 00"	42' 08"	12' 00"
No. 56		DS	1928	DE	1,174*	165' 00"	42' 04"	15' 07"
Ojibway		SB	1945	D	53*	53' 00"	28' 00"	7' 00"

Built: Great Lakes Engineering Works, Ashtabula, OH

Sioux		DS	1954	B	504*	120' 00"	50' 00"	10' 00"

Built: St. Louis Shipbuilding & Steel Co., St. Louis, MO

William C. Gaynor	8423818	TB	1956	D	187*	94' 00"	27' 00"	11' 09"

Built: Defoe Shipbuilding Co., Bay City, MI (William C. Gaynor '56-'88, Captain Barnaby '88-'02)

M-2 MacDONALD MARINE LTD., GODERICH, ON *(mactug.com)*

Debbie Lyn		TB	1950	D	10*	45' 00"	14' 00"	10' 00"

Built: Mathieson Boat Works, Goderich, ON (Skipper '50-'60)

Donald Bert		TB	1953	D	11*	45' 00"	14' 00"	10' 00"

Built: Mathieson Boat Works, Goderich, ON

Dover		TB	1931	D	70*	84' 00"	17' 00"	6' 00"

Built: Canadian Mead-Morrison Co. Ltd., Welland, ON (Earleejune, Iveyrose)

Ian Mac		TB	1955	D	12*	45' 00"	14' 00"	10' 00"

Built: Mathieson Boat Works, Goderich, ON

M-3 MADELINE ISLAND FERRY LINE INC., LaPOINTE, WI *(madferry.com)*

Bayfield {2}		PA/CF	1952	D	83*	120' 00"	43' 00"	10' 00"

Built: Chesapeake Marine Railway, Deltaville, VA (Charlotte '52-'99)

Island Queen {2}		PA/CF	1966	D	90*	75' 00"	34' 09"	10' 00"

Fleet Name / Vessel Name	IMO #	Vessel Type	Year Built	Engine Type	Cargo Cap. or Gross*	Overall Length	Breadth	Depth
Madeline		PA/CF	1984	D	94*	90' 00"	35' 00"	8' 00"
Nichevo II		PA/CF	1962	D	89*	65' 00"	32' 00"	8' 09"

M-4 MAID OF THE MIST STEAMBOAT CO. LTD., NIAGARA FALLS, ON *(maidofthemist.com)*

Fleet Name / Vessel Name	IMO #	Vessel Type	Year Built	Engine Type	Cargo Cap. or Gross*	Overall Length	Breadth	Depth
Maid of the Mist IV		ES	1976	D	74*	72' 00"	16' 00"	7' 00"
Built: Hike Metal Products Ltd., Wheatley, ON								
Maid of the Mist V		ES	1983	D	74*	72' 00"	16' 00"	7' 00"
Built: Hike Metal Products Ltd., Wheatley, ON								
Maid of the Mist VI		ES	1990	D	155*	78' 09"	29' 06"	7' 00"
Built: Duratug Shipyard & Fabricating Ltd., Port Dover, ON								
Maid of the Mist VII		ES	1997	D	160*	80' 00"	30' 00"	7' 00"
Built: Cartier Construction Inc., Belleville, ON								

M-5 MALCOLM MARINE, ST. CLAIR, MI *(malcolmmarine.com)*

Fleet Name / Vessel Name	IMO #	Vessel Type	Year Built	Engine Type	Cargo Cap. or Gross*	Overall Length	Breadth	Depth
Debbie Lee		TB	1955	D	13*	32' 00"	11' 00"	4' 04"
Huron Lady		TB		D	13*	38' 00"	12' 00"	4' 00"
Manitou {2}		TB	1942	D	199*	110' 00"	26' 02"	15' 06"
Built: U.S. Coast Guard, Curtis Bay, MD (USCGC Manitou [WYT-60] '43–'84)								

M-6 MANITOU ISLAND TRANSIT, LELAND, MI *(leelanau.com/manitou)*

Fleet Name / Vessel Name	IMO #	Vessel Type	Year Built	Engine Type	Cargo Cap. or Gross*	Overall Length	Breadth	Depth
Manitou Isle		PA/PK	1946	D	39*	52' 00"	14' 00"	8' 00"
(Namaycush '46–'59)								
Mishe Mokwa		PA/CF	1966	D	49*	65' 00"	17' 06"	8' 00"
Built: J. W. Nolan & Sons, Erie, PA								

M-7 MARINE ONE TOWING & SALVAGE LTD., ST. CLAIR SHORES, MI *(marineonetowing.com)*

Fleet Name / Vessel Name	IMO #	Vessel Type	Year Built	Engine Type	Cargo Cap. or Gross*	Overall Length	Breadth	Depth
Sheila Kaye		TB	1943	D	58*	65' 00"	18' 00"	7' 03"
Built: Sturgeon Bay Shipbuilding & Dry Dock Co., Sturgeon Bay, WI (Acushnet '43–'08)								

M-8 MARINE MUSEUM OF THE GREAT LAKES AT KINGSTON, KINGSTON, ON *(marmuseum.ca)*

Fleet Name / Vessel Name	IMO #	Vessel Type	Year Built	Engine Type	Cargo Cap. or Gross*	Overall Length	Breadth	Depth
Alexander Henry		MU	1959	D	1,674*	210' 00"	44' 00"	17' 09"
Built: Port Arthur Shipbuilding Co., Port Arthur, ON; former Canadian Coast Guard icebreaker was retired in 1985; open to the public at Kingston, ON								

M-9 MARINE TECH LLC, DULUTH, MN *(marinetechduluth.com)*

Fleet Name / Vessel Name	IMO #	Vessel Type	Year Built	Engine Type	Cargo Cap. or Gross*	Overall Length	Breadth	Depth
Callie M.		TB	1910	D	51*	64' 03"	16' 09"	8' 06"
Built: Houma Shipbuilding Co., Houma, LA (Chattanooga '10–'79, Howard T. Hagen '79–'94, Nancy Ann '94–'01)								
Dean R. Smith		DR	1985	B	338*	120' 00"	48' 00"	7' 00"
(No. 2 '85–'94, B. Yetter '94–'01)								
Miss Laura		TB	1943	D	146*	81' 01"	24' 00"	9' 10"
Built: Lawley & Son Corp., Neponset, MA (DPC-3 '43–'46, DS-43 '46–'50, Fresh Kills '50–'69, Richard K. '69–'93, Leopard '93–'03)								

M-10 MARIPOSA CRUISE LINE LTD., TORONTO, ON *(mariposacruises.com)*

Fleet Name / Vessel Name	IMO #	Vessel Type	Year Built	Engine Type	Cargo Cap. or Gross*	Overall Length	Breadth	Depth
Capt. Matthew Flinders	8883355	ES	1982	D	746*	144' 00"	40' 00"	8' 06"
Built: North Arm Slipway Pty. Ltd., Port Adelaide, Australia								
Mariposa Belle		ES	1970	D	195*	93' 00"	23' 00"	8' 00"
Built: Hike Metal Products, Wheatley, ON (Niagara Belle '70–'73)								
Northern Spirit I	8870073	ES	1983	D	489*	136' 00"	31' 00"	9' 00"
Built: Blount Marine Corp., Warren, RI (New Spirit '83–'89, Pride of Toronto '89–'92)								
Oriole	8800054	ES	1987	D	200*	75' 00"	23' 00"	8' 00"
Built: Duratug Shipyard Fabricating Ltd., Port Dover, ON								
Rosemary		ES	1960	D	52*	68' 00"	15' 06"	6' 08"
Built: Bender Ship Repairs, Mobile, AL								
Showboat Royal Grace		ES	1988	D	135*	58' 00"	18' 00"	4' 00"
Built: Herb Fraser & Associates Ltd., Port Colborne, ON								

M-11 MAXIMUS CORP., BLOOMFIELD HILLS, MI *(boblosteamers.com)*

Fleet Name / Vessel Name	IMO #	Vessel Type	Year Built	Engine Type	Cargo Cap. or Gross*	Overall Length	Breadth	Depth
Ste. Claire		PA	1910	R	870*	197' 00"	65' 00"	14' 00"
Built: Detroit Dry Dock Co., Detroit, MI; former Detroit to Bob-Lo Island passenger steamer last operated Sept. 2, 1991; undergoing restoration at Detroit, MI								

M-12 McASPHALT MARINE TRANSPORTATION LTD., SCARBOROUGH, ON *(mcasphalt.com)*

Fleet Name / Vessel Name	IMO #	Vessel Type	Year Built	Engine Type	Cargo Cap. or Gross*	Overall Length	Breadth	Depth
Everlast	7527332	ATB	1976	D	1,361*	143' 04"	44' 04"	21' 04"
Built: Hakodate Dock Co., Hakodate, Japan (Bilibino '77–'96)								
John J. Carrick	9473444	TK	2008	B	11,613	407' 06"	71' 07"	30' 00"
Built: Penglai Bohai Shipyard Co. Ltd., Penglai, China								
McAsphalt 401	8970768	TK	1966	B	7,399	300' 00"	60' 00"	23' 00"
Built: Todd Shipyards Corp., Houston, TX (Pittson 200 '66–'73, Pointe Levy '73–'87)								

Herbert C. Jackson in the ice above Port Huron, April 2010. (Andy Severson)

Fleet Name / Vessel Name	IMO #	Vessel Type	Year Built	Engine Type	Cargo Cap. or Gross*	Overall Length	Breadth	Depth
Norman McLeod	8636219	TK	2001	B	6,809*	379' 02"	71' 06"	30' 02"

Built: Jinling Shipyard, Nanjing, China

[ATB Everlast / Norman McLeod OA dimensions together]						500' 00"	71' 06"	30' 02"
Victorious	9473262	ATB	2009	D	1,299	122' 00"	44' 03"	26' 02

Built: Penglai Bohai Shipyard Co. Ltd., Penglai, China

M-13 McKEIL MARINE LTD., HAMILTON, ON (mckeilmarine.com)

Vessel Name	IMO #	Vessel Type	Year Built	Engine Type	Cargo Cap. or Gross*	Overall Length	Breadth	Depth
AGS-359	8636257	DH	1966	B	1,500	187' 00"	35' 00"	11' 00"

Built: Dravo Corp., Neville Island, PA

Alouette Spirit	8641537	DB	1969	B	10,087*	425' 02"	74' 01"	29' 05"

Built: Gulfport Shipbuilding Co., Port Arthur, TX (KTC 135 '69-'04, Lambert's Spirit '04-'05)

Bonnie B. III		TB	1969	D	308*	107' 00"	32' 00"	18' 00"

(Esso Oranjestad '69-'85, Oranjestad '85-'86, San Nicolas '86-'87, San Nicolas I '87-'88)

Carrol C. 1		TB	1969	D	307*	107' 00"	32' 00"	18' 00"

Built: Gulfport Shipbuilding Corp., Port Arthur, TX (Esso San Nicolas '69-'86, San Nicolas '86-'87, Carrol C '87-'88)

Condarrell	5083605	DH	1953	D	3,017	259' 00"	43' 06"	21' 00"

Built: Canadian Shipbuilding & Engineering, Kingston, ON; laid up at Port Colborne, ON (D. C. Everest '53-'81)

Erie-West		DB	1951	B	1,800	290' 00"	50' 00"	12' 00"

Built: Dravo Corp., Pittsburgh, PA Dover Light)

Evans McKeil	8983416	TB	1936	D	284*	110' 00"	25' 06"	14' 07"

Built: Panama Canal Co., Balboa, Panama (Alhajuela '36-'70, Barbara Ann {2} '70-'89)

Florence M.	5118797	TB	1961	D	236*	96' 03"	29' 03"	9' 00"

Built: P.K. Harris & Sons, Appledore, England (Foundation Vibert '61-'73, Point Vibert '73-'06)

General Chemical No. 37		TK	1956	D	883*	208' 09"	42' 09"	13' 09"

Built: Todd Shipyard, Houston, TX

Jarrett M	5030086	TB	1945	D	96*	82' 00"	20' 00"	10' 00"

Built: Russel Brothers Ltd., Owen Sound, ON (Atomic '45-'06)

Jarrett McKeil	8959776	TB	1956	D	197*	91' 08"	27' 04"	12' 03"

Built: Davie Shipbuilding Co., Lauzon, QC (Robert B. No. 1 '56-'97)

Jean-Raymond	8637263	DB	1941	B	6,800	389' 09"	56' 11"	21' 00"

Built: U.S. Navy Shipyard, Philadelphia, PA

John Spence	7218735	TB	1972	D	719*	171' 00"	38' 00"	15' 01"

Built: Star Shipyard, New Westminster, BC (Mary B. VI '72-'81, Mary B. '81-'82, Mary B. VI '82-'83, Artic Tuktu '83-'94)

Lambert Spirit	8641525	DB	1968	B	9,645	393' 07"	69' 08"	27' 05"

Built: Avondale Shipyards Inc., Avondale, LA (KTC 115 '68-'06)

Molly M. 1	5118838	TB	1962	D	207*	98' 06"	27' 10"	12' 02"

Built: Davie Shipbuilding Co., Lauzon, QC (Foundation Vigour '62-'74, Point Vigour '74-'07)

Niagara Spirit		TK	1984	D	418*	340' 00"	78' 00"	19' 00"

Built: FMC Corp., Portland, OR (Alaska Trader '84-'99, Timberjack '99-'08)

Salvor	5427019	TB	1963	D	407*	120' 00"	31' 00"	18' 06"

Built: Jakobson Shipyard, Oyster Bay, NY (Esther Moran '63-'00)

Stormont	8959893	TB	1953	D	108*	80' 00"	20' 00"	15' 00"

Built: Canadian Dredge & Dock Co., Kingston, ON

S/VM 86		DB	1958	B	487*	161' 01"	40' 00"	10' 00"

Built: Canadian Shipbuilding & Engineering Ltd., Collingwood, ON (S.L.S. 86)

Tony MacKay	7227786	TB	1973	D	366*	127' 00"	30' 05"	14' 05"

Built: Richard Dunston Ltd., Hessle, England (Point Carroll '73-'01)

Viateur's Spirit		DB	2004	D	253*	141' 01"	52' 03"	5' 01"

Built: Port Weller Dry Dock, Port Weller, ON (Traverse René Lavasseur '04-'06)

Wilf Seymour		TB	1961	D	442*	122' 00"	31' 00"	17' 00"

Built: Gulfport Shipbuilding, Port Arthur, TX (M. Moran '61-'70, Port Arthur '70-'72, M. Moran '72-'00, Salvager '00-'04)

Wyatt M.		TB	1948	D	123*	85' 00"	20' 00"	10' 00"

Built: Russel Brothers Ltd., Owen Sound, ON (P. J. Murer '48-'81, Michael D. Misner '81-'93, Thomas A. Payette '93-'96, Progress '96-'06)

McKEIL SHIPS LTD. – A SUBSIDIARY OF McKEIL MARINE LTD., HAMILTON, ON

Vessel Name	IMO #	Vessel Type	Year Built	Engine Type	Cargo Cap. or Gross*	Overall Length	Breadth	Depth
Kathryn Spirit	6717069	GC	1967	D	12,106	504' 05"	66' 03"	36' 07"

Built: Lindholmen Shipyard, Gothenburg, Sweden (Holmsund '67-'97, Menominee '97-'06)

MONTREAL BOATMEN LTD. – A SUBSIDIARY OF McKEIL MARINE LTD., PORT COLBORNE, ON

Vessel Name	IMO #	Vessel Type	Year Built	Engine Type	Cargo Cap. or Gross*	Overall Length	Breadth	Depth
Aldo H.		PB	1979	D	37*	56' 04"	15' 04"	6' 02"
Boatman No. 3		PB	1965	D	13*	33' 08"	11' 00"	6' 00"
Boatman No. 6		PB	1979	D	39*	56' 07"	18' 07"	6' 03"
Dredge Primrose		DR	1915	B	916*	136' 06"	42' 00"	10' 02"

Built: M. Beatty & Son Ltd., Welland, ON

Fleet Name Vessel Name	IMO #	Vessel Type	Year Built	Engine Type	Cargo Cap. or Gross*	Overall Length	Breadth	Depth
M-14	**McMULLEN & PITZ CONSTRUCTION CO., MANITOWOC, WI** *(mcmullenandpitz.net)*							
Dauntless		TB	1937	D	25*	52′ 06″	15′ 06″	5′ 03″
Erich		TB	1943	D	19*	37′ 00″	12′ 06″	5′ 07″
M-15	**McNALLY CONSTRUCTION INC., HAMILTON, ON** *(mcnallycorp.com)*							
Bagotville		TB	1964	D	65*	65′ 00″	18′ 05″	8′ 03″
Built: Verreault Navigation, Les Méchins, QC								
Beaver Delta II		TB	1959	D	14*	35′ 08″	12′ 00″	4′ 04″
Built: Allied Builders Ltd., Vancouver, BC (Halcyon Bay)								
Beaver Gamma		TB	1960	D	17*	37′ 01″	12′ 09″	6′ 00″
Built: Diesel Sales & Service (Burlington) Ltd., Burlington, ON (Burlington Bertie)								
Beaver Kay		GC	1953	B	614*	115′ 01″	60′ 00″	9′ 05″
Built: George T. Davie & Sons Ltd., Lauzon, QC								
Canadian		DR	1954	B	1,087*	173′ 08″	49′ 08″	13′ 04″
Built: Port Arthur Shipbuilding Co. Ltd., Port Arthur (Thunder Bay), ON								
Canadian Argosy		DS	1978	B	951*	149′ 09″	54′ 01″	10′ 08″
Built: Canadian Shipbuilding & Engineering Ltd., Collingwood, ON								
Cargo Carrier I		DB	1969	B	196*	89′ 09″	29′ 09″	8′ 05″
Built: Halifax Shipyards Ltd., Halifax, NS								
Cargo Master		CS	1964	B	562*	136′ 00″	50′ 00″	9′ 00″
Built: Canadian Shipbuilding & Engineering Ltd., Collingwood, ON								
Carl M.		TB	1957	D	21*	47′ 00″	14′ 06″	6′ 00″
Dapper Dan		TB	1948	D	21*	41′ 03″	12′ 07″	5′ 09″
Built: Russel Brothers Ltd., Owen Sound, ON								
F. R. McQueen		DB	1959	B	180*	79′ 09″	39′ 09″	5′ 07″
Built: Manitowoc Engineering Corp., Manitowoc, WI								
Greta V		TB	1951	D	14*	44′ 00″	12′ 00″	5′ 00″
Handy Andy		DB	1925	B	313*	95′ 09″	43′ 01″	10′ 00″
Idus Atwell		DS	1962	B	366*	100′ 00″	40′ 00″	8′ 05″
Built: Dominion Bridge Co. Ltd., Toronto, ON								
Island Sauvage		PA	1969	D	381*	86′ 03″	61′ 04″	9′ 03″
Built: Halifax Shipyards Ltd., Halifax, NS (Cargo Carrier II)								
Jamie L.		TB	1988	D	25*	36′ 04″	14′ 07″	5′ 09″
Jerry Newberry		TB	1956	D	244*	98′ 00″	28′ 02″	14′ 04″
Built: Davie Shipbuilding Co., Lauzon, QC (Foundation Victor '56-'73, Point Victor '73-'77, Kay Cole '77-'95)								
John Holden		DR	1954	B	148*	89′ 08″	30′ 01″	6′ 02″
Built: McNamara Construction Co. Ltd., Toronto, ON								
Lac Como		TB	1944	D	63*	65′ 00″	16′ 10″	7′ 10″
Built: Canadian Bridge Co., Walkerville, ON (Tanac 74 '44-'64)								
Lac Vancouver		TB	1943	D	65*	60′ 09″	16′ 10″	7′ 08″
Built: Central Bridge Co., Trenton, ON (Vancouver '43-'74)								
Mister Joe		TB	1964	D	70*	61′ 00″	19′ 00″	7′ 02″
Built: Russel Brothers Ltd., Owen Sound, ON (Churchill River - '99)								
Oshawa		TB	1969	D	24*	42′ 09″	13′ 08″	5′ 04″
Sandra Mary		TB	1962	D	97*	80′ 00″	21′ 00″	10′ 09″
Built: Russel Brothers Ltd., Owen Sound, ON (Flo Cooper '62-'00)								
Whitby		TB	1978	D	24*	42′ 19″	13′ 08″	6′ 05″
William B. Dilly		DR	1957	B	473*	116′ 00″	39′ 10″	9′ 01″
Built: Canadian Shipbuilding & Engineering Ltd., Collingwood, ON								
Willmac		TB	1959	D	16*	40′ 00″	13′ 00″	3′ 07″
M-16	**MENASHA TUGBOAT CO., SARNIA, ON**							
Menasha {2}		TB	1949	D	132*	78′ 00″	24′ 00″	9′ 08″
Built: Bludworth Marine, Houston, TX (W. C. Harms '49-'54, Hamilton '54-'86, Ruby Casho '86-'88, W. C. Harms '88-'97)								
M-17	**MERCURY CHICAGO'S SKYLINE CRUISELINE, CHICAGO, IL** *(mercuryskylinecruiseline.com)*							
Chicago's First Lady		ES	1991	D	62*	96′ 00″	22′ 00″	9′ 00″
Chicago's Little Lady		ES	1999	D	70*	69′ 02″	22′ 08″	7′ 00″
Skyline Princess		ES	1956	D	56*	59′ 04″	16′ 00″	4′ 08″
Skyline Queen		ES	1959	D	45*	61′ 05″	16′ 10″	6′ 00″
M-18	**MICHIGAN DEPARTMENT OF NATURAL RESOURCES, LANSING, MI** *(michigan.gov/dnr)*							
Channel Cat		RV	1968	D	24*	46′ 00″	13′ 06″	4′ 00″
Lake Char		RV	2006	D	26*	56′ 00″	16′ 00″	4′ 05″
Steelhead		RV	1967	D	70*	63′ 00″	16′ 04″	6′ 06″

Fleet Name Vessel Name	IMO #	Vessel Type	Year Built	Engine Type	Cargo Cap. or Gross*	Overall Length	Breadth	Depth

M-19 MICHIGAN MARITIME MUSEUM, SOUTH HAVEN, MI (michiganmaritimemuseum.org)

Friends Good Will		TV/ES	2004	D/W	54*	56' 05"	17' 00"	11' 03"

Built: Scarano Boatbuilding, Inc., Albany, NY

M-20 MICHIGAN TECHNOLOGICAL UNIVERSITY, HOUGHTON, MI

Agassiz		RV	2002	D	14*	36' 00"	13' 00"	4' 00"

M-21 MIDLAND TOURS INC., MIDLAND, ON (midlandtours.com)

Miss Midland	7426667	ES	1974	D	106*	68' 07"	19' 04"	6' 04"

Built: Marlin Yachts Co. Ltd., Gananoque, ON

M-22 MIDWEST MARITIME CORP., MILWAUKEE, WI

Leona B.		TB	1972	D	99*	59' 08"	24' 01"	10' 03"

(Kings Squire '72-'89, Juanita D. '78-'89, Peggy Ann '89-'93, Mary Page Hannah {2} '93-'04)

M-23 MILLER BOAT LINE, PUT-IN-BAY, OH (millerferry.com)

Islander {3}		PA/CF	1983	D	92*	90' 03"	38' 00"	8' 03"
Put-in-Bay {3}		PA/CF	1997	D	97*	136 00"	38' 06"	9' 06"

Built: Sturgeon Bay Shipbuilding Co., Sturgeon Bay, WI; lengthened by 40' at Cleveland, OH, in '09

South Bass		PA/CF	1989	D	95*	96' 00"	38' 00"	9' 06"
Wm. Market		PA/CF	1993	D	95*	96' 00"	38' 06"	8' 09"

Built: Peterson Builders Inc., Sturgeon Bay, WI

M-24 MILWAUKEE BOAT LINE, MILWAUKEE, WI (mkeboat.com)

Iroquois		PA	1922	D	91*	61' 09"	21' 00"	6' 04"
Vista King		ES	1978	D	60*	78' 00"	23' 00"	5' 02"
Voyageur		PA	1988	D	94*	67' 02"	21' 00"	7' 04"

M- 25 MILWAUKEE HARBOR COMMISSION, MILWAUKEE, WI (city.milwaukee.gov/port)

Harbor Seagull		TB	1961	D	23*	44' 05"	16' 04"	5' 00"

M-26 MILWAUKEE RIVER CRUISE LINE, MILWAUKEE, WI (edelweissboats.com)

Edelweiss II		ES	1989	D	95*	73' 08"	20' 00"	2' 08"

M-27 MINISTRY OF TRANSPORTATION, DOWNSVIEW, ON (www.mto.gov.on.ca)

Cassiopeia IV		PA	1957	Gas	40*	50' 00"	24' 00"	3' 070"

Built: Russel-Hipwell Engines Ltd., Owen Sound, ON

Frontenac II	5068875	PA/CF	1962	D	666*	181' 00"	45' 00"	10' 00"

Built: Chantier Maritime de Saint-Laurent, Saint-Laurent, QC (Charlevoix {2} '62-'92)

Frontenac Howe Islander		PF/CF	2004	D	130*	100' 00"	32' 03"	5' 05"

Built: Heddle Marine Service Inc., Hamilton, ON

Glenora	5358074	PA/CF	1952	D	189*	127' 00"	33' 00"	9' 00"

Built: Erieau Shipbuilding & Drydock Co. Ltd., Erieau, ON (The St. Joseph Islander '52-'74)

Jiimaan	9034298	PA/CF	1992	D	2,807*	176' 09"	42' 03"	13' 06"

Built: Port Weller Drydock, Port Weller, ON

Pelee Islander	5273274	PA/CF	1960	D	334*	145' 00"	32' 00"	10' 00"

Built: Erieau Shipbuilding & Drydock Co. Ltd., Erieau, ON

Quinte Loyalist	5358062	PA/CF	1954	D	204*	127' 00"	32' 00"	8' 00"

Built: Erieau Shipbuilding & Drydock Co. Ltd., Erieau, ON

Wolfe Islander III	7423079	PA/CF	1975	D	985*	205' 00"	68' 00"	6' 00"

Built: Port Arthur Shipbuilding Co., Port Arthur, ON

M-28 MONTREAL PORT AUTHORITY, MONTREAL, QC (port-montreal.com)

Denis M		TB	1942	D	21*	46' 07"	12' 08"	4' 01"

Built: Russel Brothers Ltd., Owen Sound, ON (Marcel D.)

Maisonneuve	7397749	PA	1972	D	84*	63' 10"	20' 07"	9' 03"

Built: Fercraft Marine Inc., Ste. Catherine D'Alexandre, QC

M-29 MUNISING BAY SHIPWRECK TOURS INC., MUNISING, MI (shipwrecktours.com)

Miss Munising		ES	1967	D	50*	60' 00"	14' 00"	4' 04"

M-30 MUSÉE MARITIME DU QUÉBEC, L' ISLET, QC (mmq.qc.ca)

Bras d'Or 400		MU	1968	D	250*	163' 11"	66' 00"	

Built: Marine Industries Limited, Sorel, QC; former Canadian Coast Guard anti-submarine warfare technology hydrofoil is on display at L'Islet, QC

Ernest Lapointe		MU	1941	R	1,179*	185' 00"	36' 00"	22' 06"

Built: Davie Shipbuilding Co., Lauzon, QC; former Canadian Coast Guard icebreaker; open to the public at L'Islet, QC

JOHN G. MUNSON

Vessel Spotlight

With a post-World War II building frenzy under way and a crisis in Korea looming, a real need for new and larger vessels on the Great Lakes became evident.

In 1950, Irvin Clymer, president of the Bradley Transportation Line, awarded a contract to the Manitowoc Shipbuilding Co. for a new, 666-foot self-unloading bulk carrier. The vessel was slated for the stone trade – limestone in particular.

Christened *John G. Munson*, the second vessel to bear that name, she was the last new vessel built for the Bradley fleet before it was merged by parent company U.S. Steel Corp., with its sister fleet , the Pittsburgh Steamship Co., in 1968, creating the USS Great Lakes Fleet.

When the *John G. Munson* entered service in 1952, it was the largest self-unloader on the Great Lakes. A new Great Lakes limestone cargo record was quickly set; on Sept. 9, 1952, the *Munson* carried a record 20,871 gross tons of limestone from Calcite to Buffington, Ind., and succeeded in breaking its own record in 1953 when on July 4 another Calcite limestone load of 21,011 gross tons was loaded for Gary, Ind. This record stood until 1966.

Following the amalgamation of the two fleets, the *Munson*'s main cargoes were iron ore, stone and coal. Today, the *Munson* is the last vessel from the Bradley Fleet still sailing for the current version of the USS Great Lakes Fleet, the Duluth-based Great Lakes Fleet.

To many people with roots in the Great Lakes shipping industry, the *John G. Munson* is still considered a "Bradley boat." Even though the hull colors have changed, many of the ports of call and cargoes remain the same, especially limestone – just as Mr. Clymer had in mind back in 1950. *– George Wharton*

John G. Munson on the St. Marys River, summer 2010. (Roger LeLievre)

Fleet Name / Vessel Name	IMO #	Vessel Type	Year Built	Engine Type	Cargo Cap. or Gross*	Overall Length	Breadth	Depth

M-31 MUSEUM SHIP COL. JAMES M. SCHOONMAKER, TOLEDO, OH *(jmschoonmaker.org)*

| Col. James M. Schoonmaker | | MU | 1911 | T | 15,000 | 617' 00" | 64' 00" | 33' 01" |

Built: Great Lakes Engineering Works, Ecorse, MI; former Shenango Furance Co./Republic Steel Co./Cleveland-Cliffs Steamship Co. bulk carrier last operated in 1980; open to the public at Toledo, OH; vessel marks its 100th anniversary in 2011 (Col. James M. Schoonmaker 1911–'69, Willis B. Boyer '69–'2011)

M-32 MUSEUM SHIP WILLIAM G. MATHER, CLEVELAND, OH *(wgmather.nhlink.net)*

| William G. Mather {2} | | MU | 1925 | T | 13,950 | 618' 00" | 62' 00" | 32' 00" |

Built: Great Lakes Engineering Works, Ecorse, MI; former Cleveland-Cliffs Steamship Co. bulk carrier last operated Dec. 21, 1980; open to the public at Cleveland, OH

M-33 MUSIQUE AQUATIQUE CRUISE LINES INC., TORONTO, ON *(citysightseeingtoronto.com)*

| Harbour Star | | ES | 1978 | D | 45* | 63' 06" | 15' 09" | 3' 09" |

Built: Eastern Equipment Ltd., LaSalle, QC (K. Wayne Simpson '78–'95)

M-34 MUSKOKA STEAMSHIP & HISTORICAL SOCIETY, GRAVENHURST, ON *(realmuskoka.com)*

| Segwun | | PA | 1887 | R | 308* | 128' 00" | 24' 00" | 7' 06" |

Built: Melancthon Simpson, Toronto, ON (Nipissing {2} 1887–'25)

| Wanda III | | PA | 1915 | R | 60* | 94' 00" | 12' 00" | 5' 00" |

Built: Poulson Iron Works Ltd., Toronto, ON

| Wenonah II | 8972003 | PA | 2001 | D | 447* | 127' 00" | 28' 00" | 6' 00" |

Built: McNally Construction Inc., Belleville, ON

N-1 NADRO MARINE SERVICES LTD., PORT DOVER, ON *(nadromarine.ca)*

| Ecosse | 8624682 | TB | 1979 | D | 142* | 91' 00" | 26' 00" | 8' 06" |

Built: Hike Metal Products Ltd., Wheatley, ON (R & L No. 1 '79–'96)

| Intrepid III | | TB | 1976 | D | 39* | 66' 00" | 17' 00" | 7' 06" |

Built: Halter Marine Ltd., Chalmette, LA

| Lac Manitoba | | TB | 1944 | D | 51* | 64' 00" | 16' 07" | 7' 10" |

Built: Central Bridge Co., Trenton, ON (Tanac 75 '44–'52, Manitoba '52–'57)

| Seahound | | TB | 1941 | D | 57* | 65' 00" | 18' 00" | 8' 00" |

Built: Equitable Equipment Co., New Orleans, LA ([Unnamed] '41–'56, Sea Hound '56–'80, Carolyn Jo '80–'00)

| Vac | | TB | 1942 | D | 36* | 65' 00" | 20' 04" | 4' 03" |

Built: George Gamble, Port Dover, ON

| Vigilant I | | TB | 1944 | D | 111* | 79' 06" | 20' 11" | 10' 02" |

Built: Russell Brothers Ltd., Owen Sound, ON (HMCS Glenlivet [W-43] '44–'75, Glenlivet II '75–'77, Canadian Franko '77–'82, Glenlivet II '82–'00)

N-2 NAUTICA QUEEN CRUISE DINING, CLEVELAND, OH *(nauticaqueen.com)*

| Nautica Queen | | ES | 1981 | D | 95* | 124' 00" | 31' 02" | 8' 09" |

Built: Blount Marine Corp., Warren, RI (Bay Queen '81–'85, Arawanna Queen '85–'88, Star of Nautica '88–'92)

N-3 NAUTICAL ADVENTURES, TORONTO, ON *(nauticaladventure.com)*

| Empire Sandy | 5071561 | ES/3S | 1943 | D/W | 338* | 140' 00" | 32' 08" | 14' 00" |

Built: Clellands Ltd., Wellington-Quay-on-Tyne, UK (Empire Sandy '43–'48, Ashford '48–'52, Chris M. '52–'79)

| Wayward Princess | | ES | 1976 | D | 325* | 92' 00" | 26' 00" | 10' 00" |

Built: Marlin Yacht Co., Summerstown, ON (Cayuga II '76–'82)

N-4 NAVY MARINE CORPS RESERVE CENTER, BUFFALO, NY

| LCU 1680 | | TV | 1943 | D | 170* | 135' 00" | 29' 00" | |

N-5 NEW YORK POWER AUTHORITY, LEWISTON, NY

Breaker		TB	1962	D	29*	43' 03"	14' 03"	5' 00"
Daniel Joncaire		TB	1979	D	25*	43' 03"	15' 00"	5' 00"
Havasu II		CS	2010	B	114*	80' 00"	34' 00"	5' 00"

N-6 NEW YORK STATE MARINE HIGHWAY TRANSPORTATION CO., TROY, NY *(nysmarinehighway.com)*

| Benjamin Elliot | | TB | 1960 | D | 27* | 47 07" | 15' 02" | 7' 02" |

Built: Gladding-Hearn Shipbuilding, Somerset, MA (El-Jean)

| Margot | 5222043 | TB | 1958 | D | 141* | 90' 00" | 25' 00" | 10' 00" |

Built: Jakobson Shipyard, Oyster Bay, NY (Jolene Rose, Margot Moran)

N-7 NORTHERN MARINE TRANSPORTATION INC., SAULT STE. MARIE, MI

Empire State		PB	1951	D	21*	41' 09"	12' 04"	6' 06"
David Allen		PB	1964	D	32*	56' 04"	13' 03"	6' 00"
Linda Jean		PB	1950	D	17*	38' 00"	10' 00"	5' 00"

Fleet Name Vessel Name	IMO #	Vessel Type	Year Built	Engine Type	Cargo Cap. or Gross*	Overall Length	Breadth	Depth

O-1 OAK GROVE & MARINE TRANSPORTATION INC., CLAYTON, NY

| Maple Grove | | PK | 1954 | D | 55* | 73' 07" | 20' 00" | 9' 00" |

O-2 OCCIDENTAL CHEMICAL CORP., LUDINGTON, MI (oxy.com)

| Spartan | 7047461 | ATB | 1969 | D | 191* | 127' 05" | 32' 01" | 14' 03" |

Built: Burton Shipyard, Bridge City, TX (Lead Horse '69-'73, Gulf Challenger '73-'80, Challenger {2} '80-'93, Mark Hannah '93-'10)

| Spartan II | | TK | 1980 | B | 8,050 | 407' 01" | 60' 00" | 21' 00" |

Built: Sturgeon Bay Shipbuilding Co., Sturgeon Bay, WI (Hannah 6301 '80-'10)

O-3 OCEAN GROUP INC., QUÉBEC, QC (groupocean.com)

| Basse-Cote | 8644620 | DB | 1932 | B | 400 | 201' 00" | 40' 00" | 12' 00" |

Built: Department of Marine and Fisheries Government Shipyard, Sorel, QC (Louis D. '32-'93)

| Betsiamites | 8644632 | SU | 1969 | B | 11,600 | 402' 00" | 75' 00" | 24' 00" |

Built: Port Weller Dry Docks Ltd., St. Catharines, ON

Coucoucache		TB	1934	D	10*	34' 01"	9' 05"	4' 02"
David T. D.		TB	1947	D	22*	42' 01"	12' 03"	5' 08"
H. E. Graham		TB	1964	D	7*	32' 09"	9' 05"	3' 05"
J. V. Perrin		TB	1958	D	10*	34' 01"	10' 00"	3' 09"
Jerry G.	8959788	TB	1960	D	202*	91' 06"	27' 03"	12' 06"

Built: Davie Shipbuilding Co., Lauzon, QC

Kim R. D.		TB	1954	D	30*	48' 07"	14' 01"	5' 08"
La Croche		TB	1940	D	7*	32' 07"	9' 05"	3' 05"
La Prairie	7393585	TB	1975	D	110*	73' 09"	25' 09"	11' 08"

Built: Georgetown Shipyard, Georgetown, PEI

| Lac St-Francois | | BC | 1979 | B | 1,200 | 195' 00" | 35' 00" | 12' 00" |

Built: Nashville Bridge Co., Nashhville, TN (TCF 505)

Le Phil D.		TB	1961	D	38*	56' 01"	16' 00"	5' 08"
Mado-Ray		TB	1954	D	12*	38' 00"	12' 01"	3' 03"
Navcomar No. 1		DB	1955	B	402*	135' 00"	35' 00"	9' 00"

Built: Sincennes-McNaughton Line Ltd., Montreal, QC (McAllister No. 1 '55-'92)

| Ocean Bertrand Jeansonne | 9521526 | TB | 2008 | D | 402* | 94' 05" | 36' 05" | 17' 02" |

Built: East Isle Shipyard, Georgetown, PEI

| Ocean Bravo | 7025279 | TB | 1970 | D | 320* | 110' 00" | 28' 06" | 17' 00" |

Built: Davie Shipbuilding Co., Lauzon, QC (Takis V. '70-'80, Donald P '80-'80, Nimue '80-'83, Donald P. '83-'98)

| Ocean Delta | 7235707 | TB | 1973 | D | 722* | 136' 08" | 35' 08" | 22' 00" |

Built: Ulstein Mek. Verksted A.S., Ulsteinvik, Norway (Sistella '73-'78, Sandy Cape '78-'80, Captain Ioannis S. '80-'99)

| Ocean Express | | PB | 1999 | D | 29* | 47' 02" | 14' 00" | 7' 05" |

Built: Industries Ocean Inc., Charlevoix, QC (H-2000 '99-'00)

| Ocean Georgie Bain | 9553892 | TB | 2009 | D | 204* | 75' 02" | 29' 09" | 12' 09" |

Built: Industries Ocean Inc., Ile-Aux-Coudres, QC

| Ocean Golf | 5146354 | TB | 1959 | D | 159* | 103' 00" | 25' 10" | 11' 09" |

Built: P.K. Harris & Sons, Appledore, England (Launched as Stranton. Helen M. McAllister '59-'97)

| Ocean Henry Bain | 9420916 | TB | 2006 | D | 402* | 94' 08" | 30' 01" | 14' 09" |

Built: East Isle Shipyard, Georgetown, PEI

| Ocean Hercule | 7525346 | TB | 1976 | D | 448* | 120' 00" | 32' 00" | 19' 00" |

(Stril Pilot '76-'81, Spirit Sky '81-'86, Ireland '86-'89, Irelandia '89-'95, Charles Antoine '95-'97)

| Ocean Intrepide | 9203423 | TT | 1998 | D | 302* | 80' 00" | 30' 01" | 14' 09" |

Built: Industries Ocean Inc., Ile-Aux-Coudres, QC

| Ocean Jupiter {2} | 9220160 | TT | 1999 | D | 302* | 80' 00" | 30' 00" | 13' 04" |

Built: Industries Ocean Inc., Ile-Aux-Coudres, QC

| Ocean K. Rusby | 9345556 | TB | 2005 | D | 402* | 94' 08" | 30' 01" | 14' 09" |

Built: East Isle Shipyard, Georgetown, PEI

| Ocean Lima | | TB | 1977 | D | 15* | 34' 02" | 11' 08" | 4' 00" |

(VM/S St. Louis III '77-'10)

| Ocean Raymond Lemay | 9420904 | TB | 2006 | D | 402* | 94' 08" | 30' 01" | 14' 09" |

Built: East Isle Shipyard, Georgetown, PEI

| Ocean Serge Genois | 9553907 | TB | 2010 | D | 204* | 75' 01" | 30' 01" | 12' 09" |

Built: Industries Ocean Inc., Ile-Aux-Coudres, QC

| Ocean Yvan Desgagnés | 9542207 | TB | 2010 | D | 402* | 94' 04" | 36' 05" | 17' 00" |

Built: East Isle Shipyard, Georgetown, PEI

| Omni-Atlas | 8644668 | CS | 1913 | B | 479* | 133' 00" | 42' 00" | 10' 00" |

Built: Sir William Arrol & Co. Ltd., Glasgow, Scotland

Mississagi unloading grain at the Kraft elevator in Toledo. (Paul C. LaMarre III)

Fleet Name / Vessel Name	IMO #	Vessel Type	Year Built	Engine Type	Cargo Cap. or Gross*	Overall Length	Breadth	Depth
Omni-Richelieu	6923084	TB	1969	D	144*	83' 00"	24' 06"	13' 06"
Built: Pictou Industries Ltd., Pictou, NS (Port Alfred II '69–'82)								
Rapide Blanc		TB	1951	D	10*	34' 00"	10' 00"	4' 03"
Roxane D		TB	1945	D	50*	60' 06"	16' 06"	6' 07"

OCÉAN REMORQUAGE TROIS-RIVIÈRES INC. – SUBSIDIARY OF OCÉAN GROUPE INC.

Fleet Name / Vessel Name	IMO #	Vessel Type	Year Built	Engine Type	Cargo Cap. or Gross*	Overall Length	Breadth	Depth
Andre H.	5404172	TB	1963	D	317*	126' 00"	28' 06"	12' 10"
Built: Davie Shipbuilding Co., Lauzon, QC (Foundation Valiant '63–'73, Point Valiant {1} '73–'95)								
Avantage	6828882	TB	1969	D	362*	116' 10"	32' 09"	16' 03"
Built: J. Boel En Zonen, Temse, Belgium (Sea Lion '69–'97)								
Duga	7530030	TB	1977	D	382*	114' 02"	32' 10"	16' 05"
Built: Langsten Slip & Båtbyggeri A/S, Lanste, Norway								
Escorte		TT	1964	D	120*	85' 00"	23' 07"	7' 05"
Built: Jakobson Shipyard, Oyster Bay, NY (USS Menasha [YTB / YTM-773, YTM-761] '64–'92, Menasha {1} '92–'95)								
Josee H.		PB	1961	D	66*	63' 50"	16' 02"	9' 50"
Built: Ferguson Industries Ltd., Pictou, NS (Le Bic '61–'98)								
Ocean Charlie	7312024	TB	1973	D	448*	123' 02"	31' 07"	16' 01"
Built: Davie Shipbuilding Co., Lauzon, QC (Leonard W. '73–'98)								
Ocean Echo II	6913091	AT	1969	D	438*	104' 08"	34' 05"	18' 00"
Built: Port Weller Dry Docks, Port Weller, ON (Atlantic '69–'75, Laval '75–'96)								
Ocean Foxtrot	7101619	TB	1971	D	700*	170' 10"	38' 09"	11' 11"
Built: Cochrane & Sons Ltd., Selby, England (Polar Shore '71–'77, Canmar Supplier VII '77–'95)								
R. F. Grant		TB	1934	D	78*	71' 00"	17' 00"	8' 00"
Built: Canadian Vickers Ltd., Montreal, QC								
Service Boat No. 1		PB	1965	D	55*	57' 08"	16' 01"	7' 06"
Built: Three Rivers Boatmen Ltd., St. Antoine de Tilly, QC								
Service Boat No. 4		PB	1959	D	26*	39' 01"	14' 02"	6' 03"
Built: Three Rivers Boatmen Ltd., St. Antoine de Tilly, QC								

O-4 OLYMPIA CRUISE LINE INC., THORNHILL, ON

Fleet Name / Vessel Name	IMO #	Vessel Type	Year Built	Engine Type	Cargo Cap. or Gross*	Overall Length	Breadth	Depth
Enterprise 2000		ES	1998	D	370*	121' 06"	35' 00"	6' 00"
Built: Galactica 001 Enterprises Ltd., Toronto, ON								

O-5 ONTARIO MINISTRY OF NATURAL RESOURCES, UPPER GREAT LAKES MANAGEMENT UNIT, PETERBOROUGH, ON *(mnr.gov.on.ca)*

Fleet Name / Vessel Name	IMO #	Vessel Type	Year Built	Engine Type	Cargo Cap. or Gross*	Overall Length	Breadth	Depth
Atigamayg		RV	1954	D	82*	43' 09"	20' 02"	5' 07"
Built: Mathieson Boat Works, Goderich, ON (Robert Henry '54–'91)								
Erie Explorer		RV	1981	D	72*	53' 05"	20' 01"	4' 08"
Built: Hopper Fisheries Ltd., Port Stanley, ON (Janice H.X. '81–'97)								
Huron Explorer I		RV	2010	D	112*	62' 00"	21' 03"	6' 00"
Built: Hike Metal Products Ltd., Wheatley, ON								
Keenosay		RV	1957	D	68*	51' 04"	20' 07"	2' 07"
Built: S.G. Powell Shipyard Ltd., Dunnville, ON								
Namaycush		RV	1954	D	28*	65' 03"	12' 00"	4' 01"
Built: Mathieson Boat Works, Goderich, ON								
Nipigon Osprey		RV	1990	D	33*	42' 04"	14' 09"	6' 08"
Built: Kanter Yachts Corp., St. Thomas, ON								
Ontario Explorer		RV	2009	D	84*	64' 09"	21' 03"	6' 00"
Built: Hike Metal Products Ltd., Wheatley, ON								

O-6 ONTARIO POWER GENERATION INC., TORONTO, ON

Fleet Name / Vessel Name	IMO #	Vessel Type	Year Built	Engine Type	Cargo Cap. or Gross*	Overall Length	Breadth	Depth
Niagara Queen II		IB	1992	D	58*	56' 01"	18' 00"	6' 08"
Built: Hike Metal Products Ltd., Wheatley, ON								

O-7 OSBORNE INC., GRAND RIVER, OH

Fleet Name / Vessel Name	IMO #	Vessel Type	Year Built	Engine Type	Cargo Cap. or Gross*	Overall Length	Breadth	Depth
Emmet J. Carey		SC	1948	D	900	114' 00"	23' 00"	11' 00"
Built: Hugh E. Lee Iron Works, Saginaw, MI; laid up at Fairport, OH (Beatrice Ottinger '48–'63, James B. Lyons '63–'88)								
F. M. Osborne {2}		SC	1910	D	500	150' 00"	29' 00"	11' 03"
Built: J. Baterman & T. Horn, Buffalo, NY (Grand Island {1} '10–'58, Lesco '58–'75)								

O-8 OWEN SOUND TRANSPORTATION CO. LTD., OWEN SOUND, ON *(ontarioferries.com)*

Fleet Name / Vessel Name	IMO #	Vessel Type	Year Built	Engine Type	Cargo Cap. or Gross*	Overall Length	Breadth	Depth
Chi-Cheemaun	7343607	PA/CF	1974	D	6,991*	365' 05"	61' 00"	21' 00"
Built: Canadian Shipbuilding and Engineering Ltd., Collingwood, ON								

P-1 PENN MARITIME INC., STAMFORD, CT *(pennmaritime.com)*

Fleet Name / Vessel Name	IMO #	Vessel Type	Year Built	Engine Type	Cargo Cap. or Gross*	Overall Length	Breadth	Depth
Caribbean	1518420	TK	1995	B	8,327*	460' 00"	72' 00"	36' 00"
Built: Alabama Shipyard Inc., Mobile, AL								

Fleet Name / Vessel Name	IMO #	Vessel Type	Year Built	Engine Type	Cargo Cap. or Gross*	Overall Length	Breadth	Depth
Lucia	8899562	AT	1995	D	254*	127' 00"	38' 00"	20' 04"

Built: Moss Point Marine, Escatawpa, MS

P-2 PERE MARQUETTE SHIPPING CO., LUDINGTON, MI (pmship.com)

Pere Marquette 41	5073894	SU	1941	B	3,413*	403' 00"	58' 00"	23' 05"

Built: Manitowoc Shipbuilding Co., Manitowoc, WI; converted from powered train/car ferry to a self-unloading barge in '97 (City of Midland 41 '41-'97)

Undaunted	8963210	AT	1943	DE	569*	143' 00"	38' 00"	18' 00"

Built: Gulfport Boiler/Welding, Port Arthur, TX (USS Undaunted [ATR-126, ATA-199] '44-'63, USMA Kings Pointer '63-'93, Krystal K. '93-'97) **[Undaunted / PM 41 OA dimensions together]** 493' 06" 58' 00" 23' 06"

P-3 PETERSEN STEAMSHIP CO., DOUGLAS, MI (keewatinmaritimemuseum.com)

Keewatin {2}		MU	1907	Q	3,856*	346' 00"	43' 08"	26' 06"

Built: Fairfield Shipbuilding and Engineering Co. Ltd., Govan, Scotland; former Canadian Pacific Railway Co. passenger vessel last operated Nov. 29, 1965; open to the public at Douglas, MI

P-4 PICTURED ROCKS CRUISES INC., MUNISING, MI (picturedrocks.com)

Grand Island {2}		ES	1989	D	52*	68' 00"	16' 01"	7' 01"
Grand Portal		ES	2004	D	76*	64' 08"	20' 00"	8' 08"
Miners Castle		ES	1974	D	82*	68' 00"	16' 06"	6' 04"
Miss Superior		ES	1984	D	83*	68' 00"	16' 09"	10' 04"
Pictured Rocks		ES	1972	D	53*	55' 07"	13' 07"	4' 04"

P-5 PLAUNT TRANSPORTATION CO. INC., CHEBOYGAN, MI (bbiferry.com)

Kristen D		CF	1987	D	83*	64' 11"	36' 00"	4' 06"

P-6 PORT CITY CRUISE LINE INC., MUSKEGON, MI (portcityprincesscruises.com)

Port City Princess		ES	1966	D	79*	64' 09"	30' 00"	5' 06"

Built: Blount Marine Corp., Warren, RI (Island Queen {1} '66-'87)

P-7 PORT CITY TUG INC., MUSKEGON, MI

Prentiss Brown	7035547	TB	1967	D	197*	123' 05"	31' 06"	19' 00"

Built: Gulfport Shipbuilding, Port Arthur, TX (Betty Culbreath, Micheala McAllister)

Susan W. Hannah	7644312	ATB	1977	D	174*	121' 06"	34' 06"	18' 02"

Built: Toche Enterprises Inc., Ocean Springs, MS (Lady Elda '77-'78, Kings Challenger '78-'78, ITM No. 1 '78-'81, Kings Challenger '81-'86)

P-8 PORT HURON MUSEUM, PORT HURON, MI (phmuseum.org)

Bramble		MU	1944	DE	1,025*	180' 00"	37' 00"	17' 04"

Built: Zenith Dredge Co., Duluth, MN; former U.S. Coast Guard buoy tender/icebreaker was retired in 2003; open to the public at Port Huron, MI (USCGC Bramble [WLB-392] '44-'03)

Huron		MU	1920	D	392*	96' 05"	24' 00"	10' 00"

Built: Charles L. Seabury Co., Morris Heights, NY; former U.S. Coast Guard lightship WLV-526 was retired Aug. 20, 1970; open to the public at Port Huron, MI (Lightship 103 – Relief [WAL-526] '20-'36)

P-9 PORTOFINO ON THE RIVER, WYANDOTTE, MI (portofinoontheriver.com)

Friendship		ES	1968	D	76*	85' 00"	23' 04"	7' 03"

Built: Hike Metal Products Ltd., Wheatley, ON (Peche Island V '68-'71, Papoose V '71-'82)

P-10 PRESQUE ISLE BOAT TOURS, ERIE, PA (piboattours.com)

Lady Kate {2}		ES	1952	D	11*	59' 03"	15' 00"	3' 09"

Built: J. W. Nolan & Sons, Erie, PA (G. A. Boeckling II, Cedar Point III, Island Trader '89-'97)

P-11 PRINCE EDWARD TUG AND BARGE CO. LTD., PICTON, ON

Husky		TB	2001	D	10*	33' 05"	13' 09"	n/a

P-12 PURE MICHIGAN BOAT CRUISES LLC, MUNISING, MI

Isle Royale Queen III		PA	1959	D	88*	74' 03"	18' 04"	6' 05"

Built: T.D. Vinette Co., Escanaba, MI (Isle Royale Queen II)

P-13 PURVIS MARINE LTD., SAULT STE. MARIE, ON (purvismarine.com)

Adanac III		TB	1913	D	108*	80' 03"	19' 03"	9' 10"

Built: Western Drydock & Shipbuilding Co., Port Arthur, ON (Edward C. Whalen '13-'66, John McLean '66-'95)

Anglian Lady	5141483	TB	1953	D	398*	132' 00"	31' 00"	14' 00"

Built: John I. Thorneycroft & Co., Southampton, England (Hamtun '53-'72, Nathalie Letzer '72-'88)

Avenger IV	5401297	TB	1962	D	291*	120' 00"	30' 00"	19' 00"

Built: Cochrane & Sons Ltd., Selby, Yorkshire, England (Avenger '62-'85)

E. M. Ford		CC	1898	Q	7,100	428' 00"	50' 00"	28' 00"

Built: Cleveland Shipbuilding Co., Cleveland, OH; converted to a self-unloading cement carrier at Christy Corp., Sturgeon Bay, WI, in '56; last operated Sept. 16, 1996; awaiting scrapping at Sault Ste. Marie, ON (Presque Isle {1} 1898-'56)

Fleet Name / Vessel Name	IMO #	Vessel Type	Year Built	Engine Type	Cargo Cap. or Gross*	Overall Length	Breadth	Depth
G.L.B. No. 2		DB	1953	B	3,215	240' 00"	50' 00"	12' 00"
Built: Ingalls Shipbuilding Corp., Birmingham, AL (Jane Newfield '53–'66, ORG 6502 '66–'75)								
Malden		DB	1946	B	1,075	150' 00"	41' 09"	10' 03"
Built: Russel Brothers Ltd., Owen Sound, ON								
Martin E. Johnson		TB	1959	D	26*	47' 00"	16' 00"	7' 00"
Built: Russel Brothers Ltd., Owen Sound, ON								
PML 357		DB	1932	B	363*	138' 00"	38' 00"	11' 00"
PML 2501		TK	1980	B	1,954*	302' 00"	52' 00"	17' 00"
Built: Cenac Shipyard, Houma, LA (CTCO 2505 '80–'96)								
PML 9000		DB	1968	B	4,285*	400' 00"	76' 00"	20' 00"
Built: Bethlehem Steel – Shipbuilding Division, San Francisco, CA (Palmer '68–'00)								
PML Alton		DB	1933	B	150	93' 00"	30' 00"	8' 00"
Built: McClintic- Marshall, Sturgeon Bay, WI								
PML Ironmaster		DB	1962	B	7,437*	360' 00"	75' 00"	25' 00"
Built: Yarrows Ltd., Esquimalt, BC (G.T. Steelmaster, Ceres, American Gulf VII, Seaspan 241, G.T. Ironmaster)								
PML Tucci		CS	1958	B	601*	150' 00"	52' 00"	10' 00"
Built: Calumet Shipyard & Drydock Co., Chicago, IL (MCD '58–'73, Minnesota '73–'88, Candace Andrie '88–'08)								
PML Tucker		DS	1971	B	477*	140' 00"	50' 00"	9' 00"
Built: Twin City Shipyard, St. Paul, MN (Illinois '71–'02, Meredith Andrie '02–'08)								
Reliance	7393808	TB	1974	D	708*	148' 03"	35' 07"	21' 07"
Built: Ulstein Hatlo A/S, Ulsteinvik, Norway (Sinni '74–'81, Irving Cedar '81–'96, Atlantic Cedar '96–'02)								
Rocket		TB	1901	D	40*	73' 00"	16' 00"	7' 00"
Built: Buffalo Shipbuilding Co., Buffalo, NY								
Sheila P.		TB	1940	D	15*	40 00"	14' 00"	5' 00"
Tecumseh II		DB	1976	B	2,500	180' 00"	54' 00"	12' 00"
(U-727 '76–'94)								
Wilfred M. Cohen	7629271	TB	1947	D	284*	102' 06"	28' 00"	15' 00"
Built: Newport News Shipbuilding and Drydock Co., Newport News, VA (A. T. Lowmaster '48–'75)								
W. I. Scott Purvis	5264819	TB	1938	D	203*	96' 00"	26' 00"	10' 00"
Built: Marine Industries, Sorel, QC (Orient Bay '38–'75, Guy M. No. 1 '75–'90)								
W.J. Isaac Purvis		TB	1962	D	71*	72' 00"	19' 00"	12' 00"
Built: McNamara Marine Ltd., Toronto, ON (Angus M. '62–'92, Omni Sorel '92–'02, Joyce B. Gardiner '02–'09)								
W. J. Ivan Purvis	5217218	TB	1938	D	190*	100' 00"	26' 00"	10' 00"
Built: Marine Industries, Sorel, QC (Magpie '38–'66, Dana T. Bowen '66–'75)								
Yankcanuck {2}	5409811	CS	1963	D	4,760	324' 03"	49' 00"	26' 00"
Built: Collingwood Shipyards, Collingwood, ON								

P-14 PUT-IN-BAY BOAT LINE CO., PORT CLINTON, OH *(jet-express.com)*

All vessels built at Gladding-Hearn Shipbuilding, Somerset, MA

Jet Express		PF/CA	1989	D	93*	92' 08"	28' 06"	8' 04"
Jet Express II		PF/CA	1992	D	85*	92' 06"	28' 06"	8' 04"
Jet Express III		PF/CA	2001	D	70*	78' 02"	27' 06"	8' 02"
Jet Express IV		PF/CA	1995	D	71*	77' 02"	28' 05"	7' 07"
(Monmouth, Theodore Roosevelt, Grey Lady)								

Q-1 QUEBEC PORT AUTHORITY, QUÉBEC, QC *(portquebec.ca)*

Beaupre		TB	1952	D	13*	37' 05"	10' 49"	4' 08"
Built: Russel-Hipwell Engines Ltd., Owen Sound, ON (W.J. Balcom)								

R-1 REBELLION TUG & BARGE INC., NIAGARA FALLS, NY *(rebelliontug.com)*

Shenandoah		TB	1941	D	29*	49' 09"	14' 00"	6' 00"
Built: Sturgeon Bay Shipbuilding Co., Sturgeon Bay, WI (Lauren E., R. H. Vaughn)								

R-2 RIO TINTO-ALCAN INC., LA BAIE, QC *(riotintoalcan.com)*

Alexis-Simard	8000056	TT	1980	D	286*	92' 00"	34' 00"	13' 07"
Built: Georgetown Shipyards Ltd., Georgetown, PEI								
Fjord Saguenay	9351012	TT	2006	D	381*	94' 00"	36' 05"	16' 04"
Built: East Isle Shipyard, Georgetown, PEI (Svitzer Njord, Stevns Iceflower)								

R-3 ROCKPORT BOAT LINE LTD., ROCKPORT, ON *(rockportcruises.com)*

Ida M.		ES	1970	D	29*	55' 00"	14' 00"	3' 00"
Built: William E. Andress & Son, Rockport, ON								
Ida M. II		ES	1973	D	121*	63' 02"	22' 02"	5' 00"
Built: Rockport Boat Lines Ltd., Rockport, ON								
Sea Prince II		ES	1978	D	172*	83' 00"	24' 02"	6' 08"
Built: Hike Metal Products Ltd., Wheatley, ON								

Joseph L. Block in the upper end of the Rock Cut. *(Mike Harting)*

Algorail downbound in the Detroit River below the Ambassador Bridge. *(Wade P. Streeter)*

Fleet Name Vessel Name	IMO #	Vessel Type	Year Built	Engine Type	Cargo Cap. or Gross*	Overall Length	Breadth	Depth
R-4	**ROEN SALVAGE CO., STURGEON BAY, WI** (roensalvage.com)							
Chas. Asher		TB	1967	D	39*	49' 02"	17' 06"	6' 10"
Built: Sturgeon Bay Shipbuilding Co., Sturgeon Bay, WI								
John R. Asher		TB	1943	D	93*	68' 09"	20' 00"	8' 00"
Built: Platzer Boat Works, Houston, TX (U. S. Army ST-71 '43-'46, Russell 8 '46-'64, Reid McAllister '64-'67, Donegal '67-'85)								
Louie S.		TB	1956	D	10*	37' 00"	12' 00"	4' 05"
Spuds		TB	1944	D	19*	42' 00"	12' 05"	5' 04"
Stephan M. Asher		TB	1954	D	60*	65' 00"	19' 01"	5' 04"
Built: Burton Shipyard Inc., Port Arthur, TX (Captain Bennie '54-'82, Dumar Scout '82-'87)								
Timmy A.		TB	1953	D	12*	33' 06"	10' 08"	5' 02"
R-5	**RUSSELL ISLAND TRANSIT CO., ALGONAC, MI**							
Islander {2}		PA/CF	1967	D	38*	41' 00"	15' 00"	3' 06"
R-6	**RYBA MARINE CONSTRUCTION CO., CHEBOYGAN, MI** (rybamarine.com)							
Amber Mae		TB	1922	D	67*	65' 00"	14' 01"	10' 00"
Built: Glove Shipyard Inc., Buffalo, NY (E. W. Sutton '22-'52, Venture '52- '00)								
Henning		TB		D	40*	46' 00"	14' 03"	6' 00"
Kathy Lynn	8034887	TB	1944	D	140*	85' 00"	24' 00"	9' 06"
Built: Decatur Iron & Steel Co., Decatur, AL (U. S. Army ST-693 '44-'79, Sea Islander '79-'91)								
Rochelle Kaye		TB	1963	D	52*	51' 06"	19' 04"	7' 00"
Built: St. Charles Steel Works Inc., Thibodeaux, LA (Jaye Anne '63-?, Katanni ?-'97)								
Tenacious	5238004	TB	1960	D	149*	79' 01"	25' 06"	12' 06"
Built: Ingalls Shipbuilding Corp., Pascagoula, MS (Mobil 8 '60-'91, Tatarrax '91-'93, Nan McKay '93-'95)								
S-1	**SAGINAW VALLEY NAVAL SHIP MUSEUM, BAY CITY, MI** (ussedson.org)							
Edson **[DD-946]**		MU	1958	D		418' 03"	45' 03"	
Built: Bath Iron Works, ME; Forrest Sherman-class destroyer was decommissioned in '88; from '89-'04 on display at the Intrepid Air and Sea Museum, New York City. Declared a U.S. National Historic Landmark in '90. Returned to U.S. Navy in '04, expected to open as a marine museum at Bay City, MI, in '11								
S-2	**SCOTLUND STIVERS, MARINETTE, WI**							
Arthur K. Atkinson		PA	1917	D	3,241*	384' 00"	56' 00"	20' 06"
Built: Great Lakes Engineering Works, Ecorse, MI; last operated in April 1982; in long-term lay-up at DeTour, MI (Ann Arbor No. 6 '17-'59)								

Robert S. Pierson in the St. Clair River. *(Dave Michelson)*

Fleet Name Vessel Name	IMO #	Vessel Type	Year Built	Engine Type	Cargo Cap. or Gross*	Overall Length	Breadth	Depth

SEAWAY MARINE TRANSPORT, ST. CATHARINES, ON
PARTNERSHIP BETWEEN ALGOMA CENTRAL CORP. (A-3) AND UPPER LAKES GROUP (U-12)
SEE RESPECTIVE FLEETS FOR VESSELS INVOLVED.

S-3 SEA SERVICE LLC, SUPERIOR, WI

Sea Bear		PB	1959	D	28*	45' 08"	13' 08"	7' 00"

Built: Gladding-Hearn Shipbuilding, Somerset, MA (Narrows)

S-4 SEAJON LLC, WILMINGTON, DE

Ken Boothe Sr.		TB	2011	D	1,179*	135' 04"	50' 00"	26' 00"

Built: Donjon Shipbuilding & Repair, Erie, PA

Seajon Enterprise		SU	2012	B	33,892	740' 04"	78' 00"	45' 00"

Built: Donjon Shipbuilding & Repair, Erie, PA; under construction, expected to enter service in 2012

S-5 SELVICK MARINE TOWING CORP., STURGEON BAY, WI

Carla Anne Selvick	5298389	TB	1908	D	191*	96' 00"	23' 00"	11' 02"

Built: Skinner Shipbuilding & Dry Dock Co., Baltimore, MD (S.O. Co. No. 19 '08-'16, S.T. Co. No. 19 '16-'18,
Socony 19 '18-'47, Esso Tug No. 4 '47-'53, McAllister 44 '53-'55, Roderick McAllister '55-'84)

Cameron O.		TB	1955	D	26*	50' 00"	15' 00"	7' 03"

Built: Peterson Builders Inc., Sturgeon Bay, WI (Escort II '55-'06)

Jacquelyn Nicole		TB	1913	D	96*	71' 00"	20' 01"	11' 02"

Built: Great Lakes Towing Co., Cleveland, OH (Michigan {4} '13-'78, Ste. Marie II '78-'81, Dakota '81-'92, Ethel E. '92-'02)

Jimmy L.		TB	1939	D	148*	110' 00"	25' 00"	13' 00"

Built: Defoe Shipbuilding Co., Bay City, MI USCGC Naugatuck [WYT / WYTM-92] '39-'80, Timmy B. '80-'84)

Mary Page Hannah {1}	7436234	TB	1950	DE	461*	143' 00"	33' 01"	14' 06"

Built: Levingston Shipbuilding, Orange, TX (U. S. Army ATA-230 '49-'72, G. W. Codrington '72-'73,
William P. Feeley {2} '73-'73, William W. Stender '73-'78)

Sharon M. Selvick		TB	1945	D	28*	45' 05"	12' 10"	7' 01"

Built: Kewaunee Shipbuilding & Engineering, Kewaunee, WI (USACE Judson)

Susan L.		TB	1944	D	133*	86' 00"	23' 00"	10' 04"

Built: Equitable Equipment Co., New Orleans, LA (U. S. Army ST-709 '44-'47, USCOE Stanley '47-'99)

William C. Selvick		TB	1944	D	142*	85' 00"	23' 00"	9' 07"

Built: Platzer Boat Works, Houston, TX (U. S. Army ST-500 '44-'49, Sherman H. Serre '49-'77)

S-6 SHELL CANADA PRODUCTS LTD., MONTREAL, QC (shell.ca)

Arca	5411761	RT	1963	D	1,296	175' 00"	36' 00"	14' 00"

Built: Port Weller Dry Docks, Port Weller, ON (Imperial Lachine '63-'03, Josee M. '03-'03)

S-7 SHEPARD MARINE CONSTRUCTION, ROSEVILLE, MI

Robin Lynn	7619769	TB	1952	D	148*	85' 00"	25' 00"	11' 00"

Built: Alexander Shipyard Inc., New Orleans, LA (Bonita '52-'85, Susan Hoey {2} '85-'95, Blackie B '95-'97,
Susan Hoey {3 } '97-'98)

S-8 SHEPLER'S MACKINAC ISLAND FERRY, MACKINAW CITY, MI (sheplersferry.com)

Capt. Shepler		PF	1986	D	71*	84' 00"	21' 00"	7' 10"
Felicity		PF	1972	D	65*	65' 00"	18' 01"	8' 03"
Sacre Bleu		PK	1959	D	98*	94' 10"	31' 00"	9' 09"

Built: Sturgeon Bay Shipbuilding Co., Sturgeon Bay, WI (Put-In-Bay {2} '59-'94)

The Hope		PF	1975	D	87*	77' 00"	20' 00"	8' 03"

Built: Bergeron Boats Inc., Lafitte, LA

The Welcome		PF	1969	D	66*	60' 06"	16' 08"	8' 02"

Built: Camcraft Inc., Crown Point, LA

Wyandot		PF	1979	D	83*	77' 00"	20' 00"	8' 00"

Built: Bergeron Boats Inc., Lafitte, LA

S-9 SHORELINE CHARTERS, GILLS ROCK, WI (shorelinecharters.net)

The Shoreline		ES	1973	D	12*	33' 00"	11' 4"	3' 00"

S-10 SHORELINE CONTRACTORS INC., WELLINGTON, OH (shorelinecontractors.com)

Eagle		TB	1943	D	31*	57' 09"	14' 05"	6' 10"

Built: Defoe Shipbuilding Co., Bay City, MI

S-11 SHORELINE SIGHTSEEING CO., CHICAGO, IL (shorelinesightseeing.com)

Cap Streeter		ES	1987	D	28*	63' 06"	24' 04"	7' 07"
Evening Star		ES	2001	D	93*	83' 00"	23' 00"	7' 00"
Marlyn		ES	1961	D	70*	65' 00"	25' 00"	7' 00"
Shoreline II		ES	1987	D	89*	75' 00"	26' 00"	7' 01"

Fleet Name / Vessel Name	IMO #	Vessel Type	Year Built	Engine Type	Cargo Cap. or Gross*	Overall Length	Breadth	Depth
Star of Chicago {2}		ES	1999	D	73*	64' 10"	22' 08"	7' 05"
Voyageur		CF	1983	D	98*	65' 00"	35' 00"	7' 00"

S-12 SOCIÉTÉ DES TRAVERSIERS DU QUÉBEC, QUÉBEC, QC *(traversiers.gouv.qc.ca)*

Alphonse-Desjardins	7109233	CF	1971	D	1,741*	214' 00"	71' 06"	20' 00"

Built: Davie Shipbuilding Co., Lauzon, QC

Armand-Imbeau	7902269	CF	1980	D	1,285*	203' 07"	72' 00"	18' 04"

Built: Marine Industries Ltd., Sorel, QC

Camille-Marcoux	7343578	CF	1974	D	6,122*	310' 09"	62' 09"	39' 00"

Built: Marine Industries Ltd., Sorel, QC

Catherine-Legardeur	8409355	CF	1985	D	1,348*	205' 09"	71' 10"	18' 10"

Built: Davie Shipbuilding Co., Lauzon, QC

Felix-Antoine-Savard	9144706	CF	1997	D	2,489*	272' 00"	70' 00"	21' 09"

Built: Davie Shipbuilding Co., Lauzon, QC

Grue-des-Iles	8011732	CF	1981	D	447*	155' 10"	41' 01"	12' 06"

Built: Bateaux Tur-Bec Ltd., Ste-Catherine, QC

Jos-Deschenes	391571	CF	1980	D	1,287*	203' 07"	72' 00"	18' 04"

Built: Marine Industries Ltd., Sorel, QC

Joseph-Savard	8409343	CF	1985	D	1,445*	206' 00"	71' 10"	18' 10"

Built: Davie Shipbuilding Co., Lauzon, QC

Lomer-Gouin	7109221	CF	1971	D	1,741*	214' 00"	71' 06"	20' 00"

Built: Davie Shipbuilding Co., Lauzon, QC

Lucien-L.	6721981	CF	1967	D	867*	220' 10"	61' 06"	15' 05"

Built: Marine Industries Ltd., Sorel, QC

Radisson {1}		CF	1954	D	1,037*	164' 03"	72' 00"	10' 06"

Built: Davie Shipbuilding Co., Lauzon, QC

S-13 SOO LOCKS BOAT TOURS, SAULT STE. MARIE, MI *(soolocks.com)*

Bide-A-Wee {3}		ES	1955	D	99*	64' 07"	23' 00"	7' 11"

Built: Blount Marine Corp., Warren, RI

Hiawatha {2}		ES	1959	D	99*	64' 07"	23' 00"	7' 11"

Built: Blount Marine Corp., Warren, RI

Holiday		ES	1957	D	99*	64' 07"	23' 00"	7' 11"

Built: Blount Marine Corp., Warren, RI

Le Voyageur		ES	1959	D	70*	65' 00"	25' 00"	7' 00"

Built: Sturgeon Bay Shipbuilding and Drydock Co., Sturgeon Bay, WI

Nokomis		ES	1959	D	70*	65' 00"	25' 00"	7' 00"

Built: Sturgeon Bay Shipbuilding and Drydock Co., Sturgeon Bay, WI

S-14 SOO RIVER MARINE LLC, WILLIAMSTON, MI

Soo River Belle		PB	1961	D	25*	40' 00"	14' 00"	6' 00"

S-15 SOUTH SHORE DREDGE & DOCK INC., LORAIN, OH

Cojak		TB	1954	D	11*	31' 07"	10' 09"	5' 06"
Southshore I		DB	1986	B	88*	60' 00"	35' 00"	5' 00"

Built: South Shore Dredge & Dock Inc., Lorain, OH

S-16 SPIRIT CRUISES LLC, CHICAGO, IL *(spiritcruises.com)*

Spirit of Chicago		ES	1988	D	92*	156' 00"	35' 00"	7' 01"

Built: Blount Marine Corp., Warren, RI

S-17 SPIRIT OF THE SOUND SCHOONER CO., PARRY SOUND, ON *(spiritofthesound.ca)*

Chippewa III		PA	1954	D	47*	65' 00"	16' 00"	6' 06"

Built: Russel-Hipwell Engines Ltd., Owen Sound, ON (Maid of the Mist III '54-'56, Maid of the Mist '56-'92)

S-18 S.S. CITY OF MILWAUKEE-NATIONAL HISTORIC LANDMARK, MANISTEE, MI *(carferry.com)*

Acacia		MU	1944	DE	1,025*	180' 00"	37' 00"	17' 04"

Built: Marine Iron and Shipbuilding Corp., Duluth, MN; former U.S. Coast Guard buoy tender/icebreaker was decommissioned in '06; (Launched as USCGC Thistle [WAGL-406])

City of Milwaukee		MU	1931	R	26 cars	360' 00"	56' 03"	21' 06"

Built: Manitowoc Shipbuilding Co., Manitowoc, WI; train ferry sailed for the Grand Trunk Railroad '31-'78 and the Ann Arbor Railroad '78-'81; open to the public at Manistee, MI

S-19 S.S. COLUMBIA PROJECT, NEW YORK, NY *(sscolumbia.org)*

Columbia {2}	5077233	PA	1902	R	968*	216' 00"	60' 00"	13' 06"

Built: Detroit Dry Dock Co, Detroit, MI; former Detroit to Bob-Lo Island passenger steamer last operated Sept. 2, 1991; laid up at Ecorse, MI, awaiting funds for renovation and relocation to the East Coast

Fleet Name Vessel Name	IMO #	Vessel Type	Year Built	Engine Type	Cargo Cap. or Gross*	Overall Length	Breadth	Depth

S-20   S.S. METEOR WHALEBACK SHIP MUSEUM, SUPERIOR, WI *(superiorpublicmuseums.org)*

| Meteor {2} | | MU | 1896 | R | 40,100 | 380' 00" | 45' 00" | 26' 00" |

Built: American Steel Barge Co., Superior, WI; former ore carrier/auto carrier/tanker is the last vessel of
whaleback design surviving on the Great Lakes; Cleveland Tankers vessel last operated in 1969;
open to the public at Superior, WI *(Frank Rockefeller 1896-'28, South Park '28-'43)*

S-21   S.S. MILWAUKEE CLIPPER PRESERVATION INC., MUSKEGON, MI *(milwaukeeclipper.com)*

| Milwaukee Clipper | | MU | 1904 | Q | 4,272 | 361' 00" | 45' 00" | 28' 00" |

Built: American Shipbuilding Co., Cleveland, OH; rebuilt in '40 at Manitowoc Shipbuilding Co., Manitowoc,
WI; former Wisconsin & Michigan Steamship Co. passenger/auto carrier last operated in 1970; undergoing
restoration at Muskegon, MI *(Juniata '04-'41)*

S-22   ST. JAMES MARINE CO., BEAVER ISLAND, MI *(stjamesmarine.com)*

American Girl		TB	1922	D	63*	62' 00"	14' 00"	6' 05"
Cisco		TB	1951	D	53*	60' 06"	16' 05"	8' 00"
Wendy Anne		TB	1955	D	89*	71' 00"	20' 00"	8' 05"

Built: Smith Basin Drydock, Port Everglades, FL *(ST-2199)*

S-23   ST. LAWRENCE CRUISE LINES INC., KINGSTON, ON *(stlawrencecruiselines.com)*

| Canadian Empress | | PA | 1981 | D | 463* | 108' 00" | 30' 00" | 8' 00" |

Built: Algan Shipyards Ltd., Gananoque, ON

S-24   ST. LAWRENCE MARINE & DREDGING LTD., LANSDOWNE, ON

| Blue Quail | | TB | 1962 | D | 14* | 39' 00" | 12' 09" | 3' 03" |

S-25   ST. LAWRENCE SEAWAY DEVELOPMENT CORP., MASSENA, NY *(www.seaway.dot.gov)*

| Grasse River | | GL | 1958 | GL | | 150 00" | 65' 08" | 5' 06" |
| Robinson Bay | | TB | 1958 | DE | 213* | 103' 00" | 26' 10" | 14' 06" |

Built: Christy Corp., Sturgeon Bay, WI

| Performance | | TB | 1997 | D | | 50' 00" | 16' 06" | 7' 05" |

Built: Marine Builders Inc., Utica, IN

S-26   ST. LAWRENCE SEAWAY MANAGEMENT CORP., CORNWALL, ON *(greatlakes-seaway.com)*

| VM/S Hercules | | GL | 1962 | D | 2,107* | 200' 00" | 75' 00" | 18' 08" |

Built: Marine Industries Ltd., Sorel, QC

| VM/S Maisonneuve | | SV | 1974 | D | 56* | 58' 03" | 20' 03" | 6' 05" |

Built: Fercraft Marine Inc., Ste-Catherine d'Alexandre, QC

| VM/S St. Lambert | | TB | 1974 | D | 20* | 30' 08" | 13' 01" | 6' 05" |

Built: Sigama Ltd., Cap-De-La-Madeleine, QC

S-27   ST. MARYS CEMENT INC. (CANADA), TORONTO, ON *(stmaryscement.com)*

| Sea Eagle II | 7631860 | ATB | 1979 | D | 560* | 132' 00" | 35' 00" | 19' 00" |

Built: Modern Marine Power Co., Houma, LA *(Sea Eagle '79-'81, Canmar Sea Eagle '81-'91)*

| St. Marys Cement II | 8879914 | CC | 1978 | B | 19,513 | 496' 06" | 76' 00" | 35' 00" |

Built: Galveston Shipbuilding Co., Galveston, TX *(Velasco '78-'81, Canmar Shuttle '81-'90)*

| St. Marys Cement III | | CC | 1980 | B | 4,800 | 355' 00" | 76' 08" | 17' 09" |

Built: Robin Shipyard Pte Ltd., Singapore, China; last operated Sept. 1, '00; former cement storage barge
is laid up at Green Bay, WI *(Bigorange XVI '80-'84, Says '84-'85, Al-Sayb-7 '85-'86, Clarkson Carrier '86-'94)*

THE FOLLOWING VESSEL MANAGED BY PORT CITY STEAMSHIP SERVICES INC., MUSKEGON, MI

| St. Marys Challenger | 5009984 | CC | 1906 | S | 10,250 | 552' 01" | 56' 00" | 31' 00" |

Built: Great Lakes Engineering Works, Ecorse, MI; repowered in '50; converted to a self-unloading cement
carrier by Manitowoc Shipbuilding Co., Manitowoc, WI, in '67; celebrated its 100th season in 2006
*(William P. Snyder '06-'26, Elton Hoyt II {1} '26-'52, Alex D. Chisholm '52-'66, Medusa Challenger '66-'99,
Southdown Challenger '99-'04)*

THE FOLLOWING VESSEL MANAGED BY PORT CITY MARINE SERVICES INC., MUSKEGON, MI

| St. Marys Conquest | 5015012 | CC | 1937 | B | 8,500 | 437' 06" | 55' 00" | 28' 00" |

Built: Manitowoc Shipbuilding Co., Manitowoc, WI; converted from a powered tanker to a self-unloading
cement barge by Bay Shipbuilding, Sturgeon Bay, WI, in '87
(Red Crown '37-'62, Amoco Indiana '62-'87, Medusa Conquest '87-'99, Southdown Conquest '99-'04)

**THE FOLLOWING VESSEL CHARTERED BY ST. MARYS CEMENT CO. FROM GREAT LAKES
& INTERNATIONAL TOWING & SALVAGE CO., BURLINGTON, ON**

| Petite Forte | 6826119 | TB | 1969 | D | 368* | 127' 00" | 32' 00" | 14' 06" |

Built: Cochrane and Sons Ltd., Selby, Yorkshire, England
(E. Bronson Ingram '69-'72, Jarmac 42 '72-'73, Scotsman '73-'81, Al Battal '81-'86)

Kaye E. Barker arrives under a double rainbow to load at Marquette. (Rod Burdick)

Fleet Name Vessel Name	IMO #	Vessel Type	Year Built	Engine Type	Cargo Cap. or Gross*	Overall Length	Breadth	Depth

S-28 ST. MARYS RIVER MARINE CENTRE, SAULT STE. MARIE, ON *(norgoma.org)*

| Norgoma | | MU | 1950 | D | 1,477* | 188' 00" | 37' 06" | 22' 06" |

Built: Collingwood Shipyards, Collingwood, ON; former Ontario Northland Transportation Commission passenger vessel last operated in 1974; open to the public at Sault Ste. Marie, ON

S-29 STAR LINE MACKINAC ISLAND FERRY, ST. IGNACE, MI *(mackinacferry.com)*

All vessels built at Gulf Craft Inc., Patterson, LA

Cadillac {5}		PF	1990	D	73*	64' 07"	20' 00"	7' 07"
Joliet {3}		PF	1993	D	83*	64' 08"	22' 00"	8' 03"
LaSalle {4}		PF	1983	D	55*	65' 00"	20' 00"	7' 05"
Marquette II {2}		PF	2005	D	65*	74' 00"	23' 06"	8' 00"
Radisson {2}		PF	1988	D	97*	80' 00"	23' 06"	7' 00"

S-30 SUPERIOR ODYSSEY, MARQUETTE, MI *(superiorodyssey.com)*

| Coaster II | | PA | 1933 | D/W | 15* | 58' 00" | 12' 03" | 6' 06" |

Built: Goudy & Stevens, East Boothbay ME (Quissett)

T-1 TGL MARINE HOLDINGS ULC, PLYMOUTH, MI

| Jane Ann IV | 7802809 | ATB | 1978 | D | 954* | 150' 11" | 42' 08" | 21' 04" |

Built: Mitsui Engineering & Shipbuilding Co., Tokyo, Japan (Ouro Fino '78-'81, Bomare '81-'93, Tignish Sea '93-'98)

| Sarah Spencer | 5002223 | SU | 1959 | B | 21,844 | 693' 10" | 72' 00" | 40' 00" |

Built: Manitowoc Shipbuilding Co., Manitowoc, WI; engine removed, converted to a self-unloading barge by Halifax Dartmouth Industries, Halifax, NS, in '89 (Adam E. Cornelius {3} '59-'89, Capt. Edward V. Smith '89-'91, Sea Barge One '91-'96)

| **[Jane Ann IV / Sarah Spencer OA dimensions together]** | | | | | | 729' 03" | 72' 00" | 40' 00" |

T-2 THOUSAND ISLANDS & SEAWAY CRUISES, BROCKVILLE, ON *(1000islandscruises.com)*

| General Brock III | | ES | 1977 | D | 56* | 56' 05" | 15' 04" | 5' 02" |

Built: Gananoque Boat Line Ltd., Gananoque, ON (Miss Peterborough)

| Island Heritage | | ES | 1929 | D | 21* | 63' 09" | 9' 08" | 4' 09" |

Built: George Cranker, Ivy Lea, ON (Miss Ivy Lea No. 1)

| Sea Fox II | | ES | 1988 | D | 55* | 39' 08" | 20' 00" | 2' 00" |

T-3 THUNDER BAY TUG SERVICES LTD., THUNDER BAY, ON

| Coastal Cruiser | | TB | 1939 | D | 29* | 65' 00" | 16' 09" | 6' 01" |

Built: George Gamble, Port Dover, ON

| Glenada | | TB | 1943 | D | 107* | 80' 06" | 25' 00" | 10' 01" |

Built: Russel Brothers Ltd., Owen Sound, ON (HMCS Glenada [W-30] '43-'45)

| Keewanis | | DB | 1959 | B | 165* | 79' 10" | 35' 00" | 6' 04" |
| Miseford | | TB | 1915 | D | 116* | 85' 00" | 20' 00" | 9' 06" |

Built: M. Beatty & Sons Ltd., Welland, ON

| Paul Becotte Sr. | | DB | 1963 | B | 167* | 79' 10" | 35' 00" | 6' 04" |
| Point Valour | | TB | 1958 | D | 246* | 97' 08" | 28' 02" | 13' 10" |

Built: Davie Shipbuilding Co., Lauzon, QC (Foundation Valour '58-'83)

| Robert W. | | TB | 1949 | D | 48* | 60' 00" | 16' 00" | 8' 06" |

Built: Russel Brothers Ltd., Owen Sound, ON

| Rosalee D. | | TB | 1943 | D | 22* | 55' 00" | 12' 07" | 4' 11" |

Built: Northern Shipbuilding & Repair Co. Ltd., Bronte, ON

T-4 TOLEDO MARITIME ACADEMY, TOLEDO, OH

| Mariner 1 | | TV | 1946 | D | | 41' 00" | 10' 00" | 4' 05" |

Built: American Boiler Works, Erie, PA (Irish Skipper)

T-5 TORONTO BRIGANTINE INC., TORONTO, ON *(tallshipadventures.on.ca)*

| Pathfinder | | W/TV | 1963 | D/W | 35* | 53' 00" | 15' 00" | 6' 09" |

Built: Canadian Shipbuilding & Engineering Ltd., Collingwood, ON

| Playfair | | W/TV | 1973 | D/W | 41* | 53' 07" | 15' 00" | 7' 04" |

Built: Canadian Dredge & Co. Ltd., Kingston, ON

T-6 TORONTO DRYDOCK LTD., TORONTO, ON *(torontodrydock.com)*

| M. R. Kane | | TB | 1945 | D | 51* | 60' 06" | 16' 05" | 6' 07" |

Built: Central Bridge Co. Ltd., Trenton, ON (Tanac V-276 '45-'47)

| Menier Consol | | FD | 1962 | B | 2,575* | 304' 05" | 49' 06" | 25' 06" |

Built: Davie Shipbuilding Co., Lauzon, QC; former pulpwood carrier is now a floating dry dock at Toronto, ON

T-7 TORONTO FIRE DEPARTMENT, TORONTO, ON *(toronto.ca/fire)*

| Wm. Lyon Mackenzie | 6400575 | FB | 1964 | D | 102* | 81' 01" | 20' 00" | 10' 00" |

Built: Russel Brothers Ltd., Owen Sound, ON

Fleet Name Vessel Name	IMO #	Vessel Type	Year Built	Engine Type	Cargo Cap. or Gross*	Overall Length	Breadth	Depth

T-8 TORONTO PADDLEWHEEL CRUISES LTD., NORTH YORK, ON

Pioneer Princess		ES	1984	D	96*	56' 00"	17' 01"	3' 09"

Built: Robin Lane Hanson, Oromocto, NB

Pioneer Queen		ES	1968	D	110*	85' 00"	30' 06"	7' 03"

Built: Hike Metal Products, Wheatley, ON (Peche Island III '68-'71, Papoose IV '71-'96)

T-9 TORONTO PORT AUTHORITY, TORONTO, ON *(torontoport.com)*

Brutus I		TB	1992	D	10*	36' 01"	11' 09"	4' 04"

Built: Mariner Jack Inc., Michigan City, IN

David Hornell VC		PA/CF	2006	D	219*	95' 10"	37' 07"	7' 05"

Built: Hike Metal Products, Wheatley, ON (TCCA 2 '09-'10)

Maple City		PA/CF	1951	D	135*	70' 06"	36' 04"	5' 11"

Built: Muir Brothers Dry Dock Co. Ltd., Port Dalhousie, ON

Marilyn Bell I		PA/CF	2009	D	270*	95' 10"	37' 07"	7' 05"

Built: Hike Metal Products, Wheatley, ON (TCCA 2 '09-'10)

William Rest		TB	1961	D	62*	65' 00"	18' 06"	10' 06"

Built: Erieau Shipbuilding & Drydock Co. Ltd., Erieau, ON

Windmill Point		PA/CF	1954	D	118*	65' 00"	36' 00"	10' 00"

Built: Kingston Shipyards Ltd., Kingston, ON

T-10 TORONTO TOURS LTD., TORONTO, ON *(torontotours.com)*

Miss Kim Simpson		ES	1960	D	33*	90' 02"	13' 04"	3' 09"

Built: Molenaar's Scheepswerf, Zaandam, Holland

New Beginnings		ES	1961	D	28*	41' 09"	13' 01"	4' 09"

Built: J.J. Taylor & Sons Ltd., Toronto, ON (Harry J. Kimber)

Shipsands		ES	1972	D	23*	58' 03"	12' 01"	4' 07"

Built: Cliff Richardson Boats Ltd., Meaford, ON

T-11 TRANSPORT NANUK INC., MONTREAL, QC *(www.logistec.com)*
THE FOLLOWING VESSELS CHARTERED TO NUNAVUT EASTERN ARCTIC SHIPPING INC.
Vessels offer service between St. Lawrence River ports and the Canadian Arctic between July and November

Aivik	7908445	HL	1980	D	4,860	359' 08"	63' 08"	38' 09"

Built: ACH - Construction Navale, Le Havre, France (Mont Ventoux '80-'90, Aivik '90-'91, Unilifter '91-'92)

Avataq	8801618	GC	1989	D	9,653	370' 07"	62' 00"	37' 00"

Built: Miho Shipbuilding Co. Ltd., Shimizu Shizuoka Prefecture, Japan; operated by Spliethoff's, Amsterdam (Poleca, Mekhanik Volkosh, Tiger Speed, Lootsgracht)

Qamutik	9081289	GC	1995	D	12,760	446' 00"	62' 00"	38' 02"

Built: Frisian Shipbuilding Welgelegen B.V., Harlingen, The Netherlands; operated by Spliethoff's, Amsterdam (Edisongracht)

Umiavut	8801591	GC	1988	D	9,653	370' 07"	63' 01"	37' 00"

Built: Miho Shipbuilding Co. Ltd., Shimizu Shizuoka Prefecture, Japan; operated by Spliethoff's, Amsterdam, Netherlands (Completed as Newca; Kapitan Silin '88-'92, Lindengracht '92-'00)

T-12 TRAVERSE TALL SHIP CO., TRAVERSE CITY, MI *(tallshipsailing.com)*

Manitou {1}		ES/2S	1983	W	78*	114' 00"	21' 00"	9' 00"

T-13 30,000 ISLANDS CRUISE LINES INC., PARRY SOUND, ON *(island-queen.com)*

Island Queen V		ES	1990	D	526*	130' 00"	35' 00"	6' 06"

Built: Herb Fraser & Associates Ltd., Port Colborne, ON

T-14 TRIDENT MARINE CORP., CLEVELAND, OH *(holidaycleveland.com)*

Holiday		PA	1964	D	25*	60' 00"	16' 01"	5' 06"

U-1 UNCLE SAM BOAT TOURS, ALEXANDRIA, NY *(usboattours.com)*

Alexandria Belle		ES	1988	D	92*	82' 00"	32' 00"	8' 00"

Built: Blount Marine Corp., Warren, RI

Island Duchess		ES	1988	D	73*	90' 03"	27' 08"	9' 00"

Built: Freeport Shipbuilding Group, Inc., Freeport, FL

Island Wanderer		ES	1971	D	57*	62' 05"	22' 00"	7' 02"

Built: Blount Marine Corp., Warren, RI (Fairport Lady, Colonial Belle)

Uncle Sam 7		ES	1976	D	55*	60' 04"	22' 00"	7' 01"

Built: Blount Marine Corp., Warren, RI

U-2 U.S. ARMY CORPS OF ENGINEERS – GREAT LAKES AND OHIO RIVER DIV., CINCINNATI, OH
(usace.army.mil) **U.S. ARMY CORPS OF ENGINEERS – BUFFALO DISTRICT**

Cheraw		TB	1970	D	356*	109' 00"	30' 06"	16' 03"

Built: Southern Shipbuilding Corp., Slidell, LA (USS Cheraw [YTB-802] '70-'96)

Fleet Name Vessel Name	IMO #	Vessel Type	Year Built	Engine Type	Cargo Cap. or Gross*	Overall Length	Breadth	Depth
McCauley		CS	1948	B		112'00"	52'00"	4'25"
Simonsen		CS	1954	B		142'00"	58'00"	5'00"

U.S. ARMY CORPS OF ENGINEERS – DETROIT DISTRICT, LAKE MICHIGAN AREA OFFICE, KEWAUNEE SUB-OFFICE

Kenosha		TB	1954	D	82*	70'00"	20'00"	9'08"

Built: Missouri Valley Bridge & Iron Works, Leavenworth, KS (U.S. Army ST-2011 '54-'65)

Manitowoc		CS	1976	B		132'00"	44'00"	8'00"
Racine		TB	1931	D	61*	66'03"	18'05"	7'08"

Built: Marine Iron & Shipbuilding Company, Duluth MN

U.S. ARMY CORPS OF ENGINEERS – DETROIT DISTRICT, DETROIT AREA OFFICE

Demolen		TB	1974	D	356*	109'00"	30'06"	16'03"

Built: Marinette Marine Corp., Marinette, WI (USS Metacom [YTB-829] '74-'01, Metacom '01-'02)

Veler		CS	1991	B	613*	150'00"	46'00"	10'06"

U.S. ARMY CORPS OF ENGINEERS – DETROIT DISTRICT, DULUTH AREA OFFICE

D. L. Billmaier		TB	1968	D	356*	109'00"	30'06"	16'03"

Built: Southern Shipbuilding Corp., Slidell, LA (USS Natchitoches [YTB-799] '68-'95)

H. J. Schwartz		DB	1995	B		150'00"	48'00"	11'00"
Hammond Bay		TB	1953	D	23*	45'00"	13'00"	7'00"

U.S. ARMY CORPS OF ENGINEERS – DETROIT DISTRICT, SOO AREA OFFICE

Harvey		DB	1961	B		120'00"	40'00"	8'00"
Nicolet		DB	1971	D		120'00"	40'00"	8'00"
Owen M. Frederick		TB	1942	D	56*	65'00"	17'00"	7'06"

Built: Sturgeon Bay Shipbuilding Co., Sturgeon Bay, WI

Paul Bunyan		GL	1945	B		150'00"	65'00"	12'06"

Built: Wiley Equipment Co., Port Deposit, MD

Whitefish Bay		TB	1953	D	23*	45'00"	13'00"	7'00"

U-3 U.S. COAST GUARD 9TH COAST GUARD DISTRICT, CLEVELAND, OH *(uscg.mil/d9)*

Alder [WLB-216]		BT	2004	D	2,000*	225'09"	46'00"	19'08"

Built: Marinette Marine Corp., Marinette, WI; stationed at Duluth, MN

Biscayne Bay [WTGB-104]		IB	1979	D	662*	140'00"	37'06"	12'00"

Built: Tacoma Boatbuilding Co., Tacoma, WA; stationed at St. Ignace, MI

Bristol Bay [WTGB-102]		IB	1979	D	662*	140'00"	37'06"	12'00"

Built: Tacoma Boatbuilding Co., Tacoma, WA; stationed at Detroit, MI

Buckthorn [WLI-642]		BT	1963	D	200*	100'00"	24'00"	4'08"

Built: Mobile Ship Repair Inc., Mobile, AL; stationed at Sault Ste. Marie, MI

CGB-12000		BT	1991	B	700*	120'00"	50'00"	6'00"
CGB-12001		BT	1991	B	700*	120'00"	50'00"	6'00"
Hollyhock [WLB-214]		BT	2003	D	2,000*	225'09"	46'00"	19'08"

Built: Marinette Marine Corp., Marinette, WI; stationed at Port Huron, MI

Katmai Bay [WTGB-101]		IB	1978	D	662*	140'00"	37'06"	12'00"

Built: Tacoma Boatbuilding Co., Tacoma, WA; stationed at Sault Ste. Marie, MI

Mackinaw [WLBB-30]		IB	2005	D	3,407*	240'00"	58'00"	15'05"

Built: Marinette Marine Corp., Marinette, WI; stationed at Cheboygan, MI

Mobile Bay [WTGB-103]		IB	1979	D	662*	140'00"	37'06"	12'00"

Built: Tacoma Boatbuilding Co., Tacoma, WA; stationed at Sturgeon Bay, WI

Morro Bay [WTGB-106]		IB	1979	D	662*	140'00"	37'06"	12'00"

Built: Tacoma Boatbuilding Co., Tacoma, WA; stationed at Yorktown, VA, but relocated to the Great Lakes as needed

Neah Bay [WTGB-105]		IB	1980	D	662*	140'00"	37'06"	12'00"

Built: Tacoma Boatbuilding Co., Tacoma, WA; stationed at Cleveland, OH

Penobscot Bay [WTGB-107]		IB	1985	D	662*	140'00"	37'06"	12'00"

Built: Tacoma Boatbuilding Co., Tacoma, WA; stationed at Bayonne, NJ, but relocated to the Great Lakes as needed

U-4 U.S. COAST GUARD TUG ASSOCIATION, CLEVELAND, OH *(76fsa.org/cgta)*

Apalachee		TB/MU	1943	DE	224*	110'00"	26'04"	15'01"

Built: Ira S. Bushey & Sons Inc., Brooklyn, NY; vessel is expected to be restored as a maritime and Coast Guard museum ship at Cleveland, OH (Apalachee WYTM-71)

U-5 U.S. ENVIRONMENTAL PROTECTION AGENCY, DULUTH, MN & CHICAGO, IL *(www.epa.gov)*

Lake Explorer II		RV	1966	D	150*	86'09"	22'00"	7'02"

Built: Jackobson Shipyard, Oyster Bay, New York (NOAA Rude '66-'08)

Lake Guardian	8030609	RV	1981	D	282*	180'00"	40'00"	11'00"

Built: Halter Marine Inc., Moss Point MS (Marsea Fourteen '81-'90)

St. Marys Challenger enters port at Grand Haven. (Mike Harting)

Fleet Name Vessel Name	IMO #	Vessel Type	Year Built	Engine Type	Cargo Cap. or Gross*	Overall Length	Breadth	Depth

U-6   **U.S. FISH & WILDLIFE SERVICE, JORDAN RIVER NATIONAL FISH HATCHERY, ELMIRA, MI**

Spencer F. Baird		RV	2006	D	256*	95' 00"	30' 00"	9' 05"

U-7   **U.S. NAT'L PARK SERVICE - ISLE ROYALE NAT'L PARK, HOUGHTON, MI** *(nps.gov/isro/ranger-iii.htm)*

Greenstone II		TK	2003	B	114*	70' 01"	24' 01"	8' 00"
Built: Fraser Shipyards Inc., Superior, WI								
Ranger III	7618234	PK	1958	D	648*	152' 08"	34' 00"	13' 00"
Built: Christy Corp., Sturgeon Bay, WI								

U-8   **U.S. NAVAL SEA CADET CORPS** *(seacadets.org)*

Grayfox **[TWR-825]**		TV	1985	D	213*	120' 00"	25' 00"	12' 00"
Built: Marinette Marine, Marinette, WI; based at Port Huron, MI (USS TWR-825 '85-'97)								
Manatra **[YP-671]**		TV	1974	D	67*	80' 05"	17' 09"	5' 04"
Based at Chicago, IL; name stands for MArine NAvigation and TRaining Association (USS YP-671 '74-'89)								
Pride of Michigan **[YP-673]**		TV	1977	D	70*	80' 06"	17' 08"	5' 03"
Built: Peterson Builders Inc., Sturgeon Bay, WI; based at Mount Clemens, MI (USS YP-673 '77-'89)								

U-9   **UNIVERSITY OF MINNESOTA-DULUTH, DULUTH, MN** *(www.d.umn.edu)*

Blue Heron		RV	1985	D	175*	87' 00"	23' 00"	11' 00"*
Built: Goudy and Stevens, E. Boothbay, ME (Fairtry '85-'97)								

U-10   **UNIVERSITY OF WISCONSIN, GREAT LAKES WATER INSTITUTE, MILWAUKEE, WI** *(glwi.uwm.edu)*

Neeskay		RV	1952	D	75*	71' 00"	17' 06"	7' 06"

U-11   **UNIVERSITY OF WISCONSIN, SUPERIOR, WI** *(uwsuper.edu)*

L. L. Smith Jr.		RV	1950	D	38*	57' 06"	16' 06"	6' 06"

U-12   **UPPER LAKES GROUP INC., TORONTO, ON** *(upperlakes.com)*

MARINELINK INC., TORONTO, ON – A DIVISION OF UPPER LAKES GROUP INC.

BIG 503		BC	2000	B	902*	190' 06"	35' 00"	14' 00"
Built: Jeffboat LLC, Jeffersonville, IN								
BIG 543, BIG 546, BIG 548, BIG 549, BIG 551								
Built: Trinity Marine Products, Ashland City, TN	BC	2003	B	916*	191' 00"	35' 00"	14' 00"	
BIG 9708 B		BC	1996	B	958*	191' 09"	35' 00"	14' 00"
Built: Trinity Marine Products, Ashland City, TN								
BIG 9917 B		BC	1999	B	958*	191' 09"	35' 00"	14' 00"
Built: Trinity Marine Products, Ashland City, TN								
Commodore Straits	6525040	TB	1966	D	566*	130' 00"	34' 01"	15' 07"
Built: Dominion Steel & Coal Corp., Halifax, NS (Haida Brave '66-'79)								
MarineLink Explorer	7700477	HL	1978	B	3,000*	300' 00"	55' 00"	27' 00"
Built: Peterson Builders, Sturgeon Bay, WI; converted to a barge in 2009 at Port Colborne, ON (John Henry)								

PROVMAR FUELS INC., HAMILTON, ON – A DIVISION OF UPPER LAKES GROUP INC.

Hamilton Energy	6517328	RT	1965	D	1,282	201' 05"	34' 01"	14' 09"
Built: Grangemouth Dockyard Co., Grangemouth, Scotland (Partington '65-'79, Shell Scientist '79-'81, Metro Sun '81-'85)								
Provmar Terminal	5376521	TK	1959	B	7,300	403' 05"	55' 06"	28' 05"
Built: Sarpsborg Mek, Verksted, Greater Norway; last operated in 1984; in use as a fuel storage barge at Hamilton, ON (Varangnes '59-'70, Tommy Wiborg '70-'74, Ungava Transport '74-'85)								
Provmar Terminal II	5159600	TK	1948	D	6,832	408' 00"	53' 00"	26' 00"
Built: Collingwood Shipyards, Collingwood, ON; last operated in1986; in use as a fuel storage barge at Hamilton, ON (Imperial Sarnia {2} '48-'89)								

UPPER LAKES SHIPPING LTD., CALGARY, AB – DIVISION OF UPPER LAKES GROUP INC.

☛ *AT PRESS TIME THESE VESSELS WERE IN THE PROCESS OF BEING SOLD TO ALGOMA CENTRAL MARINE, FLEET A-3. CHECK KNOWYOURSHIPS.COM FOR POSSIBLE RENAMES*

Canadian Enterprise	7726677	SU	1979	D	33,854	730' 00"	75' 11"	46' 07"
Built: Port Weller Dry Docks, Port Weller, ON								
Canadian Mariner	9587893	SU	2011	D	37,399	740' 00"	77' 11"	49' 03
Built: Chengxi Shipyard Co. Ltd., Jiangyin City, China								
Canadian Miner	6601674	BC	1966	D	27,853	730' 00"	75' 00"	39' 01"
Built: Canadian Vickers, Montreal, QC (Maplecliffe Hall '66-'88, Lemoyne {2} '88-'94); entered long-term lay-up at Toronto, ON, Dec. 24, 2008.								
Canadian Navigator	6707961	SU	1967	D	30,324	729' 00"	75' 10"	40' 06"
Built: J. Readhead & Sons, South Shields, England; converted from a saltwater bulk carrier in '80; converted to a self-unloader in '97; both conversions by Port Weller Dry Docks, St. Catharines, ON (Demeterton '67-'75, St. Lawrence Navigator '75-'80)								

Fleet Name / Vessel Name	IMO #	Vessel Type	Year Built	Engine Type	Cargo Cap. or Gross*	Overall Length	Breadth	Depth
Canadian Olympic	7432783	SU	1976	D	33,859	730' 00"	75' 00"	46' 06"
Built: Port Weller Dry Docks, Port Weller, ON								
Canadian Progress	6821999	SU	1968	D	31,637	730' 00"	75' 00"	46' 06"
Built: Port Weller Dry Docks, Port Weller, ON								
Canadian Provider	5407277	BC	1963	T	28,960	730' 00"	75' 00"	39' 02"
Built: Collingwood Shipyards, Collingwood, ON (Murray Bay {3} '63-'94)								
Canadian Ranger	6723771	SU	1943	D	26475	729' 10"	75' 00"	39' 03"
Canadian Ranger was built by joining the stern section (pilothouse, engine room, machinery) of the former coastal package freighter Chimo with the bow and mid-body of the laker Hilda Marjanne in '84; converted to a self- unloader in '88; all work by Port Weller Dry Docks, St. Catharines, ON **(Fore Section)** *Built: Kaiser Inc., Portland, OR (Grande Ronde '43-'48, Kate N. L. '48-'61, Hilda Marjanne '61-'84); converted from a saltwater bulk carrier in '61* **(Stern Section)** *Built: Davie Shipbuilding Co., Lauzon, QC (Chimo '67-'83)*								
Canadian Transfer	6514869	SU1943/65		D	15,719	650' 00"	60' 00"	35' 00"
Canadian Transfer was built by joining the stern section of Canadian Explorer (engine room, machinery) with the bow and mid-body of the World War II-era laker Hamilton Transfer in '98; all work by Port Weller Dry Docks, St. Catharines, ON **(Fore Section)** *Built: Great Lakes Engineering Works, Ashtabula, OH (J. H. Hillman Jr. '43-'74, Crispin Oglebay {2}'74-'95, Hamilton Transfer '95-'98); converted to a self-unloader in '74* **(Stern Section)** *Built: Davie Shipbuilding Co., Lauzon, QC as Cabot {1}'65-'83, Canadian Explorer '83-'98)*								
Canadian Transport {2}	7711737	SU	1979	D	32,678	730' 00"	75' 11"	46' 07"
Built: Port Weller Dry Docks, Port Weller, ON								
Gordon C. Leitch {2}	6815237	BC	1968	D	31,668	730' 00"	75' 00"	42' 00"
Built: Canadian Vickers, Montreal, QC; converted from a self-unloader to a bulk carrier by the builders in '77 (Ralph Misener '68-'94)								
James Norris	5169124	SU	1952	S	18,386	663' 06"	67' 00"	35' 00"
Built: Midland Shipyards, Midland, ON; converted to a self-unloader by Port Weller Dry Docks, St. Catharines, ON, in '81								
John D. Leitch	6714586	SU	1967	D	34,127	730' 00"	77' 11"	45' 00"
Built: Port Weller Dry Docks, Port Weller, ON; rebuilt with new mid-body, widened 3' by the builders in '02 (Canadian Century '67-'02)								
Montrealais	5241142	BC	1962	T	29,072	730' 00"	75' 00"	39' 02"
Built: Canadian Vickers, Montreal, QC (Launched as Montrealer)								
Quebecois	5287847	BC	1963	T	28,716	730' 00"	75' 00"	39' 01"
Built: Canadian Vickers, Montreal, QC								

U-13 UPPER LAKES TOWING CO., ESCANABA, MI

Fleet Name / Vessel Name	IMO #	Vessel Type	Year Built	Engine Type	Cargo Cap. or Gross*	Overall Length	Breadth	Depth
Joseph H. Thompson		SU	1944	B	21,200	706' 06"	71' 06"	38' 06"
Built: Sun Shipbuilding & Drydock Co., Chester, PA; converted from a saltwater vessel to a Great Lakes bulk carrier by Maryland Dry Dock, Baltimore, MD, and American Shipbuilding, South Chicago, IL, in '52; converted to a self-unloading barge by the owners in '91 (USNS Marine Robin '44-'52)								
Joseph H. Thompson Jr.		ATB	1990	D	841*	146' 06"	38' 00"	30' 00"
Built: At Marinette, WI, from steel left over from the conversion of Joseph H. Thompson (above)								

U-14 USS COD SUBMARINE MEMORIAL, CLEVELAND, OH (usscod.org)

Fleet Name / Vessel Name	IMO #	Vessel Type	Year Built	Engine Type	Cargo Cap. or Gross*	Overall Length	Breadth	Depth
Cod		MU	1943	D/V	1,525*	311' 08"	27' 02"	33' 09"
Built: Electric Boat Co., Groton, CT; former U.S. Navy Albacore (Gato) class submarine IXSS-224 open to the public at Cleveland, OH								

U-15 USS GREAT LAKES LLC, NEW YORK, NY

Fleet Name / Vessel Name	IMO #	Vessel Type	Year Built	Engine Type	Cargo Cap. or Gross*	Overall Length	Breadth	Depth
Robert F. Deegan		TK	1968	B	2,424*	225' 08"	60' 00"	18' 00"

U-16 USS LST 393 PRESERVATION ASSOCIATION, MUSKEGON, MI (lst393.org)

Fleet Name / Vessel Name	IMO #	Vessel Type	Year Built	Engine Type	Cargo Cap. or Gross*	Overall Length	Breadth	Depth
LST-393		MU	1942	D	2,100	328' 00"	50' 00"	25' 00"
Built: Newport News Shipbuilding and Dry Dock Co., Newport News, VA; former U.S. Navy / Wisconsin & Michigan Steamship Co. vessel last operated July 31, 1973; open to the public at Muskegon, MI (USS LST-393 '42-'47, Highway 16 '47-'99)								

V-1 VANENKEVORT TUG & BARGE INC., BARK RIVER, MI (apmp.com)

Fleet Name / Vessel Name	IMO #	Vessel Type	Year Built	Engine Type	Cargo Cap. or Gross*	Overall Length	Breadth	Depth
Great Lakes Trader		SU	2000	B	39,600	740' 00"	78' 00"	45' 00"
Built: Halter Marine, Pearlington, MS								
Joyce L. VanEnkevort	8973033	AT	1998	D	1,179*	135' 04"	50' 00"	26' 00"
Built: Bay Shipbuilding Co., Sturgeon Bay, WI								
[ATB VanEnkevort / GL Trader OA dimensions together]						844' 10"	78' 00"	45' 00"

V-2 VANGUARD SHIPPING (GREAT LAKES) LTD., RIDGEVILLE, ON (vanshipltd.com)

Fleet Name / Vessel Name	IMO #	Vessel Type	Year Built	Engine Type	Cargo Cap. or Gross*	Overall Length	Breadth	Depth
J.W. Shelley	6821937	BC	1968	D	28,400	730' 00"	75' 00"	39' 08"
Built: Collingwood Shipyards, Collingwood, ON (Algocen '68-'05, Valgocen '05-'08)								

Fleet Name Vessel Name	IMO #	Vessel Type	Year Built	Engine Type	Cargo Cap. or Gross*	Overall Length	Breadth	Depth
V-3 VIC POWELL, DUNNVILLE, ON								
Toni D		TB	1959	D	15*	46' 00"	15' 07"	4' 01"
V-4 VICTORIAN PRINCESS CRUISE LINES INC., ERIE, PA *(victorianprincess.com)*								
Victorian Princess		ES	1985	D	46*	67' 00"	24' 00"	4' 05"
Built: Mid-City Steel Fabricating Inc., La Crosse, WI (Rosie 1, Rosie O'Shea)								
V-5 VINCENT KLAMERUS, DRUMMOND ISLAND, MI								
Lime Island		PA	1953	D	24*	42' 08"	12' 00"	6' 00"
V-6 VISTA FLEET, DULUTH, MN *(vistafleet.com)*								
Vista Queen		ES	1987	D	97*	64' 00"	16' 00"	6' 02"
Built: Mid-City Steel Fabricating Inc., La Crosse, WI (Queen of Excelsior)								
Vista Star		ES	1987	D	95*	91' 00"	24' 09"	5' 02"
Built: Freeport Shipbuilding Inc., Freeport, FL (Island Empress '87-'88)								
V-7 VOIGHT'S MARINE SERVICES LTD., ELLISON BAY AND GILLS ROCK, WI *(islandclipper.com)*								
Island Clipper {2}		ES	1987	D	71*	65' 00"	20' 00"	8' 00"
Built: Breaux Bros. Enterprises, Loreauville, LA								
Yankee Clipper		ES	1971	D	41*	46' 06"	17' 00"	6' 00"
V-8 VOYAGEUR MARITIME TRADING INC., RIDGEVILLE, ON *(voyageurtransport.com)*								
Maritime Trader	6702301	BC	1967	D	19,093	607' 09"	62' 00"	36' 00"
Built: Collingwood Shipyards, Collingwood, ON; commercially operated under contract of affreightment to Lower Lakes Towing Ltd. (Mantadoc '67-'02, Teakglen '02-'05)								
W-1 WALPOLE-ALGONAC FERRY LINE, PORT LAMBTON, ON *(walpolealgonacferry.com)*								
City of Algonac		CF	1990	D	82*	62' 06"	27' 09"	5' 09"
Built: Duratug Shipyard & Fabricating Ltd., Port Dover, ON								
Walpole Islander		CF	1986	D	72*	54' 05"	27' 09"	6' 03"
Built: Hike Metal Products, Wheatley, ON								
W-2 WALSTROM MARINE, HARBOR SPRINGS, MI *(walstrom.com)*								
DePere		DB	1924	B	172*	118' 06"	32' 00"	5' 02"
Elizabeth		TB	1945	D	21*	42' 02"	12' 01"	5' 05"
Built: Burger Boat Co., Manitowoc, WI (Charles F. Liscomb, Jason, Lydie Rae)								

USCG cutter Hollyhock at Port Huron. (Bob Powers)

Fleet Name / Vessel Name	IMO #	Vessel Type	Year Built	Engine Type	Cargo Cap. or Gross*	Overall Length	Breadth	Depth

W-3 WARNER PETROLEUM CORP., CLARE, MI (warnerpetroleum.com)

FUEL BOAT HOLDINGS LLC, CLARE, MI

Warner Provider		TK	1962	B	1,698*	264' 00"	52' 05"	12' 00"

Built: Port Houston Iron Works, Houston, TX (Hannah 2903)

| William L. Warner | 7322055 | RT | 1973 | D | 492* | 120' 00" | 40' 00" | 14' 00" |

Built: Halter Marine, New Orleans, LA; serves vessels at southern Lake Michigan ports (Jos. F. Bigane '73-'04)

WATERFRONT PETROLEUM TERMINAL CO., DETROIT, MI (waterfrontpetroleum.com)

| Coloma L. Warner | 7337892 | TB | 1955 | D | 134* | 86' 00" | 24' 00" | 10' 00" |

Built: Sturgeon Bay Shipbuilding, Sturgeon Bay, WI (Harbor Ace '55-'61, Gopher State '61-'71, Betty Gale '71-'93, Hannah D. Hannah -'10)

W-4 WASHINGTON ISLAND FERRY LINE INC., WASHINGTON ISLAND, WI (wisferry.com)

Arni J. Richter		PA/CF	2003	D	92*	104' 00"	38' 06"	10' 11"

Built: Bay Shipbuilding Co., Sturgeon Bay, WI

| Eyrarbakki | | PA/CF | 1970 | D | 95* | 87' 00" | 36' 00" | 7' 06" |

Built: Bay Shipbuilding Co., Sturgeon Bay, WI

| Robert Noble | | PA/CF | 1979 | D | 97* | 90' 04" | 36' 00" | 8' 03" |

Built: Peterson Builders Inc., Sturgeon Bay, WI

| Washington {2} | | PA/CF | 1989 | D | 97* | 100' 00" | 37' 00" | 9' 00" |

Built: Peterson Builders Inc., Sturgeon Bay, WI

W-5 WENDELLA BOAT TOURS, CHICAGO, IL (wendellaboats.com)

Linnea		ES	2010	D	77*	85' 05"	30' 00"	7' 01"
Ouilmette		ES	2001	D	43*	65' 00"	22' 04"	4' 05"
Sunliner		ES	1961	D	35*	62' 00"	14' 04"	6' 04"
Wendella		ES	2007	D	77*	85' 05"	30' 00"	7' 01"
Wendella LTD		ES	1992	D	66*	68' 00"	20' 00"	4' 09"

W-6 WESTERN RESERVE STEAMSHIP SUPPLY, LAKEWOOD, OH

Forest City		SB	1934	D	22*	44' 04"	11' 11"	4' 09"

W-7 WINDSOR RIVER CRUISES LTD., WINDSOR, ON (windsorrivercruises.com)

Macassa Bay	8624709	ES	1986	D	210*	93' 07"	29' 07"	10' 04"

Built: Boiler Pump & Marine Works Ltd., Hamilton, ON

W-8 WOHLLEB-SOCIE CO., TOLEDO, OH

Bessie B		TB	1947	D	30*	52' 03"	13' 09"	5' 05"

W-9 WINDY OF CHICAGO LTD., CHICAGO, IL (tallshipwindy.com)

Windy		ES/4S	1996	W	75*	148' 00"	25' 00"	8' 00"

Built: Detyens Shipyards Inc., Charleston, SC

W-10 WISCONSIN DEPARTMENT OF NATURAL RESOURCES, BAYFIELD AND STURGEON BAY, WI

Coregonus		RV	2011	D		60' 00"		
Barney Devine		RV	1937	D	42*	50' 00"	14' 05"	6' 00"
Hack Noyes		RV	1947	D	50*	56' 00"		4' 00"

W-11 WISCONSIN MARITIME MUSEUM, MANITOWOC, WI (wisconsinmaritime.org)

Cobia		MU	1944	D/V	1,500*	311' 09"	27' 03"	33' 09"

Built: Electric Boat Co., Groton, CT; former U. S. Navy Gato class submarine AGSS-245 is open to the public at Manitowoc, WI

X-1 VESSELS WITH UNDETERMINED STATUS AS OF MARCH 1, 2011

Essayons		TB	1908	R	117*	85' 06"	21' 02"	11' 09"

Long-inactive steam tug sank at Duluth in 2009.

| Hannah 5101 | | TK | 1978 | B | 8,050 | 360' 00" | 60' 00" | 22' 06" |

Former Hannah Marine tug is laid up and for sale at Hamilton, ON at the McKeil yard; ownership unclear.

| Islay | | TB | 1892 | D | 19* | 60' 00" | 13' 00" | 5' 00" |

Built: American Steel Barge Co., Superior, WI; laid up at Manitowoc, WI; formerly owned by the Northeastern Maritime Historical Foundation, Superior, WI; ownership unclear (Islay 1892-1947, Bayfield {1} '47-'83)

| James A. Hannah | | TB | 1945 | D | 593* | 149' 00" | 33' 00" | 16' 00" |

Built: Marietta Manufacturing, Marietta, GA; former Hannah Marine tug is laid up and for sale at Hamilton, ON, at the McKeil yard; ownership unclear (U. S. Army LT-820 '45-'65, Muskegon {1} '65-'71)

| Reiss | | TB | 1913 | R | 99* | 71' 00" | 20' 00" | 12' 06" |

Built: Great Lakes Towing Co., Cleveland, OH; former Reiss Steamship Co. tug last operated in 1969; at anchor in the Kalamazoo River, Saugatuck, MI; formerly owned by the Northeastern Maritime Historical Foundation, Superior, WI; owner unknown, sold on eBay in late 2010 (Q. A. Gillmore '13-'32)

Canadian Enterprise meets Michipicoten in the St. Clair River. (Alain Gindroz)

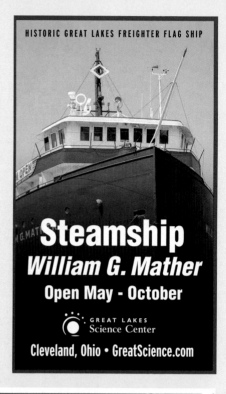

LAKER LONGEVITY

1906-'37

1906: St. Marys Challenger (re: '67) **1927**: S.T. Crapo* **1929**: Maumee (re: '61) **1936**: J.A.W. Iglehart (re: '65)* **1937**: St. Marys Conquest (re: '87)

1941-'49

1941: Pere Marquette 41 (re: '97) **1942**: Alpena (re: '91), American Victory (re: '61, '82), Lee A. Tregurtha (re: '61) **1943**: Canadian Transfer (re: '98), Cuyahoga (re: '74), Manistee (re: '64), Mississagi (re: '67) **1944**: Joseph H. Thompson (re '52 and '91), McKee Sons (re: '53, '91) **1945**: Paul H. Townsend (re: '52)* **1949**: Wilfred Sykes

1950-'59

1952: Arthur M. Anderson (re: '75, '82), Kaye E. Barker (re: '76 '81), Cason J. Callaway (re: '74, '82), Philip R. Clarke (re: '74, '82), Lewis J. Kuber (re: '06), Michipicoten (re: '57, '80), Ojibway, John G. Munson, James Norris (re: '81) **1953**: American Valor (re: '74, '82), American Fortitude (re: '81), Badger, James J. Kuber (re: '07), Pathfinder (re: '98), Saginaw **1958**: John Sherwin** **1959**: Cedarglen (re: '77), Hon. James L. Oberstar (re: '72, '81), Herbert C. Jackson (re: '75), Sarah Spencer (re: '89)

1960-'69

1960: Algontario (re: '76), Edward L. Ryerson **1961**: Canadian Ranger (re: '84), English River (re: 74) **1962**: Catherine Desgagnés, Montrealais **1963**: Canadian Provider, Halifax, (re: '80), Quebecois, Yankcanuck **1965**: Stephen B. Roman (re: '83) **1966**: Algosteel (re: '89), Canadian Miner **1967**: Algocape, Tim S. Dool (re: '96), Canadian Navigator (re: '80, '97), John D. Leitch (re: '02), Maritime Trader **1968**: Algomarine (re: '89), Algorail, Canadian Progress, Frontenac (re: '73), Gordon C. Leitch, J.W. Shelley **1969**: CSL Tadoussac (re: '01)

1971-'79

1971: Algonorth **1972**: Algoway, Roger Blough, CSL Niagara (re: '99), Stewart J. Cort **1973**: Adam E. Cornelius, Calumet, Manitowoc, John J. Boland, Rt. Hon. Paul J. Martin (re: '00), Presque Isle **1974**: Algosoo, Chi-Cheemaun, H. Lee White, Robert S. Pierson **1975**: Melissa Desgagnés, Petrolia Desgagnés, Sam Laud **1976**: James R. Barker, Joseph L. Block, Canadian Olympic, Amelia Desgagnés, Thalassa Desgagnés, St. Clair **1977**: Algoeast, Algolake, CSL Assiniboine (re: '05), CSL Laurentien (re: '01), Walter J. McCarthy Jr., Mesabi Miner **1978**: Algobay (re: '09), Algosar, American Integrity, American Spirit, Buffalo **1979**: American Courage, Canadian Enterprise, Canadian Transport, Edwin H. Gott, Indiana Harbor

1980-'87

1980: American Mariner, Burns Harbor, Salarium, Edgar B. Speer, Oakglen, Richelieu **1981**: Algowood (re: '00), American Century, American Republic, Capt. Henry Jackman (re: '96), Mapleglen, Saguenay, Paul R. Tregurtha **1982**: Atlantic Superior, Camilla Desgagnés, Peter R. Cresswell (re: '98), Michigan, Véga Desgagnés **1983**: John B. Aird, Birchglen, Spruceglen, Kaministiqua **1984**: Atlantic Huron (re: '89, '03) **1985**: Atlantic Erie, Pineglen **1986**: Anna Desgagnés, Algoma Spirit **1987**: Algoma Discovery, Algoma Guardian

1992-'99

1992: Dara Desgagnés, Esta Desgagnés **1993**: Jana Desgagnés; **1996**: Integrity **1998**: Algosea **1999**: Maria Desgagnés

2000-'11

2000: Great Lakes Trader **2001**: Norman McLeod **2004**: Algoscotia, Lake Express **2006**: Innovation **2007**: Rosaire A. Desgagnés **2008**: Algocanada, Algonova, John J. Carrick, Zelada Desgagnés **2009**: Sedna Desgagnés **2011**: Bella Desgagnés, Canadian Mariner

*(re = major rebuild; * storage barge; ** long-term lay-up)*

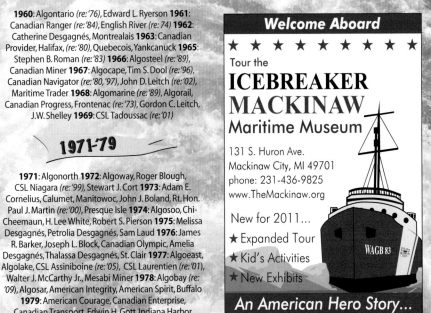

bhp: brake horsepower, a measure of diesel engine output measured at the crankshaft before entering gearbox or any other power take-out device

ihp: indicated horsepower, based on an internal measurement of mean cylinder pressure, piston area, piston stroke and engine speed; used for reciprocating engines

shp: shaft horsepower, a measure of engine output at the propeller shaft at the output of the reduction gearbox; used for steam and diesel-electric engines

cpp: controllable pitch propeller

* = tug ** = ferry

Vessel Name	Engine Manufacturer & Model #	Engine Type	Total Engines	Total Cylinders	Rated HP	Total Props	Speed MPH
Adam E. Cornelius	GM Electro-Motive Div. - 20-645-E7B	Diesel	2	20	7,200 bhp	1 cpp	16.1
Aivik	Pielstick - 8PA6L280	Diesel	3	8	5,200 bhp	1 cpp	15.0
Alder (USCG)	Caterpillar - 3608TA	Diesel	2	6	3,100 bhp	1 cpp	
Algobay	MaK - 8M32C	Diesel	2	8	10,442 bhp	1 cpp	
Algocanada	MaK - 9M32C	Diesel	1	9	6,118 bhp	1 cpp	16.1
Algocape	Sulzer - 6RND76	Diesel	1	6	9,600 bhp	1 cpp	17.3
Algoeast	B&W - 6K45GF	Diesel	1	6	5,300 bhp	1 cpp	15.8
Algolake	Pielstick - 10PC2-2V-400	Diesel	2	10	9,000 bhp	1 cpp	17.3
Algoma Dartmouth	M.A.N.-B&W - 6L23/30A	Diesel	2	6	2,310 bhp	2 cpp	13.3
Algoma Discovery	Sulzer - 6RTA62	Diesel	1	6	15,499 bhp	1 cpp	16.4
Algoma Guardian	Sulzer - 6RTA62	Diesel	1	6	15,499 bhp	1 cpp	16.4
Algoma Spirit	Sulzer - 6RTA62	Diesel	1	6	11,284 bhp	1 cpp	16.4
Algomarine	Sulzer - 6RND76	Diesel	1	6	9,600 bhp	1 cpp	17.0
Algonorth	Werkspoor - 9TM410	Diesel	2	9	12,000 bhp	1 cpp	16.1
Algonova	MaK - 9M32C	Diesel	1	9	6,118 bhp	1 cpp	16.1
Algontario	B&W - 7-74VTBF-160	Diesel	1	7	8,750 bhp	1 cpp	14.4
Algorail	Fairbanks Morse - 10-38D8-1/8	Diesel	4	10	6,662 bhp	1 cpp	13.8
Algosar	Alco - 16V251E	Diesel	2	16	5,150 bhp	2	14.4
Algoscotia	Wartsila - 6L46C	Diesel	1	6	8,445 bhp	1 cpp	16.0
Algosoo	Pielstick - 10PC2-V-400	Diesel	2	10	9,000 bhp	1 cpp	15.0
Algosea	Wartsila - 6L46A	Diesel	1	6	6,434 bhp	1 cpp	15.0
Algosteel	Sulzer - 6RND76	Diesel	1	6	9,599 bhp	1	17.0
Algoway	Fairbanks Morse - 10-38D8-1/8	Diesel	4	10	6,662 bhp	1 cpp	13.8
Algowood	MaK - 6M552AK	Diesel	2	6	10,200 bhp	1 cpp	13.8
Alpena	De Laval Steam Turbine Co.	Turbine	1	**	4,400 shp	1	14.1
Amelia Desgagnés	Allen - 12PVBCS12-F	Diesel	2	12	4,000 bhp	1	16.1
American Century	GM - Electro-Motive Div. - 20-645-E7B	Diesel	4	20	14,400 bhp	2 cpp	17.3
American Courage	GM - Electro-Motive Div. - 20-645-E7	Diesel	2	20	7,200 bhp	1 cpp	16.1
American Fortitude	General Electric Co.	Turbine	1	**	7,700 shp	1	16.7
American Integrity	GM Electro-Motive Div. - 20-645-E7	Diesel	4	20	14,400 bhp	2 cpp	18.4
American Mariner	GM Electro-Motive Div. - 20-645-E7	Diesel	2	20	7,200 bhp	1 cpp	15.0
American Republic	GM Electro-Motive Div. - 20-645-E7	Diesel	2	20	7,200 bhp	2 cpp	15.0
American Spirit	Pielstick - 16PC2-2V-400	Diesel	2	16	16,000 bhp	2 cpp	17.3
American Valor	Westinghouse Elec. Corp.	Turbine	1	**	7,700 shp	1	16.1
American Victory	Bethlehem Steel Corp.	Turbine	1	**	7,700 shp	1	19.0
Amundsen (CCG)	Alco - 16V251F	Diesel	6	16	17,700 bhp	2	18.6
Anglian Lady *	Deutz SBA12M528	Diesel		12	3,480 bhp	2 cpp	15.5
Anna Desgagnés	M.A.N. - K5SZ70/125B	Diesel	1	5	10,332 bhp	1	17.8
Arctic	M.A.N. 14V52/55A	Diesel	1	14	14,770 bhp	1 cpp	17.8
Arthur M. Anderson	Westinghouse Elec. Corp.	Turbine	1	**	7,700 shp	1	16.1
Atlantic Erie	Sulzer - 6RLB66	Diesel	1	6	11,100 bhp	1 cpp	16.1
Atlantic Huron	Sulzer - 6RLB66	Diesel	1	6	11,094 bhp	1 cpp	17.3
Atlantic Superior	Sulzer - 6RLA66	Diesel	1	6	11,095 bhp	1 cpp	17.3
Avataq	Hanshin - 6LF58	Diesel	1	6	6,000 bhp	1 cpp	16.2
Avenger IV *	British Polar	Diesel	1	9	2,700 bhp	1 cpp	12.0
Badger **	Skinner Engine Co.	Steeple Compound Uniflow	2	4	8,000 ihp	2	18.4
Barbara Andrie *	GM Electro-Motive Div. 16-645-EF	Diesel	1	16	2,000 bhp	1	
Bella Desgagnés	Wartsila - 9L20CR	Diesel	4	9	8,320 bhp	2 azimuth	17.3
Birchglen	Sulzer 4RLB76	Diesel	1	4	10,880 bhp	1cpp	13.8
Biscayne Bay (USCG)	Fairbanks Morse - 10-38D8-1/8	Diesel	2	10	2,500 bhp	1	13.8
Bristol Bay (USCG)	Fairbanks Morse - 10-38D8-1/8	Diesel	2	10	2,500 bhp	1	13.8
Buffalo	GM Electro-Motive Div. - 20-645-E7	Diesel	2	20	7,200 bhp	1 cpp	16.1
Burns Harbor	GM Electro-Motive Div. - 20-645-E7	Diesel	4	20	14,400 bhp	2 cpp	18.4
Calumet	Alco - 16V251E	Diesel	2	16	5,600 bhp	1	16.1

				Cylinders	Rated HP	Total Props	
Camilla Desgagnés	Werkspoor - 12TM410	Diesel	1	12	7,797 bhp	1 cpp	
Canadian Enterprise	M.A.N. - 7L40/45	Diesel	2	7	8,804 bhp	1 cpp	13.8
Canadian Mariner	M.A.N.-B&W - 6L48/60CR	Diesel	1	6	9,792 bhp	1 cpp	
Canadian Miner	Fairbanks Morse - 12-38D8-1/8	Diesel	4	12	8,000 bhp	1 cpp	15.0
Canadian Navigator	Doxford Engines Ltd. - 76J4	Diesel	1	4	9,680 bhp	1	16.7
Canadian Olympic	M.A.N. - 8L40/54A	Diesel	2	8	10,000 bhp	1 cpp	15.0
Canadian Progress	Caterpillar - 3612-TA	Diesel	2	12	9,000 bhp	1 cpp	15.5
Canadian Provider	John Inglis Co. Ltd.	Turbine	1	**	10,000 shp	1	17.3
Canadian Ranger	Sulzer - 5RND68	Diesel	1	5	6,100 shp	1 cpp	19.6
Canadian Transfer	Sulzer - 5RND68	Diesel	1	5	6,100 bhp	1 cpp	18.4
Canadian Transport	M.A.N. - 8L40/45	Diesel	2	8	10,000 bhp	1 cpp	13.8
Capt. Henry Jackman	MaK - 6M552AK	Diesel	2	6	9,465 bhp	1 cpp	17.3
Cason J. Callaway	Westinghouse Elec. Corp.	Turbine	1	**	7,700 shp	1	16.1
Catherine Desgagnés	Sulzer - 6SAD60	Diesel	1	6	3,841 bhp	1	15.5
Cedarglen	B&W - 7-74VTBF-160	Diesel	1	7	8,750 bhp	1 cpp	15.5
Chi-Cheemaun **	Caterpillar C280-6	Diesel	4	6	9,280 bhp	2	
Commodore Straits *	Werkspoor	Diesel	2		3,470 bhp	2	13.8
CSL Assiniboine	Pielstick - 10PC2-2V-400	Diesel	2	10	9,000 bhp	1 cpp	15.0
CSL Laurentien	Pielstick - 10PC2-2V-400	Diesel	2	10	9,000 bhp	1 cpp	16.1
CSL Niagara	Pielstick - 10PC2-2V-400	Diesel	2	10	9,000 bhp	1 cpp	15.0
CSL Tadoussac	Sulzer - 6RND76	Diesel	1	6	9,600 bhp	1	17.0
Cuyahoga	Caterpillar - 3608	Diesel	1	8	3,000 bhp	1 cpp	12.6
Daldean **	GM 671	Diesel	2	6	450 bhp		
Dara Desgagnés	B&W - 6L35MC	Diesel	1	6	5,030 bhp	1 cpp	14.4
Des Groseilliers (CCG)	Alco - 16V251F	Diesel	6	16	17,700 bhp	2	18.6
Dorothy Ann *	GM Electro-Motive Div. - 20-645-E7B	Diesel	2	20	7,200 bhp	Z-Drive	16.1
Drummond Islander IV **	Caterpillar 3508	Diesel	2	8	1,920 bhp		
Ecosse *	GM Detroit - 16V92 N	Diesel	2	16	1,800 bhp	2	13.8
Edgar B. Speer	Pielstick - 18PC2-3V-400	Diesel	2	18	19,260 bhp	2 cpp	17.0
Edward L. Ryerson	General Electric Co.	Turbine	1	**	9,900 shp	1	19.0
Edwin H. Gott	MaK 8M43C	Diesel	2	8	19,300 bhp	2 ccp	
English River	Werkspoor - TMAB-390	Diesel	1	8	1,850 bhp	1 cpp	13.8
Esta Desgagnés	B&W - 6L35MC	Diesel	1	6	5,030 bhp	1 cpp	14.4
Evans McKeil *	GM Electro-Motive Div. - 16-645C	Diesel	2	16	2,150 bhp	1	11.5
Everlast *	Daihatsu - 8DSM-32	Diesel	2	8	6,000 bhp	2	16.5
Federal Agno	Sulzer - 6RTA58	Diesel	1	6	9,500 bhp	1	16.7
Federal Asahi	B&W - 6S46MC-C	Diesel	1	6	10,710 bhp	1	16.1
Federal Hudson	B&W - 6S46MC-C	Diesel	1	6	10,710 bhp	1	15.5
Federal Hunter	B&W - 6S46MC-C	Diesel	1	6	10,710 bhp	1	15.5
Federal Kivalina	B&W - 6S46MC-C	Diesel	1	6	10,710 bhp	1	16.1
Federal Kumano	B&W - 6S46MC-C	Diesel	1	6	10,710 bhp	1	16.1
Federal Kushiro	Mitsubishi - 6UEC52LA	Diesel	1	6	9,626 bhp	1	16.6
Federal Maas	B&W - 6S50MC	Diesel	1	6	11,640 bhp	1	16.1
Federal Mackinac	B&W - 6S46MC-C	Diesel	1	6	10,540 bhp	1	16.1
Federal Margaree	B&W - 6S46MC-C	Diesel	1	6	10,686 bhp	1	16.1
Federal Nakagawa	B&W - 6S46MC-C	Diesel	1	6	10,710 bhp	1	16.1
Federal Oshima	B&W - 6S46MC-C	Diesel	1	6	10,710 bhp	1	16.1
Federal Progress	Sulzer - 7RTA58	Diesel	1	7	15,116 bhp	1 cpp	16.8
Federal Rhine	B&W - 6S50MC	Diesel	1	6	11,640 bhp	1	16.1
Federal Rideau	B&W - 6S46MC-C	Diesel	1	6	10,710 bhp	1	16.1
Federal Saguenay	B&W - 6S50MC	Diesel	1	6	11,665 bhp	1	16.1
Federal Schelde	B&W - 6S50MC	Diesel	1	6	11,640 bhp	1	16.1
Federal St. Laurent	B&W - 6S50MC	Diesel	1	6	11,640 bhp	1	16.1
Federal Venture	Sulzer - 7RTA58	Diesel	1	7	15,116 bhp	1 cpp	16.9
Federal Welland	B&W - 6S46MC-C	Diesel	1	6	10,710 bhp	1	16.1
Federal Yukon	B&W - 6S46MC-C	Diesel	1	6	10,710 bhp	1	15.5
Frontenac	Sulzer - 6RND76	Diesel	1	6	9,600 bhp	1 cpp	17.0
Frontenac II **	Caterpillar 3412	Diesel	2	12	1,344 bhp	2 cpp	
George R. Pearkes (CCG)	Alco - 16V251F	Diesel	3	16	8,973 bhp	2	13.8
Glenora **	Cummins N855M	Diesel	2	6	390 b.h.p.		
G.L. Ostrander *	Caterpillar - 3608-DITA	Diesel	2	8	6,008 bhp	2	17.3
Gordon C. Leitch	Sulzer - 6RND76	Diesel	1	6	9,600 bhp	1 cpp	17.3
Grayfox (USNCS)	Caterpillar - 3512 TAC	Diesel	2	12	2,350 bhp.	2	20.7
Griffon (CCG)	Fairbanks Morse - 8-38D8-1/8	Diesel	4	8	5,336 bhp	2	1
H. Lee White	GM Electro-Motive Div. - 20-645-E7B	Diesel	2	20	7,200 bhp	1 cpp	1

Halifax	John Inglis Co. Ltd.	Turbine	1	**	10,000 shp	1	19.6
Hamilton Energy	GM Electro-Motive Div. - 12-534-E6	Diesel	1	12	1,500 bhp	1 cpp	13.8
Herbert C. Jackson	General Electric Co.	Turbine	1	**	6,600 shp	1	16.0
Hollyhock (USCG)	Caterpillar - 3608TA	Diesel	2	6	3,100 bhp	1 cpp	
Hon. James L. Oberstar	Rolls-Royce Bergen B32:40L6P	Diesel	2	6	8,160 bhp	1 ccp	17.0
Indiana Harbor	GM Electro-Motive Div. - 20-645-E7	Diesel	4	20	14,400 bhp	2 cpp	16.1
Invincible *	GM Electro-Motive Div. - 16-645-E7B	Diesel	2	16	5,750 bhp	2	13.8
J. A. W. Iglehart	De Laval Steam Turbine Co.	Turbine	1	**	4,400 shp	1	15.0
J. S. St. John	GM Electro-Motive Div. - 8-567	Diesel	1	8	850 bhp	1	11.5
J. W. Shelley	Fairbanks Morse -10-38D8-1/8	Diesel	4	10	7,999 bhp	1cpp	13.8
James Norris	Canadian Vickers Ltd.	Uniflow	1	5	4,000 ihp	1	16.1
James R. Barker	Pielstick - 16PC2-2V-400	Diesel	2	16	16,000 bhp	2 cpp	15.5
Jana Desgagnés	B&W - 6L35MC	Diesel	1	6	5,030 bhp	1 cpp	14.4
Jane Ann IV *	Pielstick - 8PC2-2L-400	Diesel	2	8	8,000 bhp	2	15.8
Jiimaan **	Ruston Paxman Diesels Ltd.- 6RK215	Diesel	2	6	2,839 bhp	2 cpp	15.0
John B. Aird	MaK - 6M552AK	Diesel	2	6	9,460 bhp	1 cpp	13.8
John D. Leitch	B&W - 5-74VT2BF-160	Diesel	1	5	7,500 bhp	1 cpp	16.1
John G. Munson	General Electric Co.	Turbine	1	**	7,700 shp	1	17.3
John J. Boland	GM Electro-Motive Div. - 20-645-E7B	Diesel	2	20	7,200 bhp	1 cpp	15.0
John Sherwin	Conversion from steam to diesel begun in 2008, but suspended due to economy.						
John Spence *	GM Electro-Motive Div. 16-567-C	Diesel	2	16	3,280 bhp	2	13.8
Joseph H. Thompson Jr. *	Caterpillar	Diesel	2			1	
Joseph L. Block	GM Electro-Motive Div. - 20-645-E7	Diesel	2	20	7,200 bhp	1 cpp	17.3
Joyce L. VanEnkevort *	Caterpillar - 3612	Diesel	2	12	10,200 bhp	2 cpp	
Kaministiqua	Sulzer 4RLB76	Diesel	4	4	10,880 bhp	1cpp	15.5
Karen Andrie *	GM Electro-Motive Div. - 8-710G7C	Diesel	2	8	4,000 bhp	2	19
Kathryn Spirit	Pielstick 10PC2-V-400	Diesel	2		8,000 bhp	1 ccp	19
Katmai Bay (USCG)	Fairbanks Morse - 10-38D8-1/8	Diesel	2	10	2,500 bhp	1	13.8
Kaye E. Barker	De Laval Steam Turbine Co.	Turbine	1	**	7,700 shp	1	17.3
Lake Express **	M.T.U. - 16V4000M70	Diesel	4	16	12,616 bhp	4 water jet	40.0
Lee A. Tregurtha	Rolls-Royce Bergen B32:40L6P	Diesel	2	6	8,160 bhp	1 cpp	17.0
Mackinaw (USCG)	Caterpillar - 3612	Diesel	3	12	9,119 bhp	2 Azipod	17.3
Manistee	GM Electro-Motive Div. - 20-645-E6	Diesel	1	20	2,950 bhp	1	
Manitowoc	Alco - 16V251E	Diesel	2	16	5,600 bhp	1	16.1
Mapleglen	B&W - 6K67GF	Diesel	1	6	11,600 bhp	1	16.1
Maria Desgagnés	B&W - 6S42MC	Diesel	1	6	8,361 bhp	1 cpp	16.1
Maritime Trader	Fairbanks Morse -8-38D8-1/8	Diesel	4	8	5,332 bhp	1 cpp	16.1
Martha L. Black (CCG)	Alco - 16V251F	Diesel	3	16	8,973 bhp	2	13.8
Mary Page Hannah *	GM 12-278A	Diesel	2	12	1,850 bhp	2	
Maumee	Nordberg - FS-1312-H5C	Diesel	1	12	3,240 bhp	1	11.5
Melissa Desgagnés	Allen - 12PVBCS12-F	Diesel	2	12	4,000 bhp	1 cpp	13.8
Mesabi Miner	Pielstick - 16PC2-2V-400	Diesel	2	16	16,000 bhp	2 cpp	15.5
Michigan *	GM Electro-Motive Div. - 20-645-E6	Diesel	2	16	3,900 bhp	2	13.2
Michipicoten	MaK - 6M43C	Diesel	2	6	8,160 bhp	1 cpp	
Mississagi	Caterpillar - 3612-TA	Diesel	1	12	4,500 bhp	1 cpp	13.8
Mobile Bay (USCG)	Fairbanks Morse - 10-38D8-1/8	Diesel	2	10	2,500 bhp	1	13.8
Montrealais	Canadian General Electric Co. Ltd.	Turbine	1	**	9,900 shp	1	19.0
Neah Bay (USCG)	Fairbanks Morse - 10-38D8-1/8	Diesel	2	10	2,500 bhp	1	13.8
Nordik Express	GM Electro-Motive Div. 20-645-E7	Diesel	2	20	7,200 bhp	2 ccp	16.0
Oakglen	B&W - 6K67GF	Diesel	1	6	11,600 bhp	1	15.5
Ojibway	2005 GE 7FDM EFI	Diesel	1	16	4,100 bhp	1 cpp	
Olive L. Moore *	Alco - 16V251	Diesel	2	16	5,830 bhp	1	
Paul H. Townsend	Nordberg TSM-216	Diesel	1	6	2,150 bhp	1	12.1
Paul R. Tregurtha	MaK M43C	Diesel	2	6	16,080 bhp	2 cpp	
Pelee Islander **	Caterpillar 3408	Diesel	2	8	910 bhp	2	
Peter R. Cresswell	MaK - 6M552AK	Diesel	2	6	9,460 bhp	1 cpp	13.8
Petite Forte *	Ruston 8ATC	Diesel	2	8	4,200 bhp	2	15.5
Petrolia Desgagnés	B&W - 8K42EF	Diesel	1	8	5,000 bhp	1 cpp	16.4
Philip R. Clarke	Westinghouse Elec. Corp.	Turbine	1	**	7,700 shp	1	16.1
Pierre Radisson (CCG)	Alco - 16V251F	Diesel	6	16	17,700 bhp	2	18.4
Pineglen	MaK - 6M601AK	Diesel	1	6	8,158 bhp	1 cpp	15.5
Prentiss Brown *	GM Electro-Motive Div. 12-645-E2	Diesel	2	12	3,900 bhp	1	
Presque Isle*	Mirrlees Blackstone Ltd. - KVMR-16	Diesel	2	16	14,840 bhp	2 cpp	
Quebecois	Canadian General Electric Co. Ltd.	Turbine	1	**	9,900 shp	1	19.0

Name	Engine	Type	#	Cyl	Power	Prop	Speed
Quinte Loyalist **	Caterpillar 3196	Diesel	2	6	770 bhp		
Rebecca Lynn *	GM Electro-Motive Div. 16-567-BC	Diesel	2	16	3,600 bhp	2	
Reliance *	A.B. Nohab SVI 16VS-F	Diesel	2	16	5,600 bhp	1 cpp	17.6
Richelieu	B&W - 6K67GF	Diesel	1	6	11,600 bhp	1	15.4
Robert S. Pierson	Alco - 16V251E	Diesel	2	16	5,600 bhp	1	17.8
Roger Blough	Pielstick - 16PC2V-400	Diesel	2	16	14,200 bhp	1 cpp	16.7
Rosaire A. Desgagnés	MaK/Caterpillar - 6M43	Diesel	1	6	7,344 bhp	1 cpp	17.8
Rt. Hon. Paul J. Martin	Pielstick - 10PC2-V-400	Diesel	2	10	9,000 bhp	1 cpp	15.0
Saginaw	MaK - 6M43C	Diesel	1	6	8,160 bhp	1	
Saguenay	B&W - 6K67GF	Diesel	1	6	11,600 bhp	1	16.1
Salarium	Pielstick - 10PC2-2V-400	Diesel	2	10	10,700 bhp	1 cpp	13.8
Salvor *	GM Electro-Motive Div. - 16-645-E7	Diesel	2	16	5,750 bhp	2	13.8
Sam Laud	GM EMD - 20-645-E7	Diesel	2	20	7,200 bhp	1	16.1
Samuel de Champlain *	GM EMD - 20-645-E5	Diesel	2	20	7,200 bhp	2 cpp	17.3
Samuel Risley (CCG)	Wartsila - VASA 16V22HF	Diesel	2	16	7,590 bhp	2 cpp	17.3
Sarah Desgagnés	MaK - 7M43	Diesel	1	7	9,517 bhp	1 cpp	15.0
Sea Eagle II *	GM Electro-Motive Div. 20-645-E7	Diesel	2	20	7,200 bhp	2	13.8
Sedna Desgagnés	MaK/Caterpillar - 6M43	Diesel	1	6	7,344 bhp	1 cpp	17.8
Spruceglen	Sulzer 4RLB76	Diesel	1	4	10,880 bhp	1 cpp	13.8
St. Clair	GM Electro-Motive Div. - 20-645-E7	Diesel	3	20	10,800 bhp	1 cpp	16.7
St. Marys Challenger	Skinner Engine Co.	Uniflow	1	4	3,500 ihp	1	12.0
Ste. Claire	Toledo Ship Building Co.	Triple Exp.	1	3	1,083 ihp	1	
Stephen B. Roman		Diesel			5,996 bhp		18.4
(Center)	Fairbanks Morse - 10-38D8-1/8	Diesel	2	10	3,331 bhp		
(Wing)	Fairbanks Morse - 8-38D8-1/8	Diesel	2	8	2,665 bhp		
Stewart J. Cort	GM Electro-Motive Div. - 20-645-E7	Diesel	4	20	14,400 bhp	2 cpp	18.4
Sugar Islander II **	Caterpillar 3412	Diesel	2	12	1,280 bhp		
Susan W. Hannah *	GM Electro-Motive Div. - 12-645-E5	Diesel	2	12	4,320 bhp	2	11.5
Thalassa Desgagnés	B&W - 8K42EF	Diesel	1	8	5,000 bhp	1 cpp	16.4
Tim S. Dool	MaK model 8M43C	Diesel	1	8	10,750 bhp	1 cpp	17.3
Tony MacKay *	Ruston - 12C-5VM	Diesel	1	12	2,800 bhp	1 cpp	15.0
Umiak I	M.A.N.-B&W - 7S70ME-C	Diesel	1	7	29,598 bhp	1 cpp	16.5
Umiavut	Hanshin - 6LF58	Diesel	1	6	6,000 bhp	1 cpp	16.2
Undaunted *	GM Cleveland Diesel Div. - 12-278A	Diesel	1	12	2,400 bhp	1	11.5
Véga Desgagnés	Wartsila - 9R32	Diesel	2	9	7,560 bhp	1	16.1
Victorious *	MaK - 6M25	Diesel	2	6	5,384 bhp	2 cpp	12.1
Victory *	MaK - 6MU551AK	Diesel	2	6	7,880 bhp	2	16.1
Walter J. McCarthy Jr.	GM Electro-Motive Div. - 20-645-E7B	Diesel	4	20	14,400 bhp	2 cpp	16.1
Wilfred Sykes	Westinghouse Elec. Corp.	Turbine	1	**	7,700 shp	1	16.1
Wilf Seymour *	GM Electro-Motive Div. - 16-645-E7	Diesel	2	16	5,750 bhp	2	13.8
William J. Moore *	GM Electro-Motive Div. 16-645-E	Diesel	2	16	4,000 bhp	2 cpp	15.5
Wolfe Islander III **	Caterpillar 3412E	Diesel	4	12	2,284 bhp	2 x 2	13.8
Yankcanuck	Cooper-Bessemer Corp.	Diesel	1	8	1,860 bhp	1	11.5
Zélada Desgagnés	MaK/Caterpillar - 6M43	Diesel	1	6	7,344 bhp	1 cpp	17.8

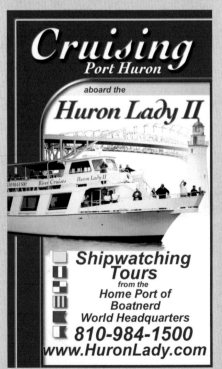
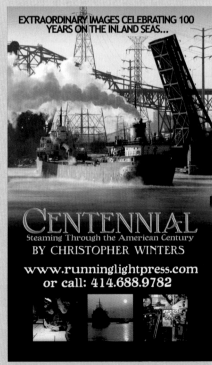

Saltwater Fleets

Island Skipper below Mission Point at Sault Ste. Marie. (Roger LeLievre)

101

PORT COLBORNE

Niagara's South Coast

The City of Port Colborne...

located on the north shore of Lake Erie, **Port Colborne** offers a thriving festival and entertainment scene that includes live theatre, white sand beaches, culinary favourites, the world class Sugarloaf Marina, fishing, golfing, recreation, and unique shopping districts along the historic Welland Canal.

Where Business and Lifestyle ARE a Perfect Match!

niagara original

1.888.PORT.FUN
PortColborne.ca

Fleet Name / Vessel Name	IMO #	Vessel Type	Year Built	Engine Type	Cargo Cap. or Gross*	Overall Length	Breadth	Depth
IA-1 **ALVARGONZALEZ NAVIGATION, GIJON, SPAIN**								
Covadonga	9300489	TK	2005	D	6,967	390' 09"	55' 05"	27' 07"
IA-2 **ALVTANK REDERI AB, DONSO, SWEDEN** *(alvtank.se)*								
Ramira	9362152	TK	2008	D	12,164	472' 07"	75' 07"	40' 08"
IA-3 **AMALTHIA MARINE INC., ATHENS, GREECE** *(www.amalmar.gr)*								
Seneca	8200486	BC	1983	D	28,788	606' 11"	75' 09"	48' 02"
(*Mangal Desai* '83-'98, *Millenium Eagle* '98-'02, *Stokmarnes* '02-'05)								
Tuscarora	8120698	BC	1983	D	28,031	639' 09"	75' 09"	46' 11"
(*Manila Spirit* '83-'86, *Rixta Oldendorff* '86-'06)								
IA-4 **ARK SHIPPING SA, PIRAEUS, GREECE**								
Polydefkis	8116984	BC	1983	D	12,334	423' 03"	65' 08"	36' 09"
(*Falknes* '83-'86, *Fitnes* '86-'88, *Falknes* '88-'93, *Uri* '93-'97, *Daisy Gren* '97-'00, *Arklow Dawn* '00-'03)								
IA-5 **ATLANTSKA PLOVIDBA D.D., DUBROVNIK, REPUBLIC OF CROATIA** *(atlant.hr)*								
FOLLOWING VESSEL UNDER CHARTER TO FEDNAV LTD.								
Orsula	9110901	BC	1996	D	34,372	656' 02"	77' 01"	48' 10"
(*Federal Calumet* {2} '96-'97)								
IB-1 **BELUGA SHIPPING GMBH, BREMEN, GERMANY** *(beluga-group.com)*								
BBC Ecuador	9222352	GC	2001	D	6,404	398' 11"	59' 09"	27' 07"
(*Beluga Satisfaction* '01-'02)								
BBC Rhine	9368338	GC	2008	D	17,323	469' 02"	70' 06"	43' 08"
(*Launched as Beluga Gratification*)								
BBC Rio Grande	9368326	GC	2008	D	17,323	469' 02"	70' 06"	43' 08"
Beluga Constellation	9273806	GC	2006	D	12,476	524' 01"	70' 06"	30' 06"
Beluga Constitution	9273791	GC	2006	D	12,477	514' 04"	70' 06"	36' 06"
Beluga Efficiency	9283954	GC	2004	D	12,806	452' 09"	68' 11"	36' 01"
(*Beluga Efficiency* '04-'06, *BBC Carolina* '06-'07)								
Beluga Elegance	9260378	GC	2004	D	12,828	452' 09"	68' 11"	36' 01"
Beluga Endeavour	9261073	GC	2004	D	12,828	452' 09"	68' 11"	36' 01"
Beluga Endurance	9312169	GC	2005	D	12,782	452' 09"	68' 11"	36' 01"
Beluga Energy	9261085	GC	2005	D	12,828	452' 09"	68' 11"	36' 01"
Beluga Expectation	9357999	GC	2005	D	12,744	452' 11"	70' 01"	36' 01"
Beluga Faculty	9443669	GC	2009	D	12,700	453' 00"	68' 11"	36' 01"
Beluga Fairy	9466996	GC	2009	D	12,700	453' 00"	68' 11"	36' 01"
Beluga Family	9381392	GC	2007	D	12,744	452' 11"	68' 11"	36' 01"
Beluga Fanfare	9388895	GC	2007	D	11,526	452' 11"	70' 01"	36' 01"
Beluga Fascination	9358022	GC	2007	D	11,526	452' 11"	70' 01"	36' 01"
Beluga Favourisation	9363546	GC	2007	D	12,744	452' 11"	68' 11"	36' 01"
Beluga Federation	9349289	GC	2006	D	11,380	452' 11"	70' 01"	36' 01"
Beluga Festival	9468097	GC	2010	D	12,744	452' 11"	68' 11"	36' 01"
(*Beluga Motion* '09-'10)								
Beluga Fidelity	9435753	GC	2007	D	12,744	452' 11"	68' 11"	36' 01"
Beluga Fighter	9388883	GC	2007	D	12,782	453' 00"	68' 11"	36' 01"
Beluga Flirtation	9358034	GC	2007	D	12,782	426' 06"	70' 01"	36' 01"
Beluga Formation	9384320	GC	2007	D	11,526	453' 00"	68' 11"	36' 01"
Beluga Fraternity	9402055	GC	2008	D	12,700	453' 00"	68' 11"	36' 01"
Beluga Frequency	9437309	GC	2007	D	12,782	452' 11"	70' 01"	36' 01"
Beluga Fusion	9358046	GC	2000	D	11,380	452' 11"	70' 01"	36' 01"
Beluga Legislation	9367073	GC	2007	D	12,000	469' 00"	62' 00"	35' 11"
(*Morgenstond II* '07-'07, *Beluga Legislation* '07-'09, *Kent Legislation* '09-'09)								

EDITOR'S NOTE: Observers will likely spot saltwater vessels not included in this book. These may be newcomers to the Great Lakes/Seaway system, recent renames or new construction. This is not meant to be an exhaustive listing of every saltwater vessel that could potentially visit the Great Lakes and St. Lawrence Seaway. To attempt to do so, given the sheer number of world merchant ships, would be space and cost prohibitive.

This list reflects vessels whose primary trade routes are on saltwater but which also regularly visit Great Lakes and St. Lawrence Seaway ports (only vessels calling into the Seaway system above the port of Montreal are listed). Fleets listed may operate other vessels worldwide than those included herein; additional vessels may be found on fleet Web sites, which have been included where available. Former names listed in boldface type indicate the vessel visited the Seaway system under that name.

Fleet Name Vessel Name	IMO #	Vessel Type	Year Built	Engine Type	Cargo Cap. or Gross*	Overall Length	Breadth	Depth
Beluga Recognition	9277280	GC	2005	D	11,380	452' 11"	70' 01"	36' 01"
Beluga Resolution	9267754	GC	2005	D	10,536	439' 04"	70' 06"	30' 06"
Beluga Revolution	9267742	GC	2005	D	10,536	439' 04"	70' 06"	30' 06"
SE Verdant	9187033	GC	2000	D	17,538	465' 10"	70' 06"	43' 08"

(Margaretha Green '00-'00, Coral Green '00-'01, Nirint Voyager '01-'02, Margaretha Green '02-'04, Newpac Cumulus '04-'05, Margaretha Green '05-'10)

SE Verdigris	9164029	GC	1999	D	17,538	465' 10"	70' 06"	43' 08"

(Marion Green '99-'10)

SE Viridian	9164017	GC	1998	D	17,538	465' 10"	70' 06"	43' 08"

(Maria Green '98-'04, BBC India '04-'08, Maria Green '08-'10)

IB-2 BERNHARD SCHULTE GROUP OF COMPANIES, HAMBURG, GERMANY (beschulte.de)

Kristina Theresa	9321641	TK	2006	D	12,972	417' 04"	66' 11"	37' 09"

(Songa Emerald '06-'06)

IB-3 BIGLIFT SHIPPING BV, ROOSENDAAL, NETHERLANDS (www.bigliftshipping.com)

Enchanter	9148116	HL	1998	D	12,950	452' 11"	74' 10"	42' 06"

(Sailor Jupiter '98-'98)

Happy Ranger	9139311	HL	1998	D	15,065	454' 01"	74' 10"	42' 04"
Happy Rover	9139309	HL	1997	D	15,700	452' 11"	74' 10"	42' 06"
Tracer	9204702	HL	2000	D	8,874	329' 09"	73' 06"	26' 11"
Tramper	9204697	HL	2000	D	8,874	329' 09"	73' 06"	26' 11"
Transporter	9204714	HL	1999	D	8,469	329' 09"	80' 01"	36' 05"
Traveller	9204726	HL	2000	D	8,874	329' 09"	73' 06"	26' 11"

IB-4 BLOUNT SMALL SHIP ADVENTURES, WARREN, RHODE ISLAND, USA (blountsmallshipadventures.com)

Grande Caribe	8978631	PA	1997	D	97*	182' 07"	39' 01"	9' 10"
Grande Mariner	8978643	PA	1998	D	97*	182' 07"	39' 01"	9' 10"
Niagara Prince	8978629	PA	1994	D	99*	174' 00"	40' 00"	9' 00"

IB-5 BLYSTAD TANKERS INC., OSLO, NORWAY (blystad.no)
   FOLLOWING VESSELS UNDER CHARTER TO SONGA SHIPMANAGEMENT

Songa Crystal	9378321	TK	2006	D	12,956	417' 04"	67' 00"	37' 09"
Songa Diamond	9460459	TK	2009	D	17,596	472' 05"	74' 02"	41' 00"
Songa Emerald	9473937	TK	2009	D	17,596	472' 05"	74' 02"	41' 00"
Songa Jade	9473925	TK	2009	D	17,596	472' 05"	74' 02"	41' 00"
Songa Opal	9473913	TK	2009	D	17,596	472' 05"	74' 02"	41' 00"
Songa Pearl	9444455	TK	2008	D	17,596	472' 05"	74' 02"	41' 00"
Songa Ruby	9444479	TK	2008	D	17,596	472' 05"	74' 02"	41' 00"
Songa Sapphire	9444467	TK	2008	D	17,596	472' 05"	74' 02"	41' 00"
Songa Topaz	9460461	TK	2009	D	17,596	472' 05"	74' 02"	41' 00"

IB-6 BOOMSMA SHIPPING BV, SNEEK, NETHERLANDS (boomsmashipping.nl)

Frisian Spring	9367774	GC	2006	D	5,023	390' 01"	44' 00"	29' 10"

Built: Port Weller Drydocks, Port Weller, ON

IB-7 BRIESE SCHIFFAHRTS GMBH & CO. KG, LEER, GERMANY (briese.de)

BBC Amazon	9303302	GC	2007	D	17,348	469' 07"	75' 11"	42' 08"
BBC Asia	9266310	GC	2003	D	7,530	393' 00"	66' 03"	32' 02"

(Embse '03-'03)

BBC Atlantic	9352743	GC	2005	D	6,192	378' 11"	54' 02"	26' 01"

(Westerriede '05-'05)

BBC Elbe	9347059	GC	2006	D	17,348	469' 07"	75' 11"	42' 08"

(Horumersiel '06-'06)

BBC Ems	9347035	GC	2006	D	17,348	469' 07"	75' 11"	42' 08"
BBC Europe	9266308	GC	2003	D	7,409	391' 09"	66' 03"	32' 02"
BBC France	9197416	GC	2005	D	4,309	324' 06"	45' 03"	24' 03"
BBC Greenland	9427079	GC	2007	D	7,530	393' 00"	66' 03"	32' 02"
BBC Jade	9421116	GC	2007	D	12,000	469' 00"	62' 00"	35' 11"
BBC Mississippi	9347061	GC	2006	D	17,348	469' 07"	75' 11"	42' 08"

(Greetsiel '06-'07)

BBC Scandinavia	9362633	GC	2007	D	7,530	393' 00"	66' 03"	32' 02"

(Rysum '07-'07)

BBC Shanghai	9224623	GC	2001	D	4,820	330' 01"	54' 06"	26' 07"

(Baltic Sea '01-'01, BBC Shanghai '01-'03, TLI Aquila '03-'03)

BBC Sweden	9278600	GC	2003	D	4,325	324' 06"	45' 03"	24' 03"

Merweborg in the St. Lawrence Seaway, summer 2010. (Ronald Dole Jr.)

Fleet Name Vessel Name	IMO #	Vessel Type	Year Built	Engine Type	Cargo Cap. or Gross*	Overall Length	Breadth	Depth
BBC Volga	9436329	GC	2009	D	17,300	469' 07"	74' 10"	43' 08"
(Ocean Breeze '09-'09)								
Kurt Paul	9435856	GC	2009	D	17,300	469' 07"	74' 10"	43' 08"
Santiago	9145114	GC	1997	D	3,525	280' 10"	42' 00"	23' 04"
Sjard	9303314	GC	2007	D	17,348	469' 07"	75' 11"	42' 08"
Skaftafell	9137741	GC	1997	D	4,820	330' 01"	54' 06"	26' 07"
*(Launched as Torum, Industrial Harmony '97-'00, **BBC Brazil** '00-'03, Brake '03-'03, BBC Brazil '04-'04)*								

IB-8 BROSTROM AB, GOTEBORG, SWEDEN (brostrom.se)

Bro Alma	9356610	TK	2008	D	17,000	472' 05"	75' 06"	40' 08"
(Ganstar '07-'08)								

IC-1 CANADA FEEDER LINES BV, GRONIGEN, NETHERLANDS (canadafeederlines.eu)

CFL Patron	9376464	GC	2008	D	6,500	388' 05"	43' 10"	29' 10"
CFL Penhar	9534365	GC	2010	D	6,500	388' 05"	43' 10"	29' 10"
CFL Perfect	9371854	GC	2009	D	6,500	388' 05"	43' 10"	29' 10"
CFL Performer	9376452	GC	2007	D	6,500	388' 05"	43' 10"	29' 10"
CFL Progress	9371828	GC	2009	D	6,500	388' 05"	43' 10"	29' 10"
CFL Promise	9371816	GC	2008	D	6,500	388' 05"	43' 10"	29' 10"
CFL Prospect	9376440	GC	2007	D	6,500	388' 05"	43' 10"	29' 10"
CFL Proud	9386433	GC	2009	D	6,500	388' 05"	43' 10"	29' 10"
CFL Prudence	9398046	GC	2008	D	6,500	388' 05"	43' 10"	29' 10"

IC-2 CALLITSIS SHIP MANAGEMENT SA, PIRAEUS, GREECE

Athanasios G. Callitsis	8101953	BC	1983	D	17,494	647' 08"	75' 09"	46' 11"
*(**Punica** '83-'96, **Pintail** '96-'07)*								

IC-3 CANADIAN FOREST NAVIGATION CO. LTD., MONTREAL, QUEBEC, CANADA (canfornav.com)

At press time, Canadian Forest Navigation Co. Ltd. had the following vessels under long-or short-term charter. Please consult their respective fleets for details: Andean, Apollon, Barnacle, Blacky, Bluebill, Brant, Bluewing, Calliroe Patronicola, Chestnut, Cinnamon, Eider, Gadwall, Garganey, Greenwing, Maccoa, Mandarin, Mottler, Olympic Melody, Olympic Mentor, Olympic Merit, Olympic Miracle, Pochard, Puffin, Redhead, Ruddy, Tufty, Whistler, Wigeon.

IC-4 CANDLER SCHIFFAHRT GMBH, BREMEN, GERMANY (candler-schiffahrt.de)

Alert	9177789	GC	1999	D	12,947	420' 01"	69' 07"	37' 01"
Glory	9378254	GC	2005	D	7,378	381' 04"	59' 01"	34' 01"
(FCC Glory '05-'06)								

Heavy-lift vessel Happy Rover. (Paul Beesley)

C

Fleet Name Vessel Name	IMO #	Vessel Type	Year Built	Engine Type	Cargo Cap. or Gross*	Overall Length	Breadth	Depth
IC-5	**CARISBROOKE SHIPPING, COWES, ISLE OF WIGHT, UNITED KINGDOM** *(carisbrookeshipping.net)*							
Vanessa-C	9267297	BC	2003	D	10,500	477' 09"	60' 03"	33' 10"
IC-6	**CHEMFLEET SHIPPING LTD., ISTANBUL, TURKEY** *(chemfleet.org)*							
Basat	9447029	TK	2008	D	10,744	432' 07"	62' 00"	33' 06"
Hulin	9447043	TK	2008	D	10,744	432' 07"	62' 00"	33' 06"
Manas	9447055	TK	2008	D	10,744	432' 07"	62' 00"	33' 06"
Sakarya	9425356	TK	2007	D	11,258	426' 06"	65' 00"	34' 01"
(Sakarya-D '07-'08)								
Zeynep A	9424223	TK	2007	D	10,500	425' 08"	64' 04"	34' 01"
IC-7	**CHEMIKALIEN SEETRANSPORT GMBH, HAMBURG, GERMANY** *(chemikalien-seetransport.de)*							
Chemtrans Alster	9439319	TK	2010	D	13,073	421' 11"	66' 11"	37' 09"
Chemtrans Elbe	9439345	TK	2008	D	13,073	421' 11"	66' 11"	37' 09"
Chemtrans Havel	9439333	TK	2009	D	13,073	421' 11"	66' 11"	37' 09"
Chemtrans Weser	9439307	TK	2009	D	13,073	421' 11"	66' 11"	37' 09"
IC-8	**CLIPPER GROUP AS, COPENHAGEN, DENMARK** *(clipper-group.com)*							
Clipper Aya	9521423	TK	2008	D	14,246	440' 02"	67' 03"	38' 01"
Clipper Golfito	9330408	TK	2006	D	14,227	440' 02"	67' 03"	38' 01"
Clipper Karen	9323003	TK	2006	D	11,259	382' 03"	65' 07"	38' 05"
Clipper Katja	9340922	TK	2006	D	11,255	382' 03"	65' 09"	37' 05"
Clipper Kira	9337286	TK	2007	D	11,259	382' 03"	66' 07"	38' 05"
Clipper Klara	9340910	TK	2004	D	11,259	382' 03"	66' 07"	38' 05"
Clipper Kristin	9322982	TK	2006	D	11,259	382' 03"	65' 07"	38' 05"
Clipper Krystal	9330020	TK	2006	D	11,259	382' 03"	65' 07"	38' 05"
Clipper Kylie	9337298	TK	2007	D	11,259	382' 03"	65' 07"	38' 05"
Clipper Lancer	9363182	TK	2006	D	10,098	388' 04"	62' 04"	33' 02"
Clipper Leader	9286451	TK	2004	D	10,098	388' 04"	62' 04"	33' 02"
(Panam Trinity '04-'06)								
Clipper Leander	9334430	TK	2006	D	10,098	388' 04"	62' 04"	33' 02"
Clipper Legacy	9307437	TK	2005	D	10,098	388' 04"	62' 04"	33' 02"
Clipper Legend	9305403	TK	2004	D	10,098	388' 04"	62' 04"	33' 02"
Clipper Loyalty	9373929	TK	2007	D	10,098	388' 04"	62' 04"	33' 02"
Clipper Mari	9422677	TK	2009	D	19,822	481' 00"	77' 10"	42' 08"
Clipper Oceanica	9317262	TK	2005	D	12,099	406' 10"	65' 07"	36' 09"
(Panam Oceanica '05-'07)								
Clipper Tobago	9209001	TK	1999	D	8,834	367' 05"	61' 08"	31' 08"
(Botany Treasure '99-'06)								
Clipper Trinidad	9191230	TK	1998	D	5,483	370' 09"	61' 08"	31' 08"
(Botany Trust '98-'06)								
Clipper Trojan	9140451	TK	1996	D	15,313	452' 09"	71' 06"	39' 08"
*(**Botany Trojan** '96-'98, **Stolt Trojan** '98-'04, **Botany Trojan** '04-'06)*								
Harbour Clear	9230012	TK	2001	D	16,875	453' 01"	75' 06"	40' 02"
(Jo Chiara D '01-'04, Chiara '04-'06, Nora '06-'09)								
Harbour Cloud	9291066	TK	2004	D	16,875	453' 01"	75' 06"	40' 02"
(Fase D '04-'04, Fase '04-'09)								
Maemi	9416044	TK	2008	D	19,822	481' 00"	77' 10"	42' 08"
(Braken '10-'10)								
Panam Atlantico	9248203	TK	2001	D	14,003	439' 08"	67' 03"	38' 01"

At press time, Clipper Group AS also had the following vessels under charter. Please consult their respective fleets for details: Eships Eagle, Magdalena Green, Marinus Green, Marion Green, Marissa Green, Marlene Green, Sloman Server.

IC-9	**COASTAL SHIPPING LTD., GOOSE BAY, NEWFOUNDLAND, CANADA** *(woodwards.nf.ca)*							
Dorsch	8007195	TK	1980	D	10,557	426' 06"	60' 08"	34' 09"
(Dorsch '81-'90, Miro '90-'98, Tellus '98-'05)								
Nanny	9051399	TK	1993	D	9,176	382' 06"	62' 04"	33' 02"
(Nathalie Sif '93-'99)								
Sibyl W.	7310521	TK	1973	D	752	170' 07"	33' 09"	15' 00"
Tuvaq	7421966	TK	1977	D	15,955	539' 08"	72' 10"	39' 04"
(Tiira '77-'02)								
IC-10	**COMMERCIAL FLEET OF DONBASS LLC, DONETSK, UKRAINE** *(www.cfd.com.ua)*							
Dobrush	8101939	BC	1982	D	28,136	644' 08"	75' 09"	46' 11"
*(**World Goodwill** '82-'85)*								

	Fleet Name Vessel Name	IMO #	Vessel Type	Year Built	Engine Type	Cargo Cap. or Gross*	Overall Length	Breadth	Depth
	Makeevka	8101927	BC	1982	D	28,136	644' 08"	75' 09"	46' 11"
	*(**World Shanghai** '82-'85)*								

IC-11 CRYSTAL POOL GROUP, HELSINKI, FINLAND *(www.crystal.fi)*

	Crystal Diamond	9327059	TK	2006	D	11,340	414' 00"	62' 04"	35' 01"
	Crystal Topaz	9327047	TK	2006	D	11,340	414' 00"	62' 04"	35' 01"

IC-12 CSL GROUP INC., MONTREAL, QUEBEC, CANADA *(csl.ca)*
    MARBULK SHIPPING INC. – MANAGED BY CSL INTERNATIONAL INC. *(cslint.com)*
    PARTNERSHIP BETWEEN CSL INTERNATIONAL INC. AND ALGOMA CENTRAL CORP.

	Ambassador	8016653	SU	1983	D	37,448	730' 00"	75' 10"	50' 00"
	*Built: Port Weller Drydocks, Port Weller, ON (**Canadian Ambassador** '83-'85, **Ambassador** '85-'00,*								
	***Algosea** {2} '00-'00)*								
	Pioneer	7925613	SU	1981	D	37,448	730' 00"	75' 10"	50' 00"
	*Built: Port Weller Drydocks, Port Weller, ON (**Canadian Pioneer** '81-'86)*								

ID-1 DE POLI TANKERS BV, SPIJKENISSE, NETHERLANDS *(www.depoli-tankers.nl)*

	Alessandro DP	9384162	TK	2007	D	17,096	453' 01"	75' 06"	40' 02"
	Giovanni DP	9261516	TK	2003	D	16,875	453' 01"	75' 06"	40' 02"
	Laguna D	9192375	TK	2000	D	15,200	446' 02"	75' 06"	40' 02"
	(Jo Laguna D '00-'05)								
	Miro D	9243382	TK	2002	D	16,875	453' 01"	75' 06"	40' 02"

ID-2 DOUN KISEN CO. LTD., OCHI EHIME PREFECTURE, JAPAN

	Bright Laker	9228265	BC	2001	D	30,778	606' 11"	77' 05"	48' 11"

IE-1 EITZEN CHEMICAL ASA, OSLO, NORWAY *(eitzen-chemical.com)*

	North Fighter	9352597	TK	2006	D	19,822	481' 00"	77' 09"	42' 08"
	Sichem Beijing	9397042	TK	2007	D	13,073	421' 11"	66' 11"	37' 09"
	Sichem Challenge	9196448	TK	1998	D	17,485	382' 06"	62' 04"	33' 02"
	*(Queen of Montreaux '98-'99, **North Challenge** '99-'06, Songa Challenge '06-'07)*								
	Sichem Defiance	9244374	TK	2001	D	17,369	442' 11"	74' 10"	41' 00"
	*(**North Defiance** '01-'06, **Songa Defiance** '06-'07)*								
	Sichem Manila	9322097	TK	2007	D	13,125	421' 11"	67' 00"	37' 09"
	Sichem Melbourne	9376921	TK	2007	D	12,936	417' 04"	67' 00"	37' 09"
	Sichem Mumbai	9322085	TK	2006	D	13,141	421' 11"	66' 11"	37' 09"
	Sichem New York	9337834	TK	2007	D	12,956	417' 04"	67' 00"	37' 09"
	Sichem Onomichi	9361471	TK	2005	D	13,091	421' 11"	66' 11"	37' 09"
	Sichem Padua	9050400	TK	1993	D	9,214	382' 06"	62' 04"	33' 02"
	(Anne Sif '93-'01, Sichem Anne '01-'02)								
	Sichem Palace	9304318	TK	2004	D	8,807	367' 05"	62' 04"	32' 10"
	Sichem Paris	9404895	TK	2008	D	13,073	421' 11"	66' 11"	37' 09"
	Sichem Peace	9311268	TK	2005	D	8,807	367' 05"	62' 04"	32' 10"
	Sichem Singapore	9322061	TK	2006	D	13,141	421' 11"	66' 11"	37' 09"

IE-2 EMIRATES SHIP INVESTMENT CO. LLC, ABU DHABI, UNITED ARAB EMIRATES *(eships.ae)*

	Eships Eagle	9353905	TK	2007	D	13,147	418' 06"	67' 00"	38' 05"

IE-3 ENERGY SHIPPING SPA, GENOA, ITALY *(energycoal.com)*

	Sunflower E	9549669	GC	2009	D	13,000	393' 08"	72' 02"	36' 01"

IE-4 ENZIAN SHIPPING AG, BERNE, SWITZERLAND *(www.enzian-shipping.com)*

	Celine	9214185	BC	2001	D	8,600	423' 03"	52' 00"	32' 00"
	Sabina	9205718	BC	2000	D	9,231	416' 08"	52' 00"	32' 00"
	SCL Bern	9304461	BC	2005	D	12,680	459' 03"	70' 06"	38' 03"
	(SCL Bern '05-'05, SITC Bern '05-'06)								

IF-1 FAIRFIELD CHEMICAL CARRIERS, WILTON, CONNECTICUT, USA *(fairfieldchemical.com)*

	Fairchem Colt	9304344	TK	2005	D	19,998	477' 04"	77' 10"	43' 10"

IF-2 FAR-EASTERN SHIPPING CO. (FESCO), VLADIVOSTOK, RUSSIA *(fesco.ru)*

	Grigoriy Aleksandrov	8610215	BC	1986	D	24,105	605' 08"	75' 02"	46' 07"
	Khudozhnik Kraynev	8521012	BC	1986	D	24,105	605' 08"	75' 02"	46' 07"

IF-3 FEDNAV LTD., MONTREAL, QUEBEC, CANADA *(fednav.com)*
    FEDNAV INTERNATIONAL LTD. - DIVISION OF FEDNAV LTD.

	Federal Agno	8316522	BC	1985	D	29,643	599' 09"	76' 00"	48' 07"
	*(**Federal Asahi** {1} '85-'89)*								
	Federal Asahi {2}	9200419	BC	2000	D	36,563	656' 02"	77' 11"	48' 09"

BBC Mississippi upbound with windmill parts. (Dave Michelson)

Sunflower E in the Welland Canal. (John C. Knecht, right)

Ramira, headed into the Great Lakes. (Paul Beesely)

Sidsel Knutsen, aground off St. Clair, Mich., in August 2010, drew plenty of curious onlookers. (Roger LeLievre)

Fleet Name Vessel Name	IMO #	Vessel Type	Year Built	Engine Type	Cargo Cap. or Gross*	Overall Length	Breadth	Depth
Federal Hudson {3}	9205902	BC	2000	D	36,563	656' 02"	77' 11"	48' 09"
Federal Hunter {2}	9205938	BC	2001	D	36,563	656' 02"	77' 11"	48' 09"
Federal Kivalina	9205885	BC	2000	D	36,563	656' 02"	77' 11"	48' 09"
Federal Kumano	9244257	BC	2001	D	32,787	624' 08"	77' 05"	49' 10"
Federal Kushiro	9284702	BC	2003	D	32,787	624' 08"	77' 05"	49' 10"
Federal Maas {2}	9118135	BC	1997	D	34,372	656' 02"	77' 01"	48' 10"
Federal Mackinac	9299460	BC	2004	D	27,000	606' 11"	77' 09"	46' 25"
Federal Margaree	9299472	BC	2005	D	27,000	606' 11"	77' 09"	46' 25"
Federal Nakagawa	9278791	BC	2005	D	36,563	656' 02"	77' 11"	48' 09"
Federal Oshima	9200330	BC	1999	D	36,563	656' 02"	77' 11"	48' 09"
Federal Progress	8806864	BC	1989	D	38,130	580' 07"	86' 07"	48' 08"
(Northern Progress '89-'02)								
Federal Rhine {2}	9110925	BC	1997	D	34,372	656' 02"	77' 01"	48' 10"
Federal Rideau	9200445	BC	2000	D	36,563	656' 02"	77' 11"	48' 09"
Federal Saguenay {2}	9110913	BC	1996	D	34,372	656' 02"	77' 01"	48' 10"
Federal Schelde {3}	9118147	BC	1997	D	34,372	656' 02"	77' 01"	48' 10"
Federal Seto	9267209	BC	2004	D	36,563	656' 02"	77' 11"	48' 09"
Federal St. Laurent {3}	9110896	BC	1996	D	34,372	656' 02"	77' 01"	48' 10"
Federal Venture	8806852	BC	1989	D	38,130	580' 07"	86' 07"	48' 08"
(Northern Venture '89-'02)								
Federal Welland	9205926	BC	2000	D	36,563	656' 02"	77' 11"	48' 09"
Federal Yukon	9205897	BC	2000	D	36,563	656' 02"	77' 11"	48' 09"

At press time, FedNav Ltd. also had the following vessels under charter. Please consult their respective fleets for details: Federal Danube, Federal Elbe, Federal Ems, Federal Fuji, Federal Kumano, Federal Kushiro, Federal Leda, Federal Manitou, Federal Matane, Federal Mattawa, Federal Miramichi, Federal Patroller, Federal Pioneer, Federal Power, Federal Polaris, Federal Seto, Federal Shimanto, Federal Weser, Federal Yoshino, Inviken, Orsula, Spar Garnet, Spar Jade, Utviken.

IF-4 **FINBETA, SAVONA, ITALY** *(www.finbeta.com)*

Acquamarina	9268631	TK	2004	D	12,004	447' 10"	66' 11"	33' 10"
Turchese	9220354	TK	1999	D	12,004	447' 10"	66' 11"	33' 10"
Zircone	9010929	TK	1993	D	8,000	409' 08"	56' 06"	29' 06"

IF-5 **FISSER & V. DOORNUM KG GMBH & CO., HAMBURG, GERMANY** *(fissership.com)*

Okapi	7129336	BC	1972	D	6,364	332' 10"	52' 07"	30' 03"
(Imela Fisser '72-'75, Boca Tabla '75-'82, Tabla '82-'86)								
Pyrgos	7203895	BC	1972	D	6,364	332' 10"	52' 07"	30' 03"
(Elisabeth Fisser '72-'79, Villiers '79-'86)								

IF-6 **FLINTER SHIPPING BV, BARENDRECHT, THE NETHERLANDS** *(flinter.nl)*

Citadel	9361380	GC	2008	D	4,500	363' 05"	45' 11"	24' 07"
Flinter Arctic	9504126	GC	2010	D	11,000	434' 08"	52' 01"	35' 04"
Flinterduin	9213882	GC	2000	D	6,359	364' 01"	49' 02"	26' 09"
Flintereems	9180865	GC	2000	D	6,200	366' 07"	48' 08"	26' 09"
Flinterland	9352339	GC	2007	D	7,705	393' 08"	49' 10"	27' 11"
Flintermaas	9180877	GC	2000	D	6,200	366' 05"	48' 10"	26' 10"
Flintermar	9327322	GC	2006	D	7,750	393' 00"	50' 07"	27' 11"
(Flintermar '06-'06, UAL Malabo '06-'09)								
Flinterrebecca	9361108	GC	2008	D	5,756	324' 02"	45' 11"	27' 11"
Flinterspirit	9229049	GC	2001	D	6,358	366' 07"	48' 08"	26' 09"
Flinterstream	9415040	GC	2009	D	6,577	424' 06"	55' 09"	32' 10"
Zeus	9190212	GC	2000	D	9,150	427' 01"	52' 01"	33' 06"

IF-7 **FRANCO COMPANIA NAVIERA SA, ATHENS, GREECE** *(franco.gr)*

Antikeri	8200503	BC	1984	D	28,788	606' 11"	75' 09"	48' 02"
*(**LT Argosy** '84-'98, **Millenium Hawk** '98-'02, **Cashin** '02-'05)*								
Barbro	8307686	BC	1984	D	29,692	599' 09"	75' 09"	48' 07"
*(**Olympic Dignity** '84-'92, **Alam Sejahtera** '92-'07)*								
Stefania I	8406925	BC	1985	D	28,269	584' 08"	75' 11"	48' 05"
*(**Astral Ocean** '85-'95, Sea Crystal '95-'97, Stefania '97-'98)*								

IF-8 **FRANK DAHL SHIPPING, CUXHAVEN, GERMANY** *(dahl-shipping.com)*
FOLLOWING VESSELS UNDER CHARTER TO WAGENBORG SHIPPING

Finex	9250397	GC	2001	D	9,857	433' 10"	52' 01"	31' 08"
*(**Volmeborg** '01-'06)*								

	Fleet Name Vessel Name	IMO #	Vessel Type	Year Built	Engine Type	Cargo Cap. or Gross*	Overall Length	Breadth	Depth
	Veerseborg	9184653	GC	1998	D	8,664	433' 10"	52' 01"	31' 08"
	(Veerseborg '98-'04, Matfen '04-'07)								
	Vossborg	9229116	GC	2000	D	8,737	433' 10"	52' 01"	31' 08"
	(Vossborg '01-'04, Morpeth '04-'07)								
IF-9	**FREESE SHIPPING, STADE, GERMANY** *(freeseship.com)*								
	Pacific Huron	9546796	GC	2010	D	30,000	623' 04"	77' 11"	47' 11"
	(Seven Islands '10-'10)								
	Three Rivers	9546796	GC	2010	D	30,000	623' 04"	77' 11"	47' 11"
IF-10	**FUKUJIN KISEN CO. LTD., OCHI EHIME PREFECTURE, JAPAN** *(fukujin-kisen.com)*								
	FOLLOWING VESSELS UNDER CHARTER TO FEDNAV LTD.								
	Federal Shimanto	9218404	BC	2001	D	32,787	624' 08"	77' 05"	49' 10"
	Federal Yoshino	9218416	BC	2001	D	32,787	624' 08"	77' 05"	49' 10"
IG-1	**GOLDEX FORTUNE LTD., MONROVIA, LIBERIA**								
	Asphodel	8316467	BC	1984	D	28,303	580' 08"	75' 09"	47' 07"
	(Vamand Wave '84-'07, Yamaska '07-'09)								
IG-2	**GREAT LAKES FEEDER LINES ULC, BURLINGTON, ONTARIO, CANADA** *(glfl.ca)*								
	Arctic Sea	8912792	BC	1991	D	3,988	320' 10"	56' 10"	23' 00"
	(Okhotskoe '91-'96, Zim Venezuela '96-'98 , Alari '98-'98 , Torm Senegal '98-'00 , Jogaila '00-'05)								
	Dutch Runner	8712075	RR	1988	D	3,056	275' 07"	52' 06"	20' 11"
	(North King '88-'88, Dutch Runner '88-'00, P&O Nedlloyd Douala '00-'02)								
IH-1	**HAPAG-LLOYD GMBH, HAMBURG, GERMANY** *(greatlakescruising.com/columbus)*								
	C. Columbus	9138329	PA	1997	D	14,903*	475' 09"	70' 06"	43' 06"
IH-2	**HARREN & PARTNER SCHIFFAHRTS GMBH, BREMEN, GERMANY** *(harren-partner.de)*								
	FOLLOWING VESSELS UNDER CHARTER TO COMBI LIFT								
	Palabora	9501875	HL	2010	D	10,052	436' 04"	75' 06"	37' 05"
	Palau	9501899	HL	2010	D	10,052	436' 04"	75' 06"	37' 05"
	Palembang	9501887	HL	2010	D	10,052	436' 04"	75' 06"	37' 05"
	Palmerton	9501863	HL	2009	D	10,052	436' 04"	75' 06"	37' 05"
	Panagia	9305295	HL	2004	D	7,846	393' 04"	66' 03"	32' 02"
	Pangani	9318943	HL	2004	D	7,846	393' 00"	66' 03"	32' 02"
	FOLLOWING VESSELS UNDER CHARTER TO CANADIAN FOREST NAVIGATION LTD.								
	Pochard	9262534	BC	2003	D	37,384	655' 10"	77' 09"	50' 02"
	Puffin	9262522	BC	2003	D	37,384	655' 10"	77' 09"	50' 02"
IH-3	**HARTMANN REEDEREI, LEER, GERMANY** *(hartmann-reederei.de)*								
	OSC Vlistdiep	9414187	GC	2007	D	7,800	388' 11"	49' 10"	27' 09"
IH-4	**HELIKON SHIPPING ENTERPRISES LTD., LONDON, UNITED KINGDOM**								
	Elikon	8001799	BC	1980	D	16,106	582' 00"	75' 02"	44' 04"
	(Bailey '80-'89)								
IH-5	**HELLAS MARINE SERVICES LTD., PIRAEUS, GREECE** *(hellasmarine.gr)*								
	Sir Henry	9151383	BC	1996	D	18,315	486' 03"	74' 10"	40' 00"
	(Rubin Lark '96-'05)								
	Sir Walter	9109550	BC	1996	D	18,315	486' 03"	74' 10"	40' 00"
	(Rubin Stork '96-'03)								
IH-6	**HERNING SHIPPING AS, HERNING, DENMARK** *(herning-shipping.dk)*								
	Jette Theresa	9406582	TK	2009	D	11,000	424' 10"	63' 00"	27' 11"
IH-7	**HERMANN BUSS GMBH, LEER, GERMANY** *(bussgruppe.de)*								
	Bornholm	9358278	BC	2006	D	7,869	388' 11"	49' 10"	27' 11"
IH-8	**HOLLAND SHIP SERVICE, THE NETHERLANDS**								
	FOLLOWING VESSELS UNDER CHARTER TO CLIPPER PROJECTS AS								
	Magdalena Green	9232462	BC	2001	D	17,538	465' 10"	70' 06"	43' 10"
	Marinus Green	9208198	BC	2000	D	17,538	465' 10"	70' 06"	43' 08"
	Marissa Green	9208203	BC	2001	D	17,538	465' 10"	70' 06"	43' 08"
	Marlene Green	9247405	BC	2001	D	17,538	465' 10"	70' 06"	43' 08"
	Sloman Server	9187045	BC	1999	D	17,538	465' 10"	70' 06"	43' 08"
	(Makiri Green '99-'10)								

Fleet Name Vessel Name	IMO #	Vessel Type	Year Built	Engine Type	Cargo Cap. or Gross*	Overall Length	Breadth	Depth
II-1 **INTERSEE SCHIFFAHRTS-GESELLSCHAFT MBH & CO., HAREN-EMS, GERMANY** *(intersee.de)*								
Aachen	9312676	GC	2004	D	5,726	348' 02"	47' 03"	26' 07"
(Lea '04-'04)								
Alexia	9369083	GC	2008	D	11,211	477' 09"	60' 03"	33' 10"
Amalia	9312717	GC	2006	D	5,726	348' 02"	47' 03"	26' 07"
(Francesca '04-'06)								
Amanda	9312688	GC	2005	D	5,726	348' 02"	47' 03"	26' 07"
Annalisa	9213727	GC	2000	D	8,737	433' 10"	52' 01"	31' 08"
(Malte Rainbow '00-'03)								
Carola	9214173	GC	2000	D	9,000	424' 08"	52' 00"	33' 04"
(Beatrice '00-'00)								
Hermann Schoening	9413901	BC	2010	D	29,635	622' 04"	77' 05"	47' 11"
Jana	9255725	GC	2001	D	8,994	433' 09"	52' 01"	31' 08'
Julia	9312729	GC	2006	D	5,726	348' 02"	47' 03"	26' 07"
Julietta	9217151	GC	2002	D	10,500	468' 02"	59' 10"	33' 04"
Katja	9235490	GC	2000	D	9,000	424' 08"	52' 00"	33' 04"
(Katja '00-'01, MSC Apapa '01-'02)								
Lara	9180853	GC	1998	D	5,500	330' 10"	49' 01"	27' 07"
Leandra	9438585	GC	2008	D	11,211	477' 09"	60' 03"	33' 10"
Luebbert	9415167	BC	2010	D	29,635	622' 04"	77' 05"	47' 11"
Maxima	9369071	GC	2007	D	11,211	477' 09"	60' 03"	33' 10"
(Maxima '07-'07, Nordana Maxima '07-'08)								
Nina	9180841	GC	1998	D	5,726	329' 09"	49' 03"	27' 07"
(Nina '98-'98, Melody '98-'02)								
Rebecca	9239288	GC	2002	D	10,500	468' 02"	59' 10"	33' 04"
Sabrina	9240471	GC	2002	D	10,500	468' 02"	59' 10"	33' 04"
(Sabrina '02-'02 , MSC Rades '02-'04 , Sabrina '04-'04 , SCM Olympic '04-'05)								
Serena	9294977	GC	2004	D	10,500	468' 02"	59' 10"	33' 04"
Sofia	9312690	GC	2005	D	5,726	348' 02"	47' 03"	26' 07"
Tatjana	9235488	GC	2000	D	9,000	424' 08"	52' 00"	33' 04"
(Tatjana '00-'02, TMC Brazil '02-'02)								
Thekla	9259020	GC	2003	D	8,994	433' 09"	52' 01"	31' 08'
(Suryawati '03-'03)								

Federal Oshima in the Detroit River, with the mailboat J.W. Westcott II at left. *(Matt Miner)*

Fleet Name Vessel Name	IMO #	Vessel Type	Year Built	Engine Type	Cargo Cap. or Gross*	Overall Length	Breadth	Depth
Uta	9369069	GC	2007	D	11,211	477' 09"	59' 10"	33' 10"
Victoria	9290074	GC	2004	D	10,500	468' 02"	59' 10"	33' 04"
Winona	9255622	GC	2003	D	10,000	433' 09"	52' 06"	32' 10"
(Vermontborg '03-'03)								
Xenia	9217163	GC	2003	D	10,500	468' 02"	59' 10"	33' 04"

II-2 INTERSHIP NAVIGATION CO. LTD., LIMASSOL, CYPRUS *(intership-cyprus.com)*
THE FOLLOWING VESSELS UNDER CHARTER TO FEDNAV LTD.

Federal Danube	9271511	BC	2003	D	37,372	652' 11"	78' 05"	50' 02"
Federal Elbe	9230000	BC	2003	D	37,372	652' 11"	78' 05"	50' 02"
Federal Ems	9229984	BC	2002	D	37,372	652' 11"	78' 05"	50' 02"
Federal Katsura	9293923	BC	2005	D	32,787	624' 08"	77' 05"	49' 10"
Federal Leda	9229996	BC	2003	D	37,372	652' 11"	78' 05"	50' 02"
Federal Patroller	9190092	BC	1999	D	17,451	469' 02"	74' 10"	43' 08"
*(Atlantic Pride '99-'01, Seaboard Rover '01-'02, **Atlantic Patroller** '02-'05, African Patroller '05-'06)*								
Federal Pioneer	9190080	BC	1999	D	17,451	469' 02"	74' 10"	43' 08"
(Atlantic Pioneer '99-'01, Seaboard Pioneer '01-'07)								
Federal Power	9190119	BC	2000	D	17,451	469' 02"	74' 10"	43' 08"
(Atlantic Power '00-'01, Seaboard Power '01-'07)								
Federal Sakura	9288291	BC	2005	D	32,787	624' 08"	77' 05"	49' 10"
Federal Weser	9229972	BC	2002	D	37,372	652' 11"	78' 05"	50' 02"
Hal Patriot	9223904	BC	2002	D	17,477	469' 02"	74' 10"	43' 08"
*(Atlantic Progress '02-'03, **BBC Russia** '03-'08, **Federal Patriot** '08-'10)*								
Hal Pendant	9223899	BC	2003	D	17,477	469' 02"	74' 10"	43' 08"
*(**Atlantic Pendant** '03-'05, **BBC Korea** '05-'08, **Federal Pendant** '08-'10)*								
Hal Pride	9190107	BC	2000	D	17,451	469' 02"	74' 10"	43' 08"
*(Atlantic Pride '00-'01, Seaboard Rover '01-'02, **Atlantic Pride** '02-'05, Seabord Chile II '05-'07,* ***Federal Pride** '07-'10)*								

II-3 ISKO MARINE SHIPPING AND TRADING, ISTANBUL, TURKEY *(www.iskomarine.com)*

Global Carrier	8111764	HL	1982	D	9,864	403' 06"	67' 08"	33' 10"
*(**Titan Scan** '82-'02, **Scan Trader** '02-'03, Global Traveller '03-'04, Taipan Scan '04-'05)*								

IJ-1 JO TANKERS BV, SPIJKENISSE, NETHERLANDS *(jotankers.com)*

Jo Spirit	9140841	TK	1998	D	6,248	352' 02"	52' 02"	30' 02"

IJ-2 JUMBO SHIPPING CO. SA, ROTTERDAM, NETHERLANDS *(jumboshipping.nl)*

Daniella	8718873	HL	1989	D	7,600	322' 09"	60' 03"	37' 02"
*(**Stellaprima** '89-'90)*								
Fairlane	9153654	HL	2000	D	7,123	361' 03"	68' 05"	44' 03"
Fairlift	8806905	HL	1990	D	7,780	330' 08"	68' 10"	43' 08"
Fairload	9083134	HL	1995	D	5,198	314' 00"	60' 03"	37' 02"
Jumbo Spirit	9083122	HL	1995	D	5,198	314' 00"	60' 03"	37' 02"
Jumbo Vision	9153642	HL	2000	D	7,123	361' 03"	68' 05"	44' 03"
Stellanova	9085730	HL	1996	D	5,198	314' 00"	60' 03"	37' 02"
Stellaprima	8912326	HL	1991	D	7,780	330' 08"	68' 10"	43' 08"

IK-1 KENT LINE, SAINT JOHN, NEW BRUNSWICK, CANADA *(kentline.com)*

Kent Sunrise	9320506	GC	2006	D	12,000	469' 00"	62' 00"	35' 11"
(Morgenstond I '06-'06, Beluga Locomotion '06-'08, Kent Locomotion '08-'08, Beluga Locomotion '08-'09, Morgenstond I '09-'10)								

IK-2 KNUTSEN O.A.S. SHIPPING AS, HAUGESUND, NORWAY *(knutsenoas.com)*

Ellen Knutsen	8910134	TK	1992	D	17,071	464' 03"	75' 07"	38' 09"
Hilda Knutsen	8716863	TK	1989	D	14,910	464' 08"	75' 07"	38' 10"
Pascale Knutsen	9070905	TK	1993	D	14,910	464' 08"	75' 07"	38' 10"
Sidsel Knutsen	9019779	TK	1993	D	22,625	533' 03"	75' 06"	48' 07"
Synnove Knutsen	9007207	TK	1992	D	17,071	464' 03"	75' 07"	38' 09"
Torill Knutsen	8806682	TK	1993	D	14,910	464' 08"	75' 07"	38' 10"
Turid Knutsen	9039884	TK	1993	D	22,625	533' 03"	75' 06"	48' 07"

IK-3 KREY SCHIFFAHRTS GMBH & CO. KG, SIMONSWOLDE, GERMANY *(krey-schiffahrt.de)*

BBC Ontario	9312157	GC	2004	D	12,711	452' 10"	68' 11"	36' 01"

IL-1 LAURANNE SHIPPING BV, GHENT, NETHERLANDS *(lauranne-shipping.com)*

LS Christine	9302009	TK	2007	D	8,400	411' 05"	59' 01"	27' 07"
(Christine H '07 -'07)								
LS Jacoba	9334428	TK	2006	D	15,602	485' 07"	70' 10"	37' 01"

Amazoneborg passing CSL Laurentien above Port Colborne. (Roger LeLievre)

Fleet Name Vessel Name	IMO #	Vessel Type	Year Built	Engine Type	Cargo Cap. or Gross*	Overall Length	Breadth	Depth
IL-2	**LEHMANN REEDEREI, LÜBECK, GERMANY** *(hans-lehmann.de)*							
Edgar Lehmann	9396543	GC	2007	D	12,000	460' 04"	64' 07"	34' 05"
Hans Lehmann	9406702	GC	2007	D	12,000	460' 04"	64' 07"	34' 05"
IL-3	**LIAMARE SHIPPING BV, MAARTENSDIJK, NETHERLANDS** *(liamareshipping.nl)*							
Liamare	9166481	GC	1999	D	5,842	351' 03"	50' 02"	27' 03"
(Ameland '99-'07)								
IL-4	**LINDOS MARITIME LTD., PIRAEUS, GREECE** *(greatlakescruiseco.com/clelia)*							
Clelia II	8708672	PA	1990	D	2,420	289' 09"	50' 03"	27' 07"
(Renaissance Four '90-'90)								
IL-5	**LLOYD FONDS SINGAPORE PTE LTD., SINGAPORE, SINGAPORE** *(lloydfonds.de)*							
Fen	9359600	TK	2006	D	12,950	417' 04"	67' 00"	37' 09"
(Launched as Songa Onyx, **Brovig Ocean** *'06-'07,* **Liquid Blue** *'07-'07)*								
Glen	9311634	TK	2005	D	12,950	417' 04"	67' 00"	37' 09"
(Launched as Songa Pearl, **Brovig Fjord** *'06-'07)*								
Moor	9359595	TK	2006	D	12,950	417' 04"	67' 00"	37' 09"
(Brovig Sea '06-'06, Songa Saphire '06-'07, **Liquid Elegance** *'07-'07)*								
Vale	9340350	TK	2007	D	13,032	421' 11"	66' 11"	37' 09"
IL-6	**LORENTZENS REDERI CO., OSLO, NORWAY**							
Songa Falcon	9482653	TK	2009	D	13,226	419' 07"	67' 00"	37' 09"
IM-1	**MARIDA TANKERS INC., NORWALK, CONNETICUT, USA** *(marida.qfleet.com)*							
Marida Mulberry	9474151	TK	2008	D	13,226	419' 07"	67' 00"	37' 09"
IM-2	**MARLOW NAVIGATION CO. LTD., LIMASSOL, CYPRUS** *(marlownavigation.com.cy)*							
BBC Rosario	9337224	GC	2007	D	12,872	452' 09"	68' 11"	36' 01"
IM-3	**MASSOEL MERIDIAN LTD., LIVERPOOL, UNITED KINGDOM** *(massoel.com)*							
Simano	9506409	GC	2008	D	7,300	370' 01"	56' 05"	29' 10"
ONEGO SHIPPING & CHARTERING								
Onego Sementina	9543328	GC	2009	D	7,300	370' 01"	56' 05"	29' 10"
(St. Kitts-Nevis '09-'09)								
IM-4	**MEGA CHEMICAL TANKERS LTD., SINGAPORE, SINGAPORE** *(mega-chemicals.ch)*							
MCT Alioth	9173094	TK	1999	D	19,996	489' 10"	77' 11"	41' 06"
***(Alioth** '99-'03)*								
MCT Almak	9173109	TK	1999	D	19,996	489' 10"	77' 11"	41' 06"
***(Almak** '99-'03)*								
MCT Altair	9173082	TK	1999	D	19,996	489' 10"	77' 11"	41' 06"
***(Altair** '99-'03)*								
MCT Arcturus	9173111	TK	2000	D	19,996	489' 10"	77' 11"	41' 06"
***(Arcturus** '99-'03)*								
IM-5	**MURMANSK SHIPPING CO., MURMANSK, RUSSIA** *(msco.ru)*							
Aleksandr Suvorov	7721237	BC	1979	D	19,885	531' 06"	75' 02"	44' 05"
Mikhail Strekalovskiy	8131881	BC	1981	D	19,252	531' 06"	75' 02"	44' 05"
Tim Buck	8319861	BC	1983	D	19,252	531' 06"	75' 02"	44' 04"
IN-1	**NAVARONE SA MARINE ENTERPRISES, LIMASSOL, CYPRUS**							
FOLLOWING VESSELS UNDER CHARTER TO CANADIAN FOREST NAVIGATION LTD.								
Andean	9413925	BC	2009	D	30,770	606' 11"	77' 09"	47' 11"
Barnacle	9409742	BC	2009	D	30,807	606' 11"	77' 09"	47' 11"
Blacky	9393149	BC	2008	D	30,801	607' 04"	77' 09"	47' 11"
Bluebill	9263306	BC	2004	D	37,200	632' 10"	77' 09"	50' 10"
Brant	9393151	BC	2008	D	30,807	606' 11"	77' 09"	47' 11"
Chestnut	9477866	BC	2009	D	30,807	606' 11"	77' 09"	47' 11"
Maccoa	9413913	BC	2009	D	30,930	606' 11"	77' 09"	47' 11"
Mottler	9477828	BC	2009	D	30,807	606' 11"	77' 09"	47' 11"
Ruddy	9459981	BC	2009	D	30,930	606' 11"	77' 09"	47' 11"
Tufty	9393163	BC	2009	D	30,807	606' 11"	77' 09"	47' 11"
IN-2	**NAVIGATION MARITIME BULGARE LTD., VARNA, BULGARIA** *(www.navbul.com)*							
Kamenitza	8006256	BC	1980	D	24,150	603' 08"	75' 02"	46' 05"
Kom	9132480	BC	1997	D	13,900	466' 04"	72' 10"	36' 06"
Malyovitza	8203359	BC	1982	D	24,456	605' 08"	75' 02"	46' 07"
Perelik	9132507	BC	1998	D	13,900	466' 04"	72' 10"	36' 06"

Fleet Name / Vessel Name	IMO #	Vessel Type	Year Built	Engine Type	Cargo Cap. or Gross*	Overall Length	Breadth	Depth
Persenk	9132519	BC	1998	D	13,900	466' 04"	72' 10"	36' 06"
Strandja	9564140	BC	2010	D	30,688	610' 03"	77' 11"	47' 11"
(Eastwind York '10-'10, Federal Yangtze '10-'10)								

IN-3   **NESTE SHIPPING OY, ESPOO, FINLAND** *(nesteoil.com)*

Futura	9255282	TK	2004	D	25,084	556' 01"	77' 11"	48' 11"

IN-4   **NICHOLAS G. MOUNDREAS SHIPPING SA, PIRAEUS, GREECE**

Spring	9416812	TK	2009	D	13,073	421' 11"	66' 11"	37' 09"

IN-5   **NOVOROSSIYSK SHIPPING CO. (NOVOSHIP), NOVOROSSIYSK, RUSSIA** *(novoship.ru)*

Vladimir Vysotskiy	8517114	TK	1988	D	16,970	497' 01"	73' 07"	39' 10"

IN-6   **NORDIC TANKERS A/S, COPENHAGEN, DENMARK** *(nordictankers.dk)*

Nordic Copenhagen	9300776	TK	2005	D	12,950	417' 04"	67' 00"	39' 09"
Nordic Stockholm	9328314	TK	2005	D	12,950	417' 04"	67' 00"	39' 09"

IO-1   **OCEAN CHALLENGE LTD., NICOSIA, CYPRUS**

Bluewing	9230919	BC	2002	D	26,747	611' 00"	77' 09"	46' 07"
Cinnamon	9239800	BC	2002	D	26,747	611' 00"	77' 09"	46' 07"
Greenwing	9230921	BC	2002	D	26,737	611' 08"	77' 09"	46' 07"
Mandarin	9239812	BC	2003	D	26,747	611' 00"	77' 09"	46' 07"

IO-2   **OCEAN TANKERS HOLDINGS PUBLIC CO. LTD., NICOSIA, CYPRUS** *(www.ocean-tankers.com)*

Stavrodromi	9169768	TK	1999	D	15,441	474' 02"	73' 11"	36' 11"
(Saint-Petersburg '99-'04, Shakhdag '04-'07)								

IO-3   **OCEANEX INC., MONTREAL, QUEBEC, CANADA** *(oceanex.com)*

Cabot {2}	7700051	RR	1979	D	7,132	564' 09"	73' 11"	45' 09"
Oceanex Avalon	9315044	CO	2005	D	14,747	481' 11"	85' 00"	45' 11"
Oceanex Sanderling	7603502	RR	1977	D	15,195	364' 01"	88' 05"	57' 07"
(Rauenfels '77-'80, Essen '80-'81, Kongsfjord '81-'83, Onno '83-'87, ASL Sanderling '87-'08)								

IO-4   **OLYMPIC SHIPPING AND MANAGEMENT SA, MONTE CARLO, MONACO** *(olyship.com)*
     FOLLOWING VESSELS UNDER CHARTER TO CANADIAN FOREST NAVIGATION LTD.

Calliroe Patronicola	8315229	BC	1985	D	29,640	599' 09"	75' 11"	48' 07"
Olympic Melody	8307674	BC	1984	D	29,640	599' 09"	75' 11"	48' 07"
(Olympic Memory '84-'84)								
Olympic Mentor	8307650	BC	1984	D	29,640	599' 09"	75' 11"	48' 07"
*(Calliroe Patronicola '84-'84, **Patricia-R.** '84-'88)*								
Olympic Merit	8315217	BC	1985	D	29,640	599' 09"	75' 11"	48' 07"
Olympic Miracle	8307662	BC	1984	D	29,640	599' 09"	75' 11"	48' 07"

IP-1   **PARAKOU SHIPPING LTD., HONG KONG, CHINA** *(parakougroup.com)*

Heloise	9498224	BC	2010	D	30,688	610' 03"	77' 11"	47' 11"

     FOLLOWING VESSELS UNDER CHARTER TO CANADIAN FOREST NAVIGATION LTD.

Eider	9285938	BC	2004	D	37,249	655' 10"	77' 09"	50' 02"
Gadwall	9358369	BC	2007	D	37,249	655' 10"	77' 09"	50' 02"
Garganey	9358383	BC	2007	D	37,249	655' 10"	77' 09"	50' 02"
Redhead	9285940	BC	2005	D	37,249	655' 10"	77' 09"	50' 02"
Whistler	9358371	BC	2007	D	37,249	655' 10"	77' 09"	50' 02"
Wigeon	9358395	BC	2007	D	37,249	655' 10"	77' 09"	50' 02"

IP-2   **PEARL SEA CRUISES LLC, GUILFORD, CT, USA** *(pearlseascruises.com)*

Pearl Mist	9412701	PA	2009	D	5,073*	335' 00"	56' 00"	12' 00"

IP-3   **PENDULUM SHIPMANAGEMENT INC., ATHENS, GREECE** *(pendulum.gr)*

Spring Breeze I	8026139	BC	1984	D	26,288	606' 11"	75' 03"	47' 03"
*(**Nand Rati** '84-'01, **Spring Breeze** '01-'06)*								

IP-4   **PEROSEA SHIPPING CO. SA, PIRAEUS, GREECE**

Sea Force	9322102	TK	2006	D	13,500	421' 11"	66' 11"	37' 09"

IP-5   **POLISH STEAMSHIP CO., SZCZECIN, POLAND** *(polsteam.com)*

Drawsko	9393450	BC	2010	D	20,603	623' 04"	77' 11"	47' 11"
Irma	9180396	BC	2000	D	34,946	655' 10"	77' 05"	50' 02"
Iryda	9180384	BC	1999	D	34,946	655' 10"	77' 05"	50' 02"
Isa	9180358	BC	1999	D	34,946	655' 10"	77' 05"	50' 02"
Isadora	9180372	BC	1999	D	34,946	655' 10"	77' 05"	50' 02"
Isolda	9180360	BC	1999	D	34,946	655' 10"	77' 05"	50' 02"

Fleet Name / Vessel Name	IMO #	Vessel Type	Year Built	Engine Type	Cargo Cap. or Gross*	Overall Length	Breadth	Depth
Miedwie	9393448	BC	2010	D	20,603	623' 04"	77' 11"	47' 11"
Nogat	9154268	BC	1999	D	17,064	488' 10"	75' 06"	39' 08"
Odra	8901597	BC	1992	D	13,756	469' 02"	68' 08"	37' 02"
(Odranes '92-'99)								
Orla	9154270	BC	1999	D	17,064	488' 10"	75' 06"	39' 08"
Pilica	9154282	BC	1999	D	17,064	488' 10"	75' 06"	39' 08"
Pomorze Zachodnie	8207783	BC	1985	D	26,696	591' 06"	75' 10"	45' 07"
Rega	8908868	BC	1995	D	17,064	488' 10"	75' 06"	39' 08"
(Fossnes '95-'02)								
Resko	9393462	BC	2010	D	20,603	623' 04"	77' 11"	47' 11"
Warta	8902929	BC	1992	D	13,756	469' 02"	68' 08"	37' 02"
(Wartanes '92-'99)								
Wicko	9393474	BC	2010	D	20,603	623' 04"	77' 11"	47' 11"

IP-6 POT SCHEEPVAART BV, DELFZIJL, NETHERLANDS (pot-scheepvaart.nl)
FOLLOWING VESSELS UNDER CHARTER TO WAGENBORG SHIPPING

Kwintebank	9234288	GC	2002	D	8,664	433' 10"	52' 01"	31' 08"
Varnebank	9213739	GC	2000	D	8,664	433' 10"	52' 01"	31' 08"

IR-1 REDERIET STENERSEN AS, BERGEN, NORWAY (stenersen.com)

Sten Aurora	9378723	TK	2008	D	16,613	472' 07"	75' 06"	40' 08"
Sten Suomi	9378723	TK	2008	D	16,611	472' 11"	76' 01"	40' 08"

IR-2 REEDEREI ECKHOFF & CO. GMBH, JORK, GERMANY (reederei-eckhoff.de)

BBC England	9258985	GC	2003	D	10,300	465' 10"	59' 10"	33' 04"
(Frida '03-'04)								

FOLLOWING VESSEL UNDER CHARTER TO CANADIAN FOREST NAVIGATION LTD.

Onego Ponza	9245263	GC	2002	D	9,900	455' 07"	52' 01"	35' 07"
(Sider Ponza '02-'02, Sider Monique '02-'03, Sider Ponza '03-'09)								

IR-3 REEDEREI ERWIN STRALMANN, MARNE, GERMANY (reederei-strahlmann.de)

Alesia	9433339	GC	2008	D	7,574	380' 10"	51' 10"	29' 02"

Polish vessel Isolda in the Welland Canal. (Matt Miner)

Fleet Name / Vessel Name	IMO #	Vessel Type	Year Built	Engine Type	Cargo Cap. or Gross*	Overall Length	Breadth	Depth
IR-4	**REEDEREI KARL SCHLUTER GMBH & CO., RENDSBURG, GERMANY** *(rks-rd.de)*							
FOLLOWING VESSEL UNDER CHARTER TO FEDNAV LTD.								
Federal Mattawa	9315537	GC	2005	D	18,825	606' 11"	77' 09"	46' 03"
IR-5	**RIGEL SCHIFFAHRTS GMBH, BREMEN, GERMANY** *(rigel-hb.com)*							
Amur Star	9480368	TK	2010	D	13,073	421' 11"	66' 11"	37' 09"
IS-1	**SARGEANT MARINE INC., BOCA RATON, FLORIDA, USA** *(sargeant.net)*							
Asphalt Carrier	9293545	TK	2010	D	9,230	356' 00"	61' 00"	34' 09"
IS-2	**SEA OBSERVER SHIPPING SERVICES SA, PIRAEUS, GREECE**							
Krios	8116996	BC	1983	D	12,319	423' 04"	65' 07"	36' 09"
(Fjordnes '83-'87, Star Jay '87-'87, Elpis '87-'90, Kamtin '90-'96, Falknes '96-'00, Demi Green '00-'01, Lia '01-'03)								
IS-3	**SEASTAR NAVIGATION CO. LTD., ATHENS, GREECE**							
FOLLOWING VESSELS UNDER CHARTER TO CANADIAN FOREST NAVIGATION CO. LTD.								
Apollon	9146821	BC	1996	D	30,855	606' 11"	77' 05"	48' 11"
(Spring Laker '96-'06)								
IS-4	**SERROMAH SHIPPING BV, ROTTERDAM, NETHERLANDS** *(serromahshipping.com)*							
Oriental Kerria	9294795	TK	2004	D	14,298	440' 02"	67' 04"	38' 01"
Oriental Protea	9330381	TK	2005	D	14,246	440' 02"	67' 03"	38' 01"
IS-5	**SHIH WEI NAVIGATION CO. LTD., TAIPEI, TAIWAN** *(www.swnav.com.tw)*							
Fodas Pescadores	9240524	BC	2001	D	11,600	387' 02"	64' 04"	36' 01"
Royal Pescadores	9151400	BC	1997	D	18,369	486' 01"	74' 10"	40' 00"
IS-6	**SICILNAVI S.R.L., PALERMO, ITALY**							
Vindemia	7723950	TK	1979	D	3,603	295' 11"	44' 07"	21' 04"
IS-7	**SIOMAR ENTERPRISES LTD., PIRAEUS, GREECE**							
Island Skipper	8312095	BC	1984	D	28,031	584' 08"	76' 02"	48' 05"
IS-8	**SPAR SHIPPING AS, BERGEN, NORWAY** *(sparshipping.com)*							
FOLLOWING VESSELS UNDER CHARTER TO FEDNAV LTD.								
Spar Garnet	8319548	BC	1984	D	30,674	589' 11"	75' 09"	50' 10"
(Mary Anne '84-'93, Federal Vigra '93-'97)								
Spar Jade	8319550	BC	1984	D	30,674	589' 11"	75' 10"	50' 11"
(Fiona Mary '84-93, Federal Aalesund '93-'97)								
IS-9	**STOLT PARCEL TANKERS INC., GREENWICH, CONNECTICUT, USA** *(stolt-nielsen.com)*							
Stolt Kite	8920555	TK	1992	D	4,735	314' 11"	49' 06"	26' 05
(Randi Terkol '92-'96)								
IS-10	**STX PAN OCEAN CO. LTD., SEOUL, SOUTH KOREA** *(stxpanocean.co.kr)*							
Pan Voyager	8309737	BC	1984	D	29,433	589' 11"	78' 01"	47' 07"
IS-11	**SUNSHIP & MLB M. LAUTERJUNG, EMDEN, GERMANY** *(sunship.de)*							
FOLLOWING VESSELS UNDER CHARTER TO FEDNAV LTD.								
Federal Manitou	9283538	BC	2004	D	27,000	606' 11"	77' 09"	46' 03"
Federal Matane	9283540	BC	2004	D	27,000	606' 11"	77' 09"	46' 03"
Federal Miramichi	9315549	BC	2004	D	27,000	606' 11"	77' 09"	46' 03"
IT-1	**TEAM SHIP MANAGEMENT GMBH & CO. KG, BREMERHAVEN, GERMANY** *(teamship.de)*							
OXL Lotus	9144471	HL	1996	D	5,147	331' 00"	62' 00"	31' 10"
(Palawan '96-'96, Scan Partner '96-'02, Palawan '02-'08)								
IT-2	**THALKAT SHIPPING SA, PIRAEUS, GREECE**							
Dora	8029636	BC	1981	D	21,951	508' 06"	75' 00"	44' 07"
(Verdant '81-'87, Luntian '87-'93, Verdin '93-'94, Oak '94-'02)								
IT-3	**THOR SHIPPING AS, SVENDBORG, DENMARK** *(thorshipping.dk)*							
Thor Athos	8703268	BC	1987	D	4,144	288' 09"	50' 09"	29' 02"
(Svenja '87-'92, Steinkirchen '92-'97, Thor Eagle '97-'01, Thor Kis '01-'07)								
IT-4	**TORVALD KLAVENESS GROUP, OSLO, NORWAY** *(klaveness.com)*							
KCL Barracuda	8317332	CC	1984	D	17,722	482' 11"	74' 11"	40' 01"
(Kiwi Star '84-'03, Thai Ho '03-'04)								
IT-5	**TRANSATLANTIC SHIPPING AB, SKÄRHAMN, SWEDEN** *(rabt.se/en)*							
Alida Gorthon	7524201	RR	1977	D	14,240	463' 10"	71' 03"	38' 09"

Fleet Name Vessel Name	IMO #	Vessel Type	Year Built	Engine Type	Cargo Cap. or Gross*	Overall Length	Breadth	Depth
Ingrid Gorthon	9213088	RR	1977	D	14,240	463' 10"	71' 03"	38' 09"
TransEagle	9213088	GC	2002	D	16,612	467' 04"	72' 02"	42' 00"
(Nordon '02-'09)								
TransOsprey	9213090	GC	2003	D	16,740	467' 03"	72' 06"	42' 00"
(Prinsenborg '03-'10)								

IT-7 TRADEWIND TANKERS SL, BARCELONA, SPAIN *(tradewindtankers.com)*

Tradewind Union	9175729	TK	1997	D	10,600	387' 02"	63' 08"	34' 01"
(Southern Lion '97-'03)								

IV-1 VIKEN SHIPPING AS, BERGEN, NORWAY *(vikenshipping.com)*
    FOLLOWING VESSELS UNDER CHARTER TO FEDNAV LTD.

Federal Fuji	8321931	BC	1986	D	29,643	599' 09"	76' 00"	48' 07"
Federal Polaris	8321929	BC	1985	D	29,643	599' 09"	76' 00"	48' 07"
Inviken	8212087	BC	1986	D	30,052	621' 05"	75' 10"	47' 11"
(Bar *'86-'97)*								
Utviken	8212099	BC	1987	D	30,052	621' 05"	75' 10"	47' 11"
(Bijelo Polje *'87-'92, C. Blanco '92-'95)*								

IW-1 W. BOCKSTIEGEL REEDEREI KG, EMDEN, GERMANY *(reederei-bockstiegel.de)*

BBC Alaska	9433262	GC	2008	D	12,840	454' 05"	68' 11"	36' 01"
BBC Chile	9210335	GC	2001	D	7,650	353' 06"	59' 09"	33' 02"
BBC Delaware	9357212	GC	2004	D	12,782	453' 00"	68' 11"	24' 07"
BBC Italy	9210347	GC	2001	D	7,650	353' 06"	59' 09"	33' 02"
(BBC Italy '99-'01, **Buccaneer** *'01-'03)*								
BBC Louisiana	9435105	GC	2008	D	12,000	453' 00"	68' 11"	36' 01"
BBC Maine	9357200	GC	2007	D	12,792	444' 05"	68' 11"	36' 01"
BBC Mexico	9197557	GC	2001	D	5,018	330' 08"	53' 10"	26' 11"
(Deborah '01-'01)								
BBC Plata	9291975	GC	2005	D	12,837	452' 09"	68' 11"	36' 01"
(Asian Voyager '05-'05)								
BBC Vermont	9357236	GC	2008	D	12,000	453' 00"	68' 11"	36' 01"
BBC Zarate	9337236	GC	2007	D	12,834	452' 09"	68' 11"	36' 01"

IW-2 WAGENBORG SHIPPING BV, DELFZIJL, NETHERLANDS *(wagenborg.com)*

Africaborg	9365661	GC	2007	D	17,323	469' 02"	70' 06"	43' 08"
(Africaborg '07-'08, Tianshan '08-'09)								
Amazoneborg	9365661	GC	2007	D	17,323	469' 02"	70' 06"	43' 08"
Americaborg	9365659	GC	2007	D	17,323	469' 02"	70' 06"	43' 08"
Asiaborg	9333553	GC	2007	D	17,323	469' 02"	70' 06"	43' 08"
Australiaborg	9397171	GC	2007	D	17,323	469' 02"	70' 06"	43' 08"
Avonborg	9429730	GC	2007	D	17,323	469' 02"	70' 06"	43' 08"
Diezeborg	9225586	GC	2000	D	8,867	437' 08"	52' 00"	32' 02"
(Diezeborg '00-'01, MSC Marmara '01-'03)								
Dintelborg	9163685	GC	1999	D	8,867	437' 07"	52' 00"	32' 02"
(Dintelborg '00-'01, MSC Dardanelles '01-'04)								
Dongeborg	9163697	GC	1999	D	8,867	437' 08"	52' 00"	32' 02"
Drechtborg	9196163	GC	2000	D	8,867	437' 08"	52' 00"	32' 02"
(Drechtborg '00-'00, MSC Skaw '00-'02, Drechtborg '02-'03, Normed Rotterdam '03-'05)								
Edenborg	9463449	GC	2010	D	10,750	452' 03"	52' 01"	36' 01"
Eemsborg	9225586	GC	2009	D	10,750	452' 03"	52' 01"	36' 01"
Fivelborg	9419307	GC	2010	D	14,595	507' 03"	56' 05"	37' 11"
Flevoborg	9419292	GC	2010	D	14,595	507' 03"	56' 05"	37' 11"
Kasteelborg	9155937	GC	1998	D	9,150	427' 01"	52' 01"	33' 06"
Keizersborg	9102904	GC	1996	D	9,150	427' 01"	52' 01"	33' 06"
Koningsborg	9155925	GC	1999	D	9,150	427' 01"	52' 01"	33' 06"
Kroonborg	9102904	GC	1995	D	9,085	428' 10"	52' 02"	33' 06"
Loireborg	9399404	GC	2008	D	7,350	401' 04"	47' 03"	26' 07"
Maineborg	9228980	GC	2001	D	9,141	441' 05"	54' 02"	32' 02"
Markborg	9142540	GC	1996	D	9,141	441' 05"	54' 02"	32' 02"
Marneborg	9142564	GC	1998	D	9,141	441' 05"	54' 02"	32' 02"
(Marneborg '98-'04, Normed Istanbul '04-'06)								
Medemborg	9142514	GC	1997	D	9,141	441' 05"	54' 02"	32' 02"
(Arion *'97-'03)*								
Merweborg	9142552	GC	1997	D	9,141	441' 05"	54' 02"	32' 02"

Fleet Name Vessel Name	IMO #	Vessel Type	Year Built	Engine Type	Cargo Cap. or Gross*	Overall Length	Breadth	Depth
Metsaborg	9243801	GC	2002	D	9,141	441' 05"	54' 02"	32' 02"
Michiganborg	9190286	GC	1999	D	9,141	441' 05"	54' 02"	32' 02"
Missouriborg	9228978	GC	2000	D	9,141	441' 05"	54' 02"	32' 02"
Morraborg	9190274	GC	1999	D	9,141	441' 05"	54' 02"	32' 02"
Munteborg	9179385	GC	1996	D	9,141	441' 05"	54' 02"	32' 02"
(**Munteborg** '96-'00, MSC Baltic '00-'04)								
Nassauborg	9248564	GC	2006	D	16,740	467' 03"	72' 06"	42' 00"
Vaasaborg	9196242	GC	1999	D	8,664	433' 10"	52' 01"	31' 08"
Vancouverborg	9213741	GC	2001	D	9,857	433' 10"	52' 01"	31' 08"
Vechtborg	9160334	GC	1998	D	8,664	433' 10"	52' 01"	31' 08"
Victoriaborg	9234276	GC	2001	D	9,857	433' 10"	52' 01"	31' 08"
Virginiaborg	9234290	GC	2001	D	9,857	433' 10"	52' 01"	31' 08"
Vlistborg	9160346	GC	1999	D	8,664	433' 10"	52' 01"	31' 08"
Voorneborg	9179373	GC	1999	D	8,664	433' 10"	52' 01"	31' 08"

At press time, Wagenborg Shipping also had the following vessels under charter. Please consult their respective fleets for details: Finex, Kwintebank, Varnebank, Veerseborg, Vossborg.

IY-1	**YARDIMCI SHIPPING GROUP, ISTANBUL, TURKEY** (www.yardimci.gen.tr)							
	CT Cork	9393060	TK	2008	D	10,303	383' 10"	68' 11"	31' 02"

IY-2	**YILMAR SHIPPING & TRADING LTD., ISTANBUL, TURKEY** (yilmar.com)							
	YM Jupiter	9291597	TK	2007	D	15,995	393' 08"	57' 09"	27' 11"
	YM Saturn	9362138	TK	2007	D	16,000	485' 07"	70' 10"	37' 01"

Saltwater vessel Serena docked at South Chicago. (Peter Groh)

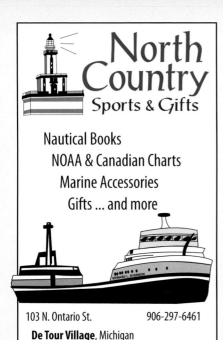

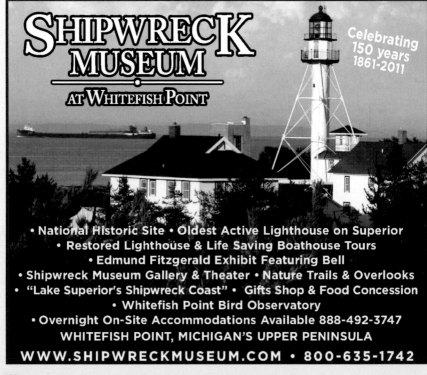

Extra Tonnage

Cement barge St. Marys Conquest enters
port at Green Bay in 2010. *(Peter Groh)*

Twin Port Paradise

Boatwatching doesn't get much better than at Duluth/Superior

Duluth, and its sister port, Superior, at the western end of Lake Superior and as far west from the Atlantic Ocean as one can safely pilot a lake boat, can be pure paradise for boatwatchers.

Hang out around Canal Park and watch the 1,000-footers pass under the Aerial Lift Bridge. Take a cruise with the Vista Fleet. Tour two historic steamships. Gorge yourself on lighthouses, if that's your pleasure. Top it all off with a museum visit, and still there's more to see and do in the Twin Ports area.

Ground zero for boatwatchers is Canal Park, in the shadow of Duluth's historic Aerial Lift Bridge. First, stop off at the adjacent Lake Superior Maritime Visitor Center and check the monitors for expected vessel arrivals and departures. You can also call the Boatwatchers Hotline at 218-722-6489 or eyeball a copy of Kenneth Newhams' Duluth Shipping News, available in printed form at clear pastic stands in the area. If the bridge sounds its horn, that's a sure sign of an oncoming vessel, although the structure goes up for small craft as well as large. Most vessels offer a salute as they leave and enter the harbor, and those horns are pretty thrilling up close.

If there's no traffic, it's worth it to spend some time in the Maritime Visitor Center, operated by the U.S. Army Corps of Engineers. The museum part of the facility houses a huge collection of superb ship models as well as life rings, pilothouse nameboards and other bits and pieces of lakers that have been scrapped in the area over the years. While you're there, sit back and enjoy the gulls, walk down the paths to its two pierhead lighthouses, take a hike on the 7.3-mile-long Lakewalk or just slurp an ice cream cone from one of the Canal Park vendors.

Continued on Page 127

James R. Barker approaches the Superior Entry Light . (Lee Rowe)

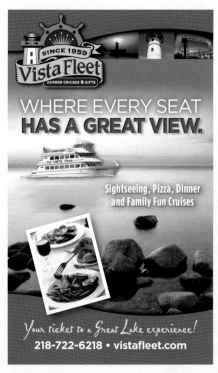

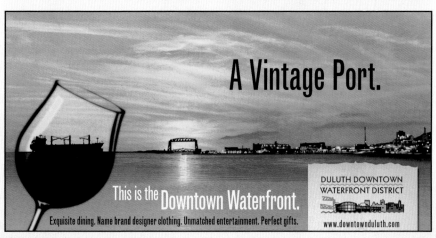

Shopping in Canal Park is also an attraction for non-boat times, with several galleries, restaurants and gift shops in the area. Just a short walk (take a shortcut over the blue-painted drawbridge spanning Minnesota Slip) away is the *William A. Irvin Ore Boat Museum*, open to the public for tours. At one time, the *Irvin* was the flagship of U.S. Steel's Great Lakes fleet, and it's worth the price of admission just to view the luxurious accommodations provided for guests of the company.

It's also worth your while to take a harbor cruise on one of the Vista Fleet's vessels (sightseeing, sunset and dinner cruises are available). The dock is located on Harbor Drive near the stern of the *Irvin* museum, and the trip includes passage under the Aerial Lift Bridge and out into Lake Superior. With luck, you'll get up close to one of the docks where a laker is loading or unloading, and the view from afloat is decidedly different from the one seen from shore.

Although most boatwatchers are interested in things above the water, the Great Lakes Aquarium offers a fascinating view of what lies beneath the surface. Visitors can learn about the geologic forces that shaped Lake Superior, watch as divers feed fish in a huge two-story tank, raise and lower locks on a scale model of the Great Lakes or pilot a virtual ore boat under the Aerial Lift Bridge.

Maritime Visitor Center at Canal Park.

Nothing beats staying overnight in the thick of the action, and South Pier Inn, next to the lift bridge on Park Point across from Canal Park, is right where you want to be. If you get the right room, you can take boat pictures from your balcony window.

Although it may be the best place to watch boats in the area, Canal Park isn't the only great vantage point. Jump on I-35 from Canal Park and take the I-535 exit toward Wisconsin and the Blatnik Bridge, then follow the signs for U.S. 53. Take the Port Terminal exit and look for an old wooden bridge span. It's now used as a fishing pier, and you can walk all the way out to the end and be almost as close to the vessels as when they go through the piers in Duluth. This is an

Continued on Page 129

Roger Blough inbound at the Duluth piers. *(Kim Nolan)*

Paul R. Tregurtha enters Duluth Harbor under the Aerial Lift Bridge. The South Pier Inn is at right. (Chris Mazzella)

especially good spot to photograph vessels headed for the Superior Midwest Energy Terminal coal dock, which will be to your right.

It's a bit of a challenge to get there, but the DMIR ore dock has a raised observation platform for viewing vessels located at the dock. From Canal Park, follow I-35 south and take the 40th Avenue West exit.

If you're looking to shoot pictures of vessels at Fraser Shipyards (mornings are best), head to Connor's Point, also off U.S. 53. Fraser is the current owner of the facility that was used to build Alexander McDougall's whalebacks more than 100 years ago. The world's last surviving example of this unique piece of maritime engineering, the 1896-built steamer *Meteor* is open to the public on Barker's Island in Superior.

If you want to see Superior Entry, through which vessels entering or leaving the BNSF ore docks generally pass on their way to and from the lake, continue east on U.S. 53 for several miles until just outside Superior. Look for the sign indicating Lake Superior and Wisconsin Point, then drive north for about a mile and take the first paved road to your left. This narrow, meandering and yes, very bumpy road will take you to Superior Entry.

After working up a hearty appetite boatwatching, sample the burgers and beer at Superior's Anchor Bar on Tower Avenue downtown. Don't let the industrial neighborhood deter you – this place, which has been featured on the "Diners, Drive-ins and Dives" TV show, serves up one of the best burgers anywhere, and the classic shipping photos and other memorabilia that cram every inch of wall space provide lots to look at while waiting for your order to arrive.

But wait, there's more …

No trip to the Twin Ports would be complete without a

Continued on Page 131

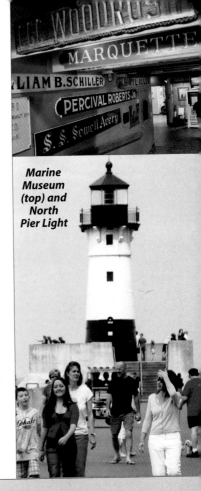

Marine Museum (top) and North Pier Light

Atlantic Huron heads into Lake Superior. (Mike Sipper)

129

Split Rock Lighthouse, on Lake Superior's north shore.

William A. Irvin museum ship, docked at Duluth. (Roger LeLievre)

Superior's whaleback musuem Meteor.

TOUR
The World's Last
WHALEBACK
SHIP

Rocky Taconite

side excursion to Lake Superior's north shore. Follow Highway 61 (made famous in song by local boy Bob Dylan) to Two Harbors to see the ore dock there, and visit the historic and beautifully restored steam tug *Edna G.* of 1896 vintage. A walk out onto the breakwater at Two Harbors allows you to look straight in on boats tied to the ore dock and loading (mornings are best for photos).

Although you need to be there at exactly the right time, it's cool to watch the vessels coming in past the Two Harbors light and making the sharp turns into the dock and out again. Continue on the route (making sure you stop by for a treat at the famous Betty's Pies) and check out the

magnificent Split Rock Lighthouse, then wind up in Silver Bay, which – in addition to a picturesque harbor – has a taconite-loading facility operated by Northshore Mining Co.

Cruise boat Vista Star.

While in Silver Bay, have your picture taken with the Rocky Taconite sculpture, an offbeat, cartoonish character complete with miner's helmet and pick, that commemorates the transition of America's steel industry from pure to pelletized ore.

One more thing: With all we've mentioned here, know that's just scratching the surface of the treats that await in the Twin Ports. – *Roger LeLievre*

131

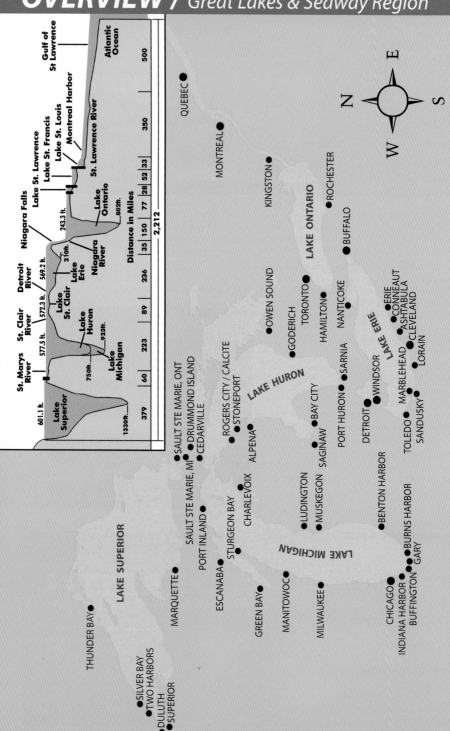

OVERVIEW / Great Lakes & Seaway Region

Gulf of St Lawrence
Atlantic Ocean

Montreal Harbor
Lake St Lawrence
Lake St Francis
Lake St Louis

St. Lawrence River

Niagara Falls

Lake Ontario 802ft.

Niagara River

Detroit River
Lake Erie 569.2 ft. / 243.3 ft. / 210ft.

St. Clair River
Lake St. Clair 572.3 ft. / 577.3 ft.

Lake Huron 923ft.

St. Marys River 577.5 ft.

Lake Superior 601.1 ft.

Lake Michigan 750ft. / 1330ft.

Distance in Miles

| 379 | 60 | 223 | 89 | 236 | 35 | 150 | 77 | 28 | 52 | 33 | 350 | 500 |

2,212

THUNDER BAY

SILVER BAY
TWO HARBORS
DULUTH
SUPERIOR

LAKE SUPERIOR

MARQUETTE

PORT INLAND

ESCANABA

STURGEON BAY

GREEN BAY

MANITOWOC

MILWAUKEE

CHICAGO
INDIANA HARBOR
BUFFINGTON
GARY
BURNS HARBOR

LAKE MICHIGAN

BENTON HARBOR

LUDINGTON
MUSKEGON

SAGINAW
BAY CITY

CHARLEVOIX
ALPENA

ROGERS CITY / CALCITE
STONEPORT

SAULT STE MARIE, ONT
DRUMMOND ISLAND
SAULT STE MARIE, MI
CEDARVILLE

LAKE HURON

GODERICH
OWEN SOUND

PORT HURON
SARNIA

DETROIT
WINDSOR

LAKE ERIE

TOLEDO
SANDUSKY
MARBLEHEAD
LORAIN
CLEVELAND
ASHTABULA
CONNEAUT
ERIE

TORONTO
HAMILTON
NANTICOKE

BUFFALO

ROCHESTER

LAKE ONTARIO

KINGSTON

MONTREAL

QUEBEC

N E
W S

Taconite ore is loaded for delivery to lower lakes steel mills at Duluth, Two Harbors and Silver Bay, Minn, as well as Superior, Wis., and Escanaba, Mich. Limestone loading ports are Port Inland, Cedarville, Drummond Island, Calcite, Rogers City and Stoneport, Mich., and Marblehead, Ohio. Coal ports are Superior, Wis., S. Chicago, Ill. and the Ohio ports of Toledo, Sandusky, Ashtabula and Conneaut. Petroleum is loaded aboard vessels at Sarnia, Ont., and E. Chicago, Ind. Grain export ports include Duluth, Minn., Milwaukee and Superior, Wis.; and the Ontario ports of Thunder Bay, Sarnia and Owen Sound.

The primary U.S. iron ore and limestone receiving ports are Cleveland, Chicago, Gary, Burns Harbor, Indiana Harbor, Detroit, Toledo, Lorain, Ashtabula and Conneaut. Nanticoke, Hamilton and Sault Ste. Marie, Ont., are major ore-receiving ports in Canada. Coal is carried by self-unloaders to power plants in the U.S. and Canada. Most grain loaded on the lakes is destined for export via the St. Lawrence Seaway. Cement from Alpena and Charlevoix, Mich., is delivered to terminals from Lake Superior to Lake Ontario. Tankers bring petroleum products to cities as diverse in size as Cleveland, Cheboygan, Detroit, Escanaba and Muskegon. Self-unloaders carry limestone, coal, road salt and sand to cities throughout the region.

Stewart J. Cort loads taconite at the BNSF dock in Superior, Wis. (Mike Sipper)

Manistee unloading coal at the Georgia Pacific slip in Green Bay. (Scott Best)

AGRICULTURAL PRODUCTS – Wheat, grain, soybeans, canola, flax and oats are shipped on the Great Lakes. Some is used domestically, but most is shipped to international markets overseas.

BUNKER C – A special grade of heavy fuel oil, also known as No. 6 fuel.

CEMENT CLINKER – A material, made by heating ground limestone and clay, that is ground up to a fine powder to produce cement.

CLINKER – The incombustible residue that remains after the combustion of coal.

COAL – Both eastern (high sulfur, used in industry) and western (low sulfer, burned at power plants) coal are shipped aboard Great Lakes vessels.

COKE – A byproduct of blended coals baked in ovens until mainly just pure carbon is left. Coke is used to generate the high heat necessary to make steel in blast furnaces.

COKE BREEZE – Byproduct of coke production.

DOLOMITE – Rock similar to limestone but somewhat harder and heavier.

FLUXSTONE – Taconite pellets premixed with limestone, so no limestone needs to be added to the mix in a blast furnace.

IRON FINES – Fines (ore less than 6mm in diameter) are created as a result of mining, crushing and processing the larger pieces of ore. See **SINTER**.

LIMESTONE – Common sedimentary rock consisting mostly of calcium carbonate used as a building stone and in the manufacture of lime, carbon dioxide and cement.

MILL SCALE – Byproduct of the shaping of iron and steel.

PETROLEUM COKE – Petroleum coke (petcoke) is the ultimate bottom end of oil refining – the parts of crude oil that will not vaporize in the refining process. It is mostly used as fuel (sometimes blended with coal) in power plants. **BUG DUST** is extremely fine coal (or coke) dust.

PIG IRON – Crude iron that is the direct product of the blast furnace and is refined to produce steel, wrought iron or ingot iron.

POTASH – A compound used for fertilizer.

SALT – Most salt shipped on the Great Lakes is used on roads and highways during the winter to melt ice.

SINTER – Broken taconite pellets, a.k.a. taconite pellet chips and fines. Small, but still useful in the blast furnace.

SLAG – Byproduct of the steelmaking process is used in the production of concrete and as seal coat cover, a base for paving, septic drain fields and railroad ballast.

TACONITE – A low-grade iron ore, containing about 27 percent iron and 51 percent silica, found as a hard rock formation in the Lake Superior region. It is pelletized for shipment to steel mills.

Why taconite pellets?

The high-grade iron ore (around 60 percent pure) that was mined on the ranges around Lake Superior was mostly exhausted in the tremendous mining efforts of World War II and in the early 1950s. There was still plenty of iron ore in the ground, but it was about 20-30 percent iron. To mine and ship all that ore in its natural form would have been expensive, so engineers developed the taconite pelletization process to increase the iron content of the product coming off the ranges headed for the steel mills.

Pellets have a number of positive attributes. Their iron content (and the content of other elements) can be precisely controlled so the steel mills know exactly what they are getting. Pellets are relatively moisture free compared with raw iron ore, so they are less prone to freeze in railcars, storage piles or dock pockets. This means the pellets can be shipped for a much longer season than natural iron ore, so companies need fewer railcars and ships to carry the same amount of pellets, thus saving money on labor and infrasructure. Pellets are also uniform in size, shape and mass, making them very easy to handle on conveyor belt systems, which makes for speedy, precise ship loading and unloading using a shipbard self-unloading system, again cutting down on costs.

TRAP ROCK – Rock, usually ground fairly fine, for use as foundations and roads or walkways. It is mined near Bruce Mines, Ont., and loaded there.

Canadian Transport unloads at the Short Cut coal dock in Detroit. (Wade P. Streeter)

CALL-IN POINTS / *Detroit-St. Clair Rivers*

Vessels transiting the St. Clair River, Lake St. Clair and the Detroit River are under the jurisdiction of Sarnia Traffic, and must radio their positions at predetermined locations. Call-in points (bold type on map) are not the same for upbound and downbound traffic. Average running times between call-in points are below. *

UPBOUND	Buoys 1&2	Black River	Stag Isl.	Salt Dock	X-32	Crib Light	Grassy Isl.
Detroit River Lt.	8:10	7:50	7:20	6:00	4:20	4:00	1:35
Grassy Island	6:45	6:25	5:55	4:35	2:55	2:35	
St. Clair Crib	4:10	3:50	3:20	2:00	0:25		
Light X-32	3:50	3:30	3:00	1:35			
Salt Dock	2:10	1:50	1:20				
Stag Isl. Upper	0:50	0:35					
Black River	0:20						

DOWNBOUND	Det. River	Grassy Isl.	Belle Isl.	Crib Light	Light 23	Salt Dock	Black River	7&8
30 min. above buoys 11&12	9:05	7:35	6:25	5:10	3:55	3:10	1:20	0:40
Buoys 7 & 8	8:15	6:55	5:45	4:30	3:15	2:30	0:40	
Black River	7:45	6:15	5:05	3:50	2:35	1:50		
Salt Dock	5:55	4:25	3:15	2:00	0:45			
Light 23	5:10	3:40	2:30	1:10				
St. Clair Crib	3:55	2:25	1:10					
USCG Belle Isle	2:40	1:10						
Grassy Isl.	1:30							

* Times can change if vessels stop for fuel or are delayed by other traffic.

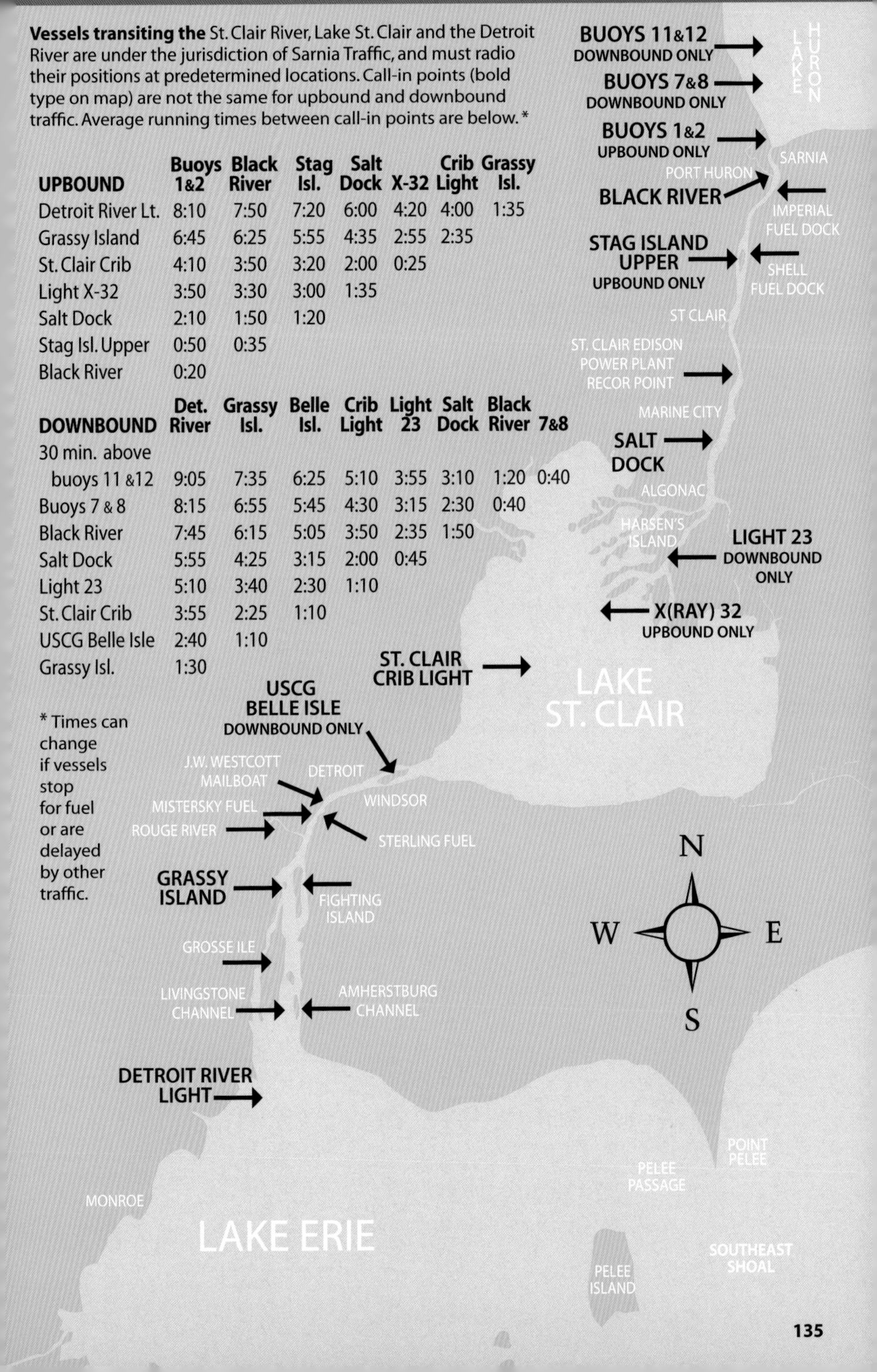

LAKE HURON

BUOYS 11&12 DOWNBOUND ONLY

BUOYS 7&8 DOWNBOUND ONLY

BUOYS 1&2 UPBOUND ONLY

PORT HURON

SARNIA

BLACK RIVER

IMPERIAL FUEL DOCK

STAG ISLAND UPPER UPBOUND ONLY

SHELL FUEL DOCK

ST CLAIR

ST. CLAIR EDISON POWER PLANT RECOR POINT

MARINE CITY

SALT DOCK

ALGONAC

HARSEN'S ISLAND

LIGHT 23 DOWNBOUND ONLY

X(RAY) 32 UPBOUND ONLY

ST. CLAIR CRIB LIGHT

LAKE ST. CLAIR

USCG BELLE ISLE DOWNBOUND ONLY

J.W. WESTCOTT MAILBOAT

DETROIT

WINDSOR

MISTERSKY FUEL

ROUGE RIVER

STERLING FUEL

GRASSY ISLAND

FIGHTING ISLAND

GROSSE ILE

LIVINGSTONE CHANNEL

AMHERSTBURG CHANNEL

DETROIT RIVER LIGHT

N
W   E
S

MONROE

LAKE ERIE

POINT PELEE

PELEE PASSAGE

SOUTHEAST SHOAL

PELEE ISLAND

The St. Marys River flows out of the southeast corner of Lake Superior in a southeasterly direction to Lake Huron. Vessels transiting the St. Marys River system are under jurisdiction of Soo Traffic, part of the U.S. Coast Guard at Sault Ste. Marie, Mich., and must radio their positions on VHF Ch. 12 (156.600 MHz) at predetermined locations. Vessels in the vicinity of the Soo Locks fall under jurisdiction of the lockmaster, who must be contacted on VHF Ch. 14 (156.700 MHz) for lock assignments.

Call-in points (bold type on map) are not the same for upbound and downbound traffic. Approximate running times between call-in points at left; times may vary due to other traffic and weather. Because of their size, 1,000-footers take more time to transit the system than smaller vessels.

Arrival times at the Soo Locks are available at the Information Center located in the locks park. Upbound vessels must make a pre-call to Soo Traffic one hour before entering the river at DeTour and downbound traffic is required to make a one-hour pre-call above Ile Parisienne.

** Upbound traffic passes Neebish Island on the east side. Downbound traffic passes the island to the west, through the Rock Cut, a channel dynamited out of solid rock in the early 1900s.

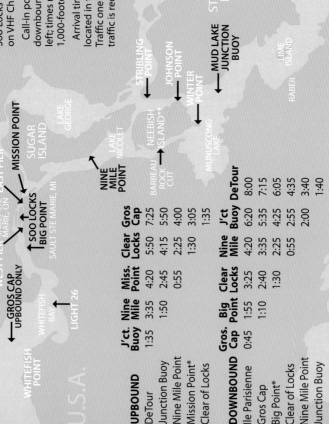

UPBOUND	J'ct. Buoy	Nine Mile	Miss. Point	Clear Locks	Gros Cap
DeTour	1:35	3:35	4:20	5:50	7:25
Junction Buoy		1:50	2:45	4:15	5:50
Nine Mile Point			0:55	2:25	4:00
Mission Point*				1:30	3:05
Clear of Locks					1:35

DOWNBOUND	Gros. Cap	Big Point	Clear Locks	Nine Mile	J'ct Buoy	DeTour
Ile Parisienne	0:45	1:55	3:25	4:20	6:20	8:00
Gros Cap		1:10	2:40	3:35	5:35	7:15
Big Point*			1:30	2:25	4:25	6:05
Clear of Locks				0:55	2:55	4:35
Nine Mile Point					2:00	3:40
Junction Buoy						1:40

* Lockmaster only

136

The Soo Locks at Sault Ste. Marie, Mich., overcome a 21-foot difference in water levels between Lake Superior and lakes Huron, Michigan and Erie.

Under the jurisdiction of the U.S. Army Corps of Engineers, the locks operate on gravity, as do all locks in the St. Lawrence Seaway system. No pumps are used to empty or fill the lock chambers; valves are opened, and water is allowed to seek its own level. All traffic passes through the locks toll-free.

Traffic is dispatched by radio to the appropriate lock according to size, other vessels in the locks area and the time the captain first calls in to the lockmaster. All vessels longer than 730 feet and/or wider than 76 feet are restricted by size to the Poe, or second, lock. A vessel is under engine and thruster control at all times, with crews ready to drop mooring lines over bollards on the lock wall to stop its movement.

As soon as the vessel is in position, engines are stopped and mooring lines made fast. If the vessel is being lowered, valves at the lower end of the lock chamber are opened to allow the water inside to flow out. If the vessel is being raised, valves at the upper end of the chamber are opened to allow water to enter. When the water reaches the desired level, the valves are closed, the protective boom is raised, the gates are opened, and the vessel leaves the lock.

The first ship canal on the American side was built from 1853-55. That canal was destroyed in 1888 by workers making way for newer and bigger locks.

MacArthur Lock
Named after World War II Gen. Douglas MacArthur, the MacArthur Lock is 800 feet long (243.8 meters) between inner gates, 80 feet wide (24.4 meters) and 31 feet deep (9.4 meters) over the sills. The lock was built in 1942-43 and opened to traffic on July 11, 1943. Vessel size is limited to 730 feet long (222.5 meters) by 76 feet wide (23 meters).

Poe Lock
The Poe Lock is 1,200 feet long (365.8 meters), 110 feet wide (33.5 meters) and has a depth over the sills of 32 feet (9.8 meters). Named after Col. Orlando M. Poe, it was built in the years 1961-68. The lock's vessel size limit is 1,100 feet long (335.3 meters) by 105 feet wide (32 meters).

Davis and Sabin locks
Dating from the first two decades of the 20th century, these two locks are no longer used. Work began in 2009 to replace them with one new Poe-sized lock, at an estimated cost of more than $500 million.

Canadian Lock
The Canadian Lock at Sault Ste. Marie, Ont., has its origin in a canal constructed from 1887-95. The present lock, operated by Parks Canada, is used by pleasure craft, tugs and tour boats.

Soo Locks facts

The Empire State Building is 1,250 feet tall. The largest vessel using the Soo Locks, the *Paul R. Tregurtha*, is 1,014 feet long.

The Great Lakes shipping season typically runs from late March to early January.

A vessel traveling from the Atlantic Ocean to Lake Superior through the St. Lawrence Seaway and the Soo Locks rises nearly 600 feet. The first lift, a total of 224 feet, is provided by the seven St. Lawrence Seaway locks that begin at Montreal. The Welland Canal raises vessels an additional 326 feet. The Soo Locks complete the process with a 21-foot lift.

One short blast of a vessel's whistle while in the lock means "cast off lines."

A red-and-white flag flying from a vessel's mast indicates a pilot is on board. Saltwater vessels must pick up Great Lakes pilots at various points in their voyage.

No tolls are charged at the Soo Locks.

The Great Lakes shipping season runs from late March to late December. In the spring and fall, a small fleet of icebreakers operated by the U.S. and Canadian coast guards, as well as commercial tugs, helps keep navigation channels open.

There are about 150 major cargo carriers engaged almost exclusively in the Great Lakes and Seaway trade.

 As part of its mission of building and maintaining the country's ports and waterways, the U.S. Army Corps of Engineers operates and maintains the Soo Locks, as well as all of the Great Lakes' connecting channels.

The 27-mile-long (43.7 km) Welland Canal, built to bypass Niagara Falls, overcomes a difference in water level of 326.5 feet (99.5 meters) between lakes Erie and Ontario. Each of the seven Welland Canal locks has an average lift of 46.5 feet (14.2 meters). All locks (except Lock 8) are 859 feet (261.8 meters) long, 80 feet (24.4 meters) wide and 30 feet (9.1 meters) deep. Lock 8 measures 1,380 feet (420.6 m) long.

The largest vessel that may transit the canal is 740 feet (225.5 meters) long, 78 feet (23.8 meters) wide and 26 feet, 6 inches (8.08 meters) in draft. Locks 1, 2 and 3 are at St. Catharines, Ont., on the Lake Ontario end of the waterway. At Lock 3, the Welland Canal Viewing Center and Museum houses an information desk (which posts a list of vessels expected at the lock), a gift shop and restaurant. At Thorold, Locks 4, 5 and 6, twinned to help speed passage of vessels, are controlled with an elaborate interlocking system for safety. These locks (positioned end to end, they resemble a short flight of stairs) have an aggregate lift of 139.5 feet (42.5 meters). Just south of Locks 4, 5 and 6 is Lock 7. Lock 8, seven miles (11.2 km) upstream at Port Colborne, completes the process, making the final adjustment to Lake Erie's level. In 1973, a new channel was constructed to replace the section of the canal that bisected the city of Welland. The Welland bypass eliminated long delays for navigation, road and rail traffic.

The average passage time for the canal is about 12 hours, with the majority of the time spent transiting Locks 4-7. Vessels passing through the Welland Canal and St. Lawrence Seaway must carry a qualified pilot. All vessel traffic though the Welland Canal is regulated by a control center, which also remotely operates the locks and the traffic bridges over the canal.

The St. Lawrence Seaway is a waterway extending some 2,038 miles (3,701.4 km) from the Atlantic Ocean to the head of the Great Lakes at Duluth, Minn., including Montreal harbor and the Welland Canal. More specifically, it is a system of locks and canals (U.S. and Canadian), built between 1954 and 1958 at a cost of $474 million and opened in 1959, that allows vessels to pass from

Olympic Miracle passing Federal Yukon in the Welland Canal. (Alain Gindroz)

Montreal to the Welland Canal at the western end of Lake Ontario. The vessel size limit within this system is 740 feet (225.6 meters) long, 78 feet (23.8 meters) wide and 26 feet (7.9 meters) draft.

Closest to the ocean is the St. Lambert Lock, which lifts ships some 15 feet (4.6 meters) from Montreal harbor to the level of the Laprairie Basin, through which the channel sweeps in a great arc 8.5 miles (13.7 km) long to the second lock. The Côte Ste. Catherine Lock, like the other six St. Lawrence Seaway locks, is built to the dimensions shown in the table below. The Côte Ste. Catherine lifts ships from the level of the Laprairie Basin 30 feet (9.1 meters) to the level of Lake Saint-Louis, bypassing the Lachine Rapids. Beyond it, the channel runs 7.5 miles (12.1 km) before reaching Lake Saint-Louis.

LOCK DIMENSIONS

Length	766' (233.5 meters)
Width	80' (24 meters
Depth	30' (9.1 meters)

The Lower Beauharnois Lock, bypassing the Beauharnois Power House, lifts ships 41 feet (12.5 meters) and sends them through a short canal to the Upper Beauharnois Lock, where they are lifted 41 feet (12.5 meters) to reach the Beauharnois Canal. After a 13-mile (20.9 km) trip in the canal and a 30-mile (48.3 km) passage through Lake Saint Francis, vessels reach the U.S. border and the Snell Lock, which has a lift of 45 feet (13.7 meters) and empties into the 10-mile (16.1 km) Wiley-Dondero Canal.

After passing through the Wiley-Dondero, ships are raised another 38 feet (11.6 meters) by the Dwight D. Eisenhower Lock, after which they enter Lake St. Lawrence, the pool upon which nearby power-generating stations draw for their turbines located a mile to the north.

At the western end of Lake St. Lawrence, the Iroquois Lock allows ships to bypass the Iroquois Control Dam. The lift here is only about one foot (0.3 meters). Once in the waters west of Iroquois, the channel meanders through the Thousand Islands to Lake Ontario and beyond.

A laker enters the St. Lambert Lock near Montreal. (Eric Treece)

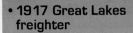

With an inexpensive VHF scanner, boatwatchers can tune to ship-to-ship and ship-to-shore traffic using the following frequency guide.

Calling/distress only	Ch. 16 – 156.800 MHz	Calling/distress only
Commercial vessels only	Ch. 06 – 156.300 MHz	Working channel
Commercial vessels only	Ch. 08 – 156.400 MHz	Working channel
DeTour Reef – Lake St. Clair Light	Ch. 11 – 156.550 MHz	Sarnia Traffic - Sect. 1
Long Point Light – Lake St. Clair Light	Ch. 12 – 156.600 MHz	Sarnia Traffic - Sect. 2
Montreal – mid-Lake St. Francis	Ch. 14 – 156.700 MHz	Seaway Beauharnois – Sect. 1
Mid-Lake St. Francis – Bradford Island	Ch. 12 – 156.600 MHz	Seaway Eisenhower – Sect. 2
Bradford Island – Crossover Island	Ch. 11 – 156.550 MHz	Seaway Iroquois – Sect. 3
Crossover Island to Cape Vincent	Ch. 13 – 156.650 MHz	Seaway Clayton – Sect. 4 St. Lawrence River portion
Cape Vincent – mid-Lake Ontario	Ch. 12 – 156.600 MHz	Seaway Sodus – Sect. 4 Lake Ontario portion
Seaway Pilot Office – Cape Vincent	Ch. 14 – 156.700 MHz	Pilotage Traffic
Mid-Lake Ontario – Welland Canal	Ch. 11 – 156.550 MHz	Seaway Newcastle – Sect. 5
Welland Canal	Ch. 14 – 156.700 MHz	Seaway Welland – Sect. 6
Welland Canal to Long Point Light	Ch. 11 – 156.550 MHz	Seaway Long Point – Sect. 7
Montreal Traffic	Ch. 10 – 156.500 MHz	Vessel traffic
Soo Traffic	Ch. 12 – 156.600 MHz	Soo Traffic, Sault Ste. Marie, MI
Lockmaster, Soo Locks	Ch. 14 – 156.700 MHz	Soo Lockmaster (WUE-21)
Coast Guard traffic	Ch. 21 – 157.050 MHz	United States Coast Guard
Coast Guard traffic	Ch. 22 – 157.100 MHz	United States Coast Guard
U.S. mailboat, Detroit, MI	Ch. 10 – 156.500 MHz	Mailboat *J. W. Westcott II*

These prerecorded messages help track vessel arrivals and departures.

Boatwatcher's Hotline	(218) 722-6489	Superior, Wis.; Duluth, Two Harbors, Taconite Harbor and Silver Bay, Minn.
CSX Coal Docks/Torco Dock	(419) 697-2304	Toledo, Ohio, vessel information
Eisenhower Lock	(315) 769-2422	Eisenhower Lock vessel traffic
Michigan Limestone docks	(989) 734-2117	Calcite, Mich., vessel information
Michigan Limestone docks	(906) 484-2201	Press 1 – Cedarville, Mich., passages
Presque Isle Corp.	(989) 595-6611	Stoneport, Mich., vessel information Ext. 7
Seaway Vessel Locator	(450) 672-4115	
Soo Traffic	(906) 635-3224	Previous day – St. Marys River
Superior Midwest Energy Terminal (SMET)	(715) 395-3559	Superior, Wis., vessel information
Thunder Bay Port Authority	(807) 345-1256	Thunder Bay, Ont., vessel info
Great Lakes Fleet	(800) 328-3760	Ext. 4389 – GLF vessel movements
Vantage Point, Boatnerd HQ	(810) 985-9057	St. Clair River traffic
Welland Canal tape	(905) 688-6462	Welland Canal traffic

The Welland Canal

Lock up the perfect fun day out!

The **Welland Canals** were built to circumvent the mighty Niagara Falls. Marvel as lake and ocean freighters are raised and lowered in the locks on their journey between Lake Erie and Lake Ontario.

Welland Canals Centre at Lock 3
1932 Welland Canals Parkway,
St. Catharines, ON L2R 7K6
t 905-984-8880 ext. 226
toll free 1-800-305-5134
e museuminfo@stcatharines.ca
w www.stcatharines.ca

THOROLD

Lock 7 Viewing Complex
50 Chapel Street South,
Thorold, ON L2V 2C6
t 905-680-9477
toll free 1-888-680-9477
e thoroldtourism@bellnet.ca
w www.thoroldtourism.ca

Call daily for ship schedules (April - December)

Motorcoach/Group Friendly!
Ship Viewing Platform - Always FREE!

A.B.M. Marine
Thunder Bay, ON

Algoma Central Corp.
St. Catharines, ON

Algoma Central Corp.
St. Catharines, ON

American Marine Constructors
Benton Harbor, MI

American Steamship Co.
Williamsville, NY

Andrie Inc.
Muskegon, MI

ArcelorMittal Mines Canada
Port Cartier, QC

Arnold Transit Co.
Mackinac Island, MI

Basic Marine Inc.
Escanaba, MI

Bay City Boat Lines
Bay City, MI

Bay Shipbuilding Co.
Sturgeon Bay, WI

Beaver Island Boat Co.
Charlevoix, MI

Blue Heron Co.
Tobermory, ON

Buffalo Dept. of Public Works
Buffalo, NY

Busch Marine Inc.
Carrollton, MI

Calumet River Fleeting Inc.
Chicago, IL

Canada Steamship Lines Inc.
Montreal, QC

Canada Steamship Lines Inc.
Montreal, QC

Canadian Coast Guard
Ottawa, ON

Central Marine Logistics Inc.
Operator for ArcelorMittal
Griffith, IN

Chicago Fire Department
Chicago, IL

Chicago Marine Asset
Management
Chicago, IL

Cleveland Fire Department
Cleveland, OH

Cooper Marine Ltd.
Selkirk, ON

Croisières AML Inc.
Québec, QC

Dann Marine Towing
Chesapeake City, MD

Dean Construction Co.
Belle River, ON

Detroit City Fire Department
Detroit, MI

Diamond Jack's River Tours
Detroit, MI

Dragage Verreault Inc.
Les Méchins, QC

Durocher Marine
Cheboygan, MI

Eastern Upper Peninsula
Transportation Authority
Sault Ste. Marie, MI

Edward E. Gillen Co.
Milwaukee, WI

Equipments Verreault Inc.
Les Méchins, QC

Erie Sand & Gravel Co.
Erie, PA

Essroc Canada Inc.
Seaway Marine Transport – Mgr.
Mississauga, ON

Fraser Shipyards Inc.
Superior, WI

Gaelic Tugboat Co.
Detroit, MI

Gallagher Marine
Construction Co. Inc.
Escanaba, MI

Gananoque Boat Line
Gananoque,ON

Geo. Gradel Co.
Toledo, OH

Goodtime Cruise Line Inc.
Cleveland, OH

Grand Portage /
Isle Royale Transportation Line
Superior, WI

Gravel & Lake Services Ltd.
Thunder Bay, ON

Great Lakes Dock & Materials
Muskegon, MI

Great Lakes Fleet Inc.
Key Lakes Inc. – Mgr.
Duluth, MN

Great Lakes & International
Towing & Salvage
Burlington, ON

Great Lakes Maritime Academy
Northwestern Michigan College
Traverse City, MI

Great Lakes Towing Co.
Cleveland, OH

Groupe C.T.M.A.
Cap-Aux-Meules, QC

Groupe Desgagnés Inc.
Québec, QC

Groupe Desgagnés Inc.
Québec, QC

Hamilton Port Authority
Hamilton, ON

Heritage Marine
Two Harbors, MN

Hornbeck Offshore Services
Covington, LA

Horne Transportation Ltd.
Wolfe Island, ON

Inland Lakes Management Inc.
Alpena, MI

Interlake Steamship Co.
Lakes Shipping Co.
Richfield, OH

K-Sea Canada Corp.
Halifax, NS

Kindra Lake Towing LP
Chicago, IL

King Co. Inc.
Holland, MI

KK Integrated Shipping LLC
Menominee, MI

Lafarge Canada Inc.
Montreal, QC

Lafarge North America Inc.
Bingham Farms, MI

Lake Erie Island Cruises LLC
Sandusky, OH

Lake Michigan Carferry
Service Inc.
Ludington, MI

Latitude 45° Nord Inc.
Salaberr-de-Valleyfield, QC

Lee Marine Ltd.
Port Lambton, ON

Lower Lakes Towing Ltd.
Port Dover, ON
Lower Lakes Transportation Co.
Williamsville, NY

Luedtke Engineering Co.
Frankfort, MI

MCM Marine Inc.
Sault Ste Marie, MI

MacDonald Marine Ltd.
Goderich, ON

Madeline Island
Ferry Line Inc.
LaPointe, WI

Malcom Marine
St. Clair, MI

Manitou Island Transit
Leland, MI

MarineLink Inc.
A Div. of Upper Lakes Group
Toronto, ON

Marine Tech LLC
Duluth, MN

Mariposa Cruise Line
Toronto, ON

Maximus Corp.
Bloomfield Hills, MI

McAsphalt Marine
Transportation
Scarborough, ON

McKeil Marine Ltd.
Hamilton, ON

McKeil Marine Ltd.
Hamilton, ON

McNally Construction Inc.
Hamilton, ON

Midwest Maritime Corp.
Milwaukee, WI

Miller Boat Line
Put-in-Bay, OH

Ministry of Transportation
Downsview, ON

Montreal Port Authority
Montreal, QC

Museum Tug John Purves
Sturgeon Bay, WI

Museum Ship
CCGC Alexander Henry
Kingston, ON

Museum Tug Edna G
Two Harbors, MN

Museum Ship
HMCS Haida
Hamilton, ON

Museum Ship
City of Milwaukee
Manistee, MI

Museum Ship
Col. James M. Schoonmaker
Toledo, OH

Museum Ship
Keewatin
Douglas, MI

Museum Ships
USS Little Rock
USS The Sullivans
Buffalo, NY

Museum Ship
Meteor
Superior, WI

Museum Ship
Milwaukee Clipper
Muskegon, MI

Museum Ships
Norgoma (Sault Ste. Marie,ON)
Norisle (Manitowaning,ON)

Museum Ship
Valley Camp
Sault Ste. Marie, MI

Museum Ship
William A. Irvin
Duluth, MN

Museum Ship
William G. Mather
Cleveland, OH

Muskoka Steamship
& Historical Society
Gravenhurst, ON

Nadro Marine Services Ltd.
Port Dover, ON

Nautica Queen
Cruise Dining
Cleveland, OH

New York State Marine
Highway Transportation Co.
Troy, NY

Ocean Group Inc.
Québec, QC

Osborne Inc.
Grand River, OH

Owen Sound
Transportation Co. Ltd.
Owen Sound, ON

Pere Marquette Shipping Co.
Tug Undaunted
Ludington, MI

Port City Tug Inc.
Muskegon, MI

Provmar Fuels Inc.
Div. of Upper Lakes Group Inc.
Hamilton, ON

Purvis Marine Ltd.
Sault Ste. Marie, ON

Purvis Marine Ltd.
Sault Ste. Marie, ON

Rebellion Tug & Barge
Niagara Falls, NY

Roen Salvage Co.
Sturgeon Bay, WI

Ryba Marine Construction Co.
Cheboygan, MI

Selvick Marine Towing Corp.
Sturgeon Bay, WI

Shoreline Sightseeing Co.
Chicago, IL

Société des Traversiers Du Québec
Québec, QC

Soo Locks Boat Tours
Sault Ste. Marie, MI

St. James Marine Co.
Beaver Island, MI

St. Lawrence Cruise Lines Inc.
Kingston, ON

St. Lawrence Seaway Development Corp.
Massena, NY

St. Lawrence Seaway Management Corp.
Cornwall, ON

St. Marys Cement Inc.
Toronto, ON

TGL Marine Holdings ULC
Plymouth, MI

Thousand Islands & Seaway Cruises
Brockville, ON

Thunder Bay Tug Services Ltd.
Thunder Bay, On

Thunder Bay Tug Services Ltd.
Thunder Bay, ON

Toronto Parks & Recreation Department
Toronto, ON

Transport Nanuk Inc. Spliethoff's Bevrachtingskantoor B.V.(Owner)
Montreal, QC

U.S. Army Corps of Engineers Great Lakes & Ohio River Div.
Cincinnati, OH

United States Coast Guard 9th Coast Guard District
Cleveland, OH

United States Environmental Protection Agency
Duluth, MN / Chicago, IL

United States National Park Service
Houghton, MI

Upper Lakes Group Inc.
Toronto, ON

Upper Lakes Towing Co.
Escanaba, MI

Vanguard Shipping Ltd.
Ridgeville, ON

Voyageur Maritime Trading Inc.
Ridgeville, ON

Warner Petroleum Corp.
Clare, MI

MEANINGS OF BOAT WHISTLES

1 SHORT: I intend to leave you on my port side (answered by same if agreed upon).

2 SHORT: I intend to leave you on my starboard side (answered by same if agreed upon). (Passing arrangements may be agreed upon by radio. If so, no whistle signal is required.)

1 PROLONGED: Vessel leaving dock.

3 SHORT: Operating astern propulsion.

1 PROLONGED, SOUNDED AT INTERVALS OF NOT MORE THAN 2 MINUTES: Vessel moving in restricted visibility.

1 SHORT, 1 PROLONGED, 1 SHORT: Vessel at anchor in restricted visibility (optional). May be accompanied by the ringing of a bell on the forward part of the ship and a gong on the aft end.

3 PROLONGED and 2 SHORT: Salute (formal).

1 PROLONGED and 2 SHORT: Salute (commonly used).

3 PROLONGED and 1 SHORT: International Shipmasters' Association member salute.

5 OR MORE SHORT BLASTS SOUNDED RAPIDLY: Danger.

Algoma Central Corp.
St. Catharines, ON

American Steamship Co.
Williamsville, NY

Andrie Inc.
Muskegon, MI

Beluga Shipping GMBH
Bremen, Germany

Canada Steamship Lines Inc.
Montreal, QC

Canadian Forest Navigation Co. Inc.
Montreal, QC

Fednav Ltd.
Montreal, QC

Flinter Groningen BV
Groningen, The Netherlands

Gaelic Tugboat Co.
Detroit, MI

**Great Lakes Fleet Inc.
Key Lakes Inc. – Mgr.**
Duluth, MN

Great Lakes Maritime Academy
Traverse City, MI

Great Lakes Towing Co.
Cleveland, OH

Groupe Desgagnés Inc.
Québec City, QC

Inland Lakes Management Inc.
Alpena, MI

**Interlake Steamship Co.
Lakes Shipping Co.**
Richfield, OH

J.W. Westcott Co.
Detroit, MI

Lafarge Canada Inc
Montreal, QC

Lake Michigan Carferry Service Inc.
Ludington, MI

**Lower Lakes Towing Ltd.
Lower Lakes Transportation Co.**
Port Dover, ON / Williamsville, NY

McAsphalt Marine Transportation Ltd.
Scarborough, ON

McKeil Marine Ltd.
Hamilton, ON

McNally Construction Inc.
Hamilton, ON

Ocean Group Inc.
Québec, QC

Owen Sound Transportation Co. Ltd.
Owen Sound, ON

Pere Marquette Shipping Co.
Ludington, MI

Purvis Marine Ltd.
Sault Ste. Marie, ON

Seaway Marine Transport
St. Catharines, ON

Upper Lakes Group Inc.
Toronto, ON

Vanguard Shipping (Great Lakes) Ltd.
Ridgeville, ON

Voyageur Maritime Trading Inc.
Ridgeville, ON

W. Bockstiegel Reederei KG
Emden, Germany

Wagenborg Shipping BV
Delfzijl, Netherlands

Alvtank Rederi AB
Donso, Sweden

Amalthia Maritime Inc.
Athens, Greece

Ark Shipping SA
Piraeus, Greece

Atlantska Plovidba
Dubrovnik, Croatia

Beluga Shipping GMBH
Bremen, Germany

Bernhard Schulte Group
Hamburg, Germany

Biglift Shipping BV
Roosendaal, Netherlands

Blystad Tankers Inc.
Oslo, Norway

Briese Schiffahrts GMBH & Co. KG
Leer, Germany

Brostrom AB
Goteburg, Sweden

Callitsis Ship Management SA
Piraeus, Greece

Canadian Forest Navigation Co. Ltd.
Montreal, QC, Canada

Carisbrooke Shipping
Cowes, UK

Chemikalien Seetransport GMBH
Hamburg, Germany

Clipper Group AS
Copenhagen, Denmark

Coastal Shipping Ltd.
Goose Bay, NL, Canada

Commercial Fleet of Donbass
Donetsk, Ukraine

Crystal Pool Group
Helsinki, Finland

De Poli Tankers BV
Spijkenisse, Netherlands

Eitzen Chemical ASA
Oslo, Norway

Enzian Shipping AG
Berne, Switzerland

Energy Shipping SPA
Genoa, Italy

Far-Eastern Shipping Co.
Vladivostok, Russia

Fednav International Ltd.
Montreal, QC, Canada

Fednav International Ltd.
Montreal, QC, Canada

Finbeta
Savona, Italy

Fisser & V. Doornum Kg GMBH
Hamburg, Germany

Flinter Shipping BV
Barendrecht, Netherlands

Franco Compania Naviera SA
Athens, Greece

Great Lakes Feeder Lines
Burlington, ON, Canada

Hapag Lloyd GMBH
Hamburg, Germany

Harren & Partner Schiffahrts GMBH
Bremen, Germany

Holland Ship Service
The Netherlands

Intersee Schiffahrts-Gesellschaft MbH & Co.
Haren-Ems, Germany

Intership Navigation Co. Ltd.
Limassol, Cyprus

IskoMarine Shipping Co.
Piraeus, Greece

Jo Tankers BV
Spijkenisse, Netherlands

Jumbo Shipping Co. SA
Rotterdam, Netherlands

Kent Line
Saint John, NB, Canada

Knutsen O.A.S. Shipping
Haugesund, Norway

Krey Schiffahrts GMBH & Co.
Simonswolde, Germany

Lehmann Reederei
Lübeck, Germany

Liamare Shipping BV
Maartensdijk, Netherlands

Lindos Maritime Ltd.
Piraeus, Greece

Lloyd Fonds Singapore
Singapore, Singapore

Mega Chemical Tankers Ltd.
Singapore, Singapore

Murmansk Shipping Co.
Murmansk, Russia

Murmansk Shipping Co.
Murmansk, Russia

**Navigation Maritime
Bulgare Ltd.**
Varna, Bulgaria

Nordic Tankers A/S
Copenhagen, Denmark

**Novorossiysk Shipping
(Novoship)**
Novorossiysk, Russia

Oceanex Inc.
Montreal, QC, Canada

**Olympic Shipping and
Management SA**
Monte Carlo, Monaco

Parakou Shipping Ltd.
Hong Kong, China

Perosea Shipping Co. SA
Piraeus, Greece

Polish Steamship Co.
Szczecin, Poland

Pot Scheepvaart BV
Delfzijl, Netherlands

Reederei Eckhoff & Co. GMBH
Jork, Germany

Rederiet Stenersen AS
Bergen, Norway

Sargeant Marine Inc.
Boca Raton, Florida USA

**Sea Observer Shipping
Services**
Piraeus, Greece

Seastar Navigation Co. Ltd.
Athens, Greece

Shih Wei Navigation Co.
Taipei, Taiwan

Siomar Enterprises Ltd.
Piraeus, Greece

Spar Shipping AS
Bergen, Norway

Stolt Parcel Tankers
Greenwich, CT, USA

Thor Shipping AS
Svendborg, Denmark

Torvald Klaveness Group
Oslo, Norway

Transatlantic Shipping AB
Skärhamn, Sweden

Union Marine Enterprises SA
Piraeus, Greece

Viken Shipping AS
Bergen, Norway

W. Bockstiegel Reederei KG
Emden, Germany

Wagenborg Shipping BV
Delfzijl, Netherlands

Yardimci Shipping Group
Istanbul, Turkey

Yilmar Shipping & Trading Ltd.
Istanbul, Turkey

149

FLAGS OF MAJOR NATIONS IN THE LAKES & SEAWAY TRADE

 Bahamas

 Barbados

 Belgium

 Bermuda

 Brazil

 Bulgaria

 Canada

 People's Republic of China

 Croatia

 Cyprus

 Denmark

 Egypt

 Finland

 France

 Germany

 Greece

 Hong Kong

 Iceland

 India

 Isle of Man

 Israel

 Italy

 Japan

 Korea-South

 Liberia

 Lithuania

 Malta

 Monaco

 Netherlands

 Norway

 Panama

 Philippines

 Poland

 Portugal

 Romania

 Russia

 Singapore

 Spain

 St. Vincent & The Grenadines

 Sweden

 Switzerland

 Taiwan

 Turkey

 United Kingdom

 United States

 Vanuatu

 Ukraine

 Yugoslavia

Other Frequently Seen Flags

International Shipmaster's Association – Member Pennant

Canadian Coast Guard Ensign

Dangerous Cargo On Board

Pilot On Board

U.S. Coast Guard Auxiliary Ensign

U.S. Coast Guard Ensign

U.S. Army Corps of Engineers

St. Lawrence Seaway Development Corp.

St. Lawrence Seaway Management Corp.

150

SHIP SIGHTINGS

Record your own vessel observations here

DATE	NAME	LOCATION / DETAILS

THE MAN WHO KNEW HIS SHIPS

"Know Your Ships" was published for the first time in 1959 by vessel enthusiast and photographer Thomas Manse of Sault Ste. Marie, Mich., with the support of his wife, Mabel, and their daughters, Judy and Cindy.

Tom started shooting pictures of the passing freighter parade through the Soo Locks and on the St. Marys River in the 1950s, and set a goal for himself of getting at least one photograph of all the ships sailing the lakes. Thomas Manse passed away in 1994, having surpassed his goal many times over.

Since then, **"Know Your Ships"** has been published by Roger LeLievre, with the help of a crew of volunteers from around the Great Lakes and St. Lawrence Seaway. All are dedicated to keeping the passion for boatwatching alive for future generations.

Tom Manse

152

Know Your SHIPS 2011

An Historic Gallery

N.M. Paterson & Sons
grain boat Canadoc
at the Soo Locks.
(Tom Manse)

Plenty of steam from Wilson Marine Transit Co.'s C.L. Austin, June 1969. (Roger LeLievre)

USCG Naugatuck and A.H. Ferbert during winter navigation experiments in the 1970s. (Tom Manse)

Armco downbound on Lake St. Clair. (Gary R. Clark)

T.R. McLagan in the 1960s. *(Peter Worden)*

USCG icebreaker Mackinaw pours on the power. *(Tom Manse)*

Cars wait in line for the City of Petoskey ferry before the Mackinaw Bridge opened in 1957.
(Tom Manse Coll.)

CITY OF PETOSKEY

Cleveland-Cliffs' steamer Frontenac flying her name pennant. (Tom Manse Coll.)

Inland Steel's Clarence B. Randall in 1974.
(Roger LeLievre)

Charles M. White heads out of the Soo Locks in 1957. (Tom Manse Coll.)

American Oil Co.
Whiting, IN

Bethlehem Steel Corp.
Cleveland, OH

Bethlehem Steel Corp.
Cleveland, OH

Buckeye Steamship Co.
Hutchinson & Co.
Cleveland, OH

Carryore Ltd.
Nipigon Transport Ltd.
Montreal, QC

Detroit
& Cleveland
Navigation Co.
Detroit, MI

Cleveland-Buffalo
Navigation Co.
Cleveland, OH

Cleveland-Cliffs
Iron Co.
Cleveland, OH

Columbia Transportation Co.
Div. Oglebay Norton Co.
Cleveland, OH

Ford Motor Co.
Dearborn, MI

M.A. Hanna Co.
National Steel Corp.
Cleveland, OH

Hindman
Transportation Co.
Owen Sound, ON

Inland Steel Co.
Chicago, IL

Kinsman Marine
Transit Co.
Cleveland, OH

T.J. McCarthy Steamship Co.
Detroit, MI

Scott Misener
Steamship Co.
Colonial Steamship Ltd.
Port Colborne, ON

N.M. Paterson & Sons
Thunder Bay, ON

Pringle Transit Co.
Cleveland, OH

Reiss Steamship Co.
Sheboygan, WI

Republic Steel Corp.
Cleveland, OH

Soo River Company
Thorold, ON

U.S. Steel Corp.
Great Lakes Fleet
Duluth, MN

White Star Line
Detroit, MI

Wilson MarineTransit Co.
Cleveland, OH

BUILT FOR SPEED

The stylish *Cliffs Victory* – built for the demands of one war and rebuilt for the needs of a second – was one of the most unusual vessels to ever sail the Great Lakes.

Built in 1945 as a Victory-class cargo ship for the U.S. Maritime Administration under the name *Notre Dame Victory*, she was declared surplus in 1948 and laid up. The cargo demands of the Korean War saw the vessel sold to the Cleveland-Cliffs Iron Co., which adapted her for Great Lakes service and renamed her *Cliffs Victory* in 1951.

She was known for her distinctive profile, which featured a high, flared bow, five deck hatches and a second hatch crane aft of her rear cabin. Her high speed earned *Cliffs Victory* the informal title "Speed Queen of the Lakes."

Cliffs Victory was scrapped in South Korea in 1987, doomed by high operating costs. The photo shows her under the Hulett unloaders in Cleveland, circa 1965. *(Tom Manse Coll.)*

Crewmen relax in the 1920s aboard Col. James M. Schoonmaker. (Capt. William Wilcox)

Pittsburgh fleet's James A. Farrell in Little Rapids cut, 1920s. (Vanderlinden Coll., Acheson Ventures.)

Crew of Charles M. Warner after an icy trip. (A.E. Young photo)

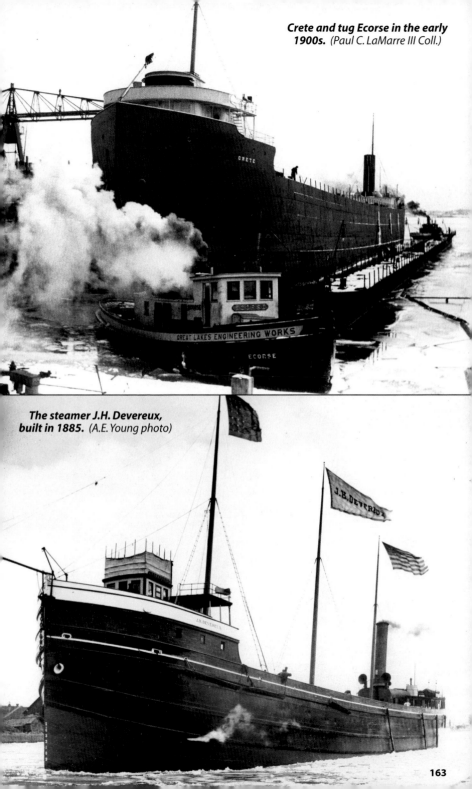

Crete and tug Ecorse in the early 1900s. (Paul C. LaMarre III Coll.)

The steamer J.H. Devereux, built in 1885. (A.E. Young photo)

Henry R. Platt Jr. of the Gartland Steamship Co. in the early 1960s. (Tom Manse)

Edward B. Greene in spring ice above the Soo Locks, 1975. (Roger LeLievre)

*Smoke and flowers mix aboard
the Kinsman Independent.*
(Paul C. LaMarre Jr.)

EDWARD B. GREENE
THE CLEVELAND - CLIFFS STEAMSHIP CO.

Chart your course as a Merchant Marine Officer aboard the ships of the world. The Academy offers an exciting Bachelor's degree program which includes three semesters at sea and 100% job placement.

INDEX TO ADVERTISERS

*Thank you for supporting
our advertisers!*

**Back cover: Wilfred Sykes upbound on
windy Lake Michigan.** *(Roger LeLievre)*

Marine Publishing Co.
Box 68, Sault Ste. Marie, MI 49783
(734) 668-4734

Back issues
1978–'79
1982–2010
$8.50

**Complete
catalog
online**

We cover the waterfront!

knowyourships.com

S.S. BADGER

HISTORIC
LAKE MICHIGAN CARFERRY

A little history, a lot of fun!

800-841-4243
www.ssbadger.com

MANITOWOC ★ LUDINGTON